The eWorld Handbook

Internet Resources and Opportunities for You, Your Family and Your Business

Who so neglects learning in his youth, loses the past and is dead for the future.
EURIPIDES
486–406 BC

The eWorld Handbook

Internet Resources and Opportunities for You, Your Family and Your Business

Christopher Lynas

Prentice Hall

An imprint of Pearson Education

Harlow, England · London · New York · Reading, Massachusetts · San Francisco
Toronto · Don Mills, Ontario · Sydney · Tokyo · Singapore · Hong Kong · Seoul
Taipei · Cape Town · Madrid · Mexico City · Amsterdam · Munich · Paris · Milan

Pearson Education Limited

Head Office:
Edinburgh Gate
Harlow CM20 2JE
Tel: +44 (0)1279 623623
Fax: +44 (0)1279 431059

London Office:
128 Long Acre, London WC2E 9AN
Tel: +44 (0)207 447 2000
Fax: +44 (0)207 240 5771

First published in Great Britain 2000

ISBN: 0–13–027044–X

British Library Cataloguing in Publication Data
A CIP catalogue record for this book can be obtained from the British Library.

Library of Congress Cataloging in Publication Data
Applied for.

10 9 8 7 6 5 4 3 2 1

Typeset by Pantek Arts, Maidstone, Kent
Printed and bound in Great Britain by Redwood Books Ltd, Trowbridge

The Publishers' policy is to use paper manufactured from sustainable forests.

About the author

Christopher Lynas is a globally acknowledged Internet consultant and commentator. He has seen the Internet evolve at an astounding rate as a business tool. He has challenged audiences from many industries in many countries to acknowledge, consider and comprehend the massive changes in their market sectors. Always entertaining and inspirational, his presentations are insights to the future. How will we do business as the twenty-first century unfolds? What will consumers' needs be? What will we experience in our family and leisure time? With in-depth research to customize presentations, Christopher Lynas is thought-provoking, educational, motivational, amusing and unique. He effectively bridges the gap between the technology and the layperson, enlightening his audiences and encouraging them to study and respect the new and emerging technology.

With humour and finesse, he confronts his audiences with the truth of what they need to do, and how they need to think, to move into the future with success and optimism. Christopher Lynas is one of the most sought-after speakers in the world today, dealing with how to adapt to the eWorld society, and how to develop the skills to succeed with current and future change.

He is a member of The Writers Guild and CimTech – The Chartered Institute of Marketing's Technology Interest Group.

Media activity

His list of media coverage is extensive and impressive – he has been often quoted and profiled in publications such as the *Financial Times*, *Investors Chronicle*, *Real Business*, *Business First*, *The Mail on Sunday*, *Scotland on Sunday*, *The Express* and various print media across Europe. In a two-week period he spoke to over 200 European journalists. He was featured in the *Newsweek International* edition that coincided with the C-bit exhibition in Hanover, Germany in March 1999. He regularly writes for *The Guardian* and *The Herald*.

He can be contacted by email: **lynas@eworldhandbook.com** or visit his Web site **http://www.eworldhandbook.com.**

Acknowledgements

First of all I would like to thank all at Pearson Education for the professional and dedicated manner they have shown in the publishing of this book.

My special thanks goes to Acquisitions Editor, Steve Temblett, for expertly managing the complete project. Thanks also go to Development Editor, Katherin Ekstrom; Senior Product Manager, Jonathan Hardy; and Publishing Co-ordinator, Alison Birtwell; as well as to all others who have been involved.

My deepest thanks go to all my family, especially my mother Connie who is greatly missed today and to my father, who through failing eyesight will not be able to read this book, but I will read it to him; to my brother Brian for shepherding me in; to my sister Josephine Crichton who was there when I needed her, and also to my brother Michael; and to Jason and Josephine Main.

Thanks are also due to all who have directly and indirectly contributed to this book: Billy, Michael and Martin Tracey, Marion and John H. Stewart, Drew Crawford, Bob Paton, Michael Coyle, Jamie Moore, Caroline Chappell, John Heron, David Dalglish, Les Lawson, Eddie MacKechnie, Harry Marsden, Paul Neary, Ed Griffiths, Sandy Pettigrew, Ed Griffiths, John Sweeney and, last but by no means least, Graeme Houston.

For Sabine
You have all my love
I could not have done it without you

Foreword

There have been very few things which have come along in our lifetimes which will end up having as much impact on the way we communicate, share information and do business as the Internet. It may still seem like early days when we consider how many people are actively using the Internet today, but the fact is that Internet usage is growing faster than any other new technology to date.

Just a few years ago, it would have been hard to imagine that we would be able to access so much information so easily through a device as small as a personal computer. But thanks to the Internet and the World Wide Web with its billions of pages of information, what once may have taken days or weeks to find is increasingly instantly available at our fingertips.

The implications for change in our daily lives are enormous. Today the Internet can be accessed from computers, through the TV, and even via mobile telephones. Very soon, using technology which has already been developed, we'll be able to customize our view of the world through almost any device to reflect our own personal interests and needs more closely. Imagine having your own specialist news channel or being able to watch your favourite TV programmes when you want to, not when the networks broadcast them. The fridge will be linked to the Internet to update our home delivery grocery orders, and we'll be able to choose our own camera angles to zoom in on our favourite sports on TV.

Companies like Excite which are working hard to make these experiences part of everyday life are increasingly working together as the boundaries between the Internet, telecommunications, entertainment and commerce blur. The Internet is after all just another medium which we can choose to use for our own convenience. It will not entirely replace the way we communicate or do business, only enhance the number of choices of where, when and what and how we communicate and consume.

Its power lies in the fact that it can turn traditional ways of doing things on their head. By connecting buyers and sellers directly, the Internet can strip out layers of inefficiency in traditional supply chains to open up new markets. It's a great leveller, small companies can achieve the same world-wide reach as their biggest competitors and groups of people from all over the world who share similar interests can find each other and work as a community. Anyone who has come into contact with the Internet to date is aware of the growing number of internet or eBusinesses which are springing up almost daily as business people and entrepreneurs grasp opportunities to create new ways of doing business.

And as exciting as these developments seem today, in five years' time there will be no such thing as eBusiness as the Internet becomes inextricably woven into our daily lives.

Evan Rudowski
VP and Managing Director of Excite Europe
http://www.excite.co.uk

Trademark Notice

Contents

Introduction and systems used in this handbook

Carrier of news and knowledge, instrument of trade and promoter of mutual acquaintance, of peace and goodwill among men and nations. Messenger of sympathy and love, servant of parted friends, consoler of the lonely, bond of the scattered family, enlarger of the common life.

INSCRIPTIONS FROM THE EAST & WEST PAVILIONS, POST OFFICE
WASHINGTON D.C.

This plaque, still there today, was placed in the mid-1850s to describe the benefits of communication by letter. These same words would have also been appropriate in the early 1900s to herald the introduction of the telephone. People at that time would have found it hard to understand the enormous changes, which have influenced their lifestyles, brought about by the introduction of the telephone. Nearly 100 years later we have a massive global telephone network, which allows us to communicate to anywhere in the world, with any one of several hundred million people, simply by dialling a few numbers. Dealing with change is a disagreeable subject for many people; it is much simpler to hope that the ramifications of change will not affect us. This is true when it comes to computers and telecommunications: just as people in the early twentieth century could not begin to comprehend how telephone systems would evolve then, many of us today cannot conceive what communication systems will be available to us in five or ten years time. We do the safe thing; we hope that the world of tomorrow will be just the same as it is today. To adopt this attitude is a foolish approach; we must open our eyes and intellect to the technological change that is evolving around us.

Can we even begin to comprehend what is going to happen to the way we work, rest and play, as the eWorld of the future takes hold of our lives? The reality is we are in an age of remarkable change, and it is those individuals who are willing to comprehend, acknowledge and interact with the changing environment in our daily lives that will survive and be prosperous. Those who are unwilling to adapt will have a far less predictable future.

It is imperative to acknowledge what is happening around us. When speaking to large groups of people, I use the term 'eWorld' to describe this new world we are entering. A world in which the total knowledge, information and ideas possessed by civilization can be shared and made accessible to everyone in the world on their individual computer screens by simply accessing the Internet.

The effect of the eWorld will be sensational, but only for those of us who accept these changes; they will prosper from the benefits that it holds. We are at the beginning of a new age; the children of this decade understand this – they are full of excitement and perception about this technology. To them it is their friend who will carry them into their future. They will be able to search for new careers and opportunities as they experiment with this new eWorld surrounding them. Adults who have welcomed this new technology are taking the same perspective; they are turning a threat into an opportunity. All of us should follow their example.

As we look back in time, we find that technological change has had an enormous effect on our lifestyles. Everything from computers to automobiles has had a serious effect on our lifestyles. The eWorld is going to have an even more dramatic effect. If you consider the last decade when the eWorld was in its infancy and the first white collar recession was in full swing, we saw massive redundancies; in some organizations, two and even three tiers of management were removed as companies restructured and re-engineered. We saw the age of the mega-merger, in which companies merged to consolidate their research and talents.

The number of full-time jobs is beginning to decrease alarmingly. The period of the job for life has definitely come to an end. New thinking is emerging in the corporate world, based on an unwillingness to increase staff levels, with a consequence that we are developing into an economy of consultants who peddle their skills and talents to business on an as-needed premise.

Companies will now hire the best talent they can, regardless of where that person might live. In the eWorld, the only thing that holds any influence is knowledge. If the knowledge is accessible from anywhere in the world, then companies will find themselves in the position of being able to pick out the most suitable talent they need to do a specific task from a selection of global, skilled consultants. A new era of competition is about to evolve as highly skilled workers sell their knowledge and talents to a global marketplace of business organizations. Lifestyle choice will come to dictate career decisions because they can supply their skills from anywhere through the tools of the eWorld; this array of professionals will impose their terms and conditions. They will make lifestyle decisions that will let them maintain their national and global customer base from a rural electronic cottage, and as a result they will enjoy the fruits of the eWorld economy. A new generation of career decisions built upon lifestyle choices is approaching us.

The matter of location is quickly becoming irrelevant, with the upsurge of telecommunication networks, fax machines, voice mail, email and other methods of communication. The office of the future will look like your study; we are entering the era of the home office.

Business competition will increase dramatically. We are at the crossroads of a new competitive economy; the impact of equality and 'eCompetition' is playing havoc with old-school business strategies. The continued evolution of the eWorld will mean that senior management, not technical staff, must guide their organizations through an increasingly complicated networked economy.

A generation's battle for economic control and survival is with us. It won't be easy; our economic systems are ruled by the older generation, comfortable in their ways, who are now faced with a new and technically sophisticated generation. Increasingly, economic survival is dependent upon mastery of technology and this requires a new style of business thinking among senior managers, who must also have some insight into the key aspects of the technology itself. To ensure that you set your organization in the right direction in the future, you should be prepared to get more familiar with technology.

Business and government will face an unprecedented consumer and electorate rebellion. Armed with new and powerful information technologies, the eWorld consumer is discovering a unique and exceptional power and influence over the decisions and activities undertaken by traditional business organizations and government. Executives will come to admire and respect this raw strength of the eWorld, but will struggle to interpret how they can use it to their advantage.

With an increasingly complex world, the ability to access and comprehend knowledge will become an important survival skill. Those who can modify their talents and skill, through knowledge, will be the true survivors in the coming eWorld. Knowledge will be crucial to success.

Embracing the eWorld is about more than building a Web site. Business success will come to those business executives who recognize that the emerging eWorld economy is all about re-engineering business relationships through the use of information technology, which when done properly gives genuine, endurable and profitable advantage. Opportunity will come to the strategic thinkers.

There are those who think that success in the eWorld is all too easy. Those individuals, who believe they have conquered the eWorld, by jumping in with much excitement but very little commitment, will discover that success comes not from technology, but from knowledge, understanding and vision.

The words on that plaque in the Post Office in Washington are still applicable to the Internet, as we enter the twenty-first century. The eWorld and the Internet will be the communication device of the individual and of business. The very nature of the corporate model is changing and that should make us all very eager about the opportunities in this new era. The eWorld is set to become far more than a tool by which we can conduct research, collect market intelligence, market our services, or conduct online transactions. In addition to all these things, the eWorld is emerging as the mechanism that will connect the ordinary person, from his or her isolated computer, to the global world that is evolving in the economy of the twenty-first century. That, more than any other influence, is why we must take the time to grasp the significant opportunities that the eWorld presents.

This handbook is written for those who want to learn about the eWorld and be able to use it as a strategic resource. It will show how the eWorld opens up new personal and business opportunities. It will help to de-mystify the many overwhelming aspects of computers and the Internet. Whether you are an experienced Web user or a first-time novice, it will help you unravel the many social, economic and political issues everyone must understand about the eWorld and how to use this knowledge in your daily lives.

One of the remarkable things about the eWorld is that every day there are new tools to discover: tips, software and systems to improve your utilization of the eWorld, to make your time a little less puzzling, to make you more productive, efficient and skilled in your time spent in the eWorld. I have split this book into five sections or themes. I have focused on the five issues which I believe will be of considerable importance to everyone as we enter the twenty-first century:

1. Eliminating doubts and fears about the Internet
2. Small businesses and the Internet
3. Internet users who have special needs
4. A pan-European guide to the Internet
5. The future of the eWorld

You will find in each section a wealth of information that will make you a more proficient and competent user of the resources and knowledge that awaits you in the eWorld. I am confident that you will find information that you never knew existed. This book is not so much a 'How To' guide but more of an illustration of how everyone can use the eWorld more effectively and productively as we begin to comprehend the effect it is having on our daily lives.

Systems used in this book

Data pointers

Throughout this book there are data pointers to sites on the World Wide Web, for example:

http://…http://www.eworldhandbook.com

Occasionally the **http://** prefix is omitted and the address will be illustrated like this

www…www.eworldhandbook.com

These will be the addresses you can use to reach the referenced site on the World Wide Web. As the Internet is in a constant state of change, all the WWW addresses listed were verified at the time of printing. Inevitably some sites will change their address, move location or just disappear. Although unable to guarantee that all listings will remain in effect, updates and corrections will be available at the eWorld Handbook World Wide Web Site on **http://www.eworldhandbook.com.**

Tips, tricks and trivia

You will find within this book "Tips, tricks and trivia" in boxes. These boxes will provide you with information relevant to the Internet and computers. You will find they have an entertainment and educational value. They are rarely pertinent to the part of the text where they appear. They look like this (this example is from Chapter 3).

Tips, tricks and trivia

A Prediction From 1949 'Computers in the future will weigh no more than 1.5 tons' *Popular Mechanics*

Tell me about your experiences

To help improve future editions of this book your feedback is welcomed. If you have any suggestions or comments, please let me have them. I am also interested as to how small businesses around the world are using the Internet. How has the Internet helped you? What Internet resources did you find most helpful? Has the Internet helped you research specific markets, products or industries?

If you wish to share your online experiences with me email me at the address below. Also, if you are aware of any small organization that is developing any products or services for the online marketplace please let me know so that I can mention them in future editions of this handbook.

I try to respond to all emails sent to me.

Christopher Lynas can be contacted on: **lynas@eworldhandbook.com.**

A first in the eWorld – a gift that's different

If you wish to have a signed copy of this handbook, either for yourself or maybe to give to a friend or relative then you can order this handbook from our Web site **http://www.eworldhandbook.com.** There will be provision to incorporate your message and name of recipient and the book will be signed by the author. We believe this is the first time this service has ever been available in the eWorld.

Part I

Eliminating doubts and fears about the Internet

1

The reality of the Internet

The only thing to fear is fear itself.

JOHN F. KENNEDY 1917–1963

- Getting started
- A brief history of the Internet
- Should I get involved?
- Who is the eWorld for?
- How do I use the eWorld to my advantage?
- Why would you want to learn about the eWorld?
- Welcome to the eWorld

Welcome to the eWorld, a world that is set to change the evolution of mankind. Knowledge will be the key to success in the twenty-first century. To obtain that knowledge you will have to have at least a working knowledge of both the Internet and computers. If you have no awareness of either, this may seem an overwhelming task. In reality it is very easy. If you are a complete novice to what I call the eWorld then this is my first tip for you. Find out where your nearest Internet cafe is, go along, have a coffee, introduce yourself, and say you have no knowledge of either computers or the Internet, but you would like them to explain the basics and let you 'surf' the Web for an hour. It will cost you maybe €5, but it will be the best €5 you will ever spend. I have been in Internet cafes throughout the world and have always found the staff in them to be both knowledgeable and helpful. You will soon realize that this hour will give you a better basic and practical knowledge than the reading alone of three books on the subject would have given you.

> **Tips, tricks and trivia**
>
> **Begins with an 'S' and ends with an 'X'**
>
> Which word occurs more than any other on the World Wide Web? You probably know the answer, but you can actually research the question, using the Altameter, at
>
> **http://altameter.x42.com**
>
> Enter a word, and this one-page site tells you how many times that word occurs on the Web; enter two words (each preceded by a plus sign), and you get a bar chart comparing the occurrence of one to another. The comparisons are great fun; when you find a word that occurs more often than you-know-what, be sure to let me know.

Getting started

To become a citizen of the eWorld you will need:

- a computer;
- a modem and a communications program;
- a browser.

It is not important what kind of computer you have, though you may discover that it is an advantage to have an up-to-date model.

A modem is a small piece of equipment that translates the internal, electrical signals of the computer to sound codes. These codes can be sent over an ordinary telephone line. In some places, a computer can be connected to the Internet and other networks through cable television networks. Cable modems use the same lines that transmit cable television.

A browser is a software program, like Netscape Navigator or Microsoft Internet Explorer.

There are also ISDN and ASDL modems. Sometimes these are called terminal adapters to differentiate them from the traditional modem.

What speed of modem do you need?

Speed is measured in many ways. One method is to use baud. Another is to use characters per second (cps) or bits per second (bps).

Bps is a measure of how many data bits are transferred over a modem in one second. The relationship between baud and bits per second is complex, and often mistreated. Bits per second is undeniable.

We can estimate the number of characters per second by dividing the number of bps by ten. For example, 56,000 bps is roughly 5,600 cps.

You will find that the majority of new computers today have 56k modems pre-installed. They will also have either Microsoft Internet Explorer or Netscape Communicator pre-installed to use as your communication program.

V.90 56 Kbits/sec receives up to 56,000 bits/s over ordinary telephone lines. The faster the modem and the more modern your computer, the more marked the improvement on your browsing and downloading times will be.

Internet Service Provider (ISP)

Your on/off switch to the eWorld

Think of your ISP as your eWorld on/off switch; the Internet Service Provider is the first thing we deal with when we get on the Internet and, unfortunately, it is one of the main reasons many people get frustrated with the Internet. As the eWorld grows the experience level of the average Internet user is going DOWN, while the complexity of the Internet is going UP.

Finding a reputable provider is one of the most difficult things about this business.

A critical look at Internet Service Providers

New Internet service providers (ISPs) are constantly opening up for business around the world. Most major cities have several local providers willing to bring the global Internet to your home computer, allowing you to reach out and explore the vast expanse of information and services available. Even in rural areas there are often providers that are only a local telephone call away. This mass infiltration of Internet providers into our society allows almost anybody with a computer, phone connection and modem to connect, establish a presence and reap the benefits of the eWorld.

Every Tom, Dick and Harry

Unfortunately, with the rapid growth of the eWorld, every Tom, Dick and Harry is setting up their own ISP companies, and there has been a tremendous influx of incompetent providers. These people learn just enough to struggle through the basics of Internet administration, and set up a barely workable system. These systems are often unreliable, don't provide needed services, and are prone to all sorts of problems. The vast majority of Internet service providers, probably as many as 70 per cent, are incompetent and are doing a disservice to their users.

People searching for a provider should always be extremely critical of the ability of various providers to follow through on what they claim to offer. Individuals looking for a provider for home Internet use probably don't have a need for 'top of the line' network gurus setting up the system and being on call for reliable, advanced technical support, but they do need to make sure their provider is knowledgeable enough to keep the system running, and provide smooth, consistent network access. Companies looking for access and individuals with advanced needs almost certainly need to find assurance that their provider is highly technically competent, and is well connected to the rest of the Internet.

Most people, however, have no easy way of discerning whether a provider is technically competent or not, simply because they are unaware of the criteria needed to judge their selection properly.

Similarly, most people don't have the technical background to judge Internet providers appropriately. The first thing to do is ask around, and try to find people who have had experiences with multiple providers in the area and are able to give an objective view.

What capabilities do they offer?

It is also important to learn about the capabilities of the provider's system. How fast is their connection to the Internet? This is not how fast the provider advertises your connection will be to them, but rather the total bandwidth the provider has to the Internet. Some providers will get their Internet link from the cheapest generic off-brand network providers, which are themselves connected to the Internet via several other cheap poorly maintained providers. Internet traffic from users of these providers has to make quite a few hops before it reaches the mainstream of the network. The impact of this is poor response times due to bandwidth bottlenecks, and poor reliability due to many points of potential failure.

As the eWorld progresses, bandwidth is set to become a very important issue.

The competence of the staff is perhaps the most important issue. If the staff are technically competent, chances are the previously mentioned criteria will not be an issue. If the staff are incompetent, though, users may be in for a tough time. Whenever a problem arises that the staff don't know how to handle, essential network services may be down until help is found.

If you are knowledgeable about the technical workings of the Internet, incompetents are quickly spotted. Most people, however, will have to rely on signs and careful observations before coming to a decision. The hundreds of inferior, incompetent Internet providers thrive on consumers who choose a provider without intelligently comparing the possibilities. If you are in the market for a provider, be sure to protect yourself against these unskilled providers

IBM/AT&T Global Network Services

There are many freeserve providers in the marketplace today. For just gaining entry to the eWorld they are acceptable, but if you wish to do business or rely on the eWorld in your daily life then the old saying 'you only get what you pay for' does come into play. For many years I have used IBM as my ISP and can honestly say I have never experienced any problems with their service. No engaged tones and never a break in service, which can be very frustrating if you are trying to achieve something in a hurry. I can also use their 'travelling user' service in over 50 countries in the world. IBM has just sold their Global Network to AT&T for $5 billion. The IBM network was truly superb and I am assured it will get even better with AT&T's telecommunications expertise. From the CD at the back of this book you will be able to install the AT & T Business Internet Services diallers. Try it and I am sure you will not be disappointed.

Selecting an ISP

When selecting an ISP always consider the following: speed of access, reliability, technical support, Web hosting and, if you travel a lot, 'travelling user' availability.

- **Speed of access**
  There are many alternatives becoming available to allow you to access the eWorld at speeds far greater than that of a normal modem. These new technologies are continually being developed and these services will get faster and faster. You should contact your local phone or cable company to inquire what high-speed Internet access is available in your area. Your usage will determine the access speed you require. Business users should always opt for the fastest access speed that is available to them. As competition increases, the cost is coming down at a steady rate. Always keep an eye on prices. The cost today may seem high, but in six months the same service may be 50 per cent less!
- **Reliability**
  As you start to use and rely on the eWorld, the reliability of your ISP is a major issue. You most certainly do not want a service that is frequently down, or when you try to access all you get is the engaged tone. Do a little research on the company you are thinking of connecting with. Check out the following:
  - How long has the company been in business?
  - What is their service like and can their systems cope with the increased demand, as more and more people are using the Internet?

Technical support

What hours is technical support available? Is it available at the weekends? Some ISPs offer 24-hour 7 days a week service and if you are relying on your connection, most certainly opt for this service. Also investigate the quality of the technical support. It is most frustrating when you have a problem and someone is being abrupt and rude with you through no fault of your own.

Web hosting

Does your ISP offer any Web hosting services? Some people use one company for email and Web access and another company for hosting their Web site. It could be more convenient for you if you used one company for all your eWorld services. The decision will be up to you, but to assist you in considering all the options to satisfy your own objectives, do bear in mind that we are now seeing emerging e-commerce service providers; their services are detailed in Chapter 6. I believe this service is the no-risk option for anyone considering a Web site. The following checklist will give you a sound understanding on how to evaluate a company for purely Web site hosting:

- **Backup** This is most important, as you can imagine if you have ever lost data on a computer. You must have a duplicate copy of your Web site in case of any malfunction in their systems. It could involve hours or even days to reconstruct your Web site. Always ensure there is a backup. Your Web hosting company should be doing this and if they are negligent and any data is lost they should be responsible for any loss.
- **Cost of disk space** The normal practice is for Web hosting companies to provide a certain amount of disk space which is measured in megabytes (MB). Check their prices and enquire about the cost of upgrading as your Web site grows; you will require more and more space. The more graphics, pictures, etc. you have, the more space you will require.
- **Limits on data transfer** When someone visits your Web site, data is transferred from your Web site to the visitor's computer; this movement of information is called data transfer. The more graphics and text you have on your site, the more data you will be transferring. Also, the more visitors you have, the greater your data transfer. Enquire if there is any limit and, if there is, what are the charges? The majority of Web hosting companies offer various packages that include varying levels of data transfer. They should be in a position to offer you a suitable package, but ensure that you can upgrade to another package if you find you are constantly exceeding your limits.
- **Design services** Enquire if any design assistance is included in their price. If not, ascertain what their charges will be.
- **Access to log files** A log file is a traffic report on the activity of your Web site. These reports will give you an assortment of valuable information on what the most popular pages on your Web site are, how many hits (visitors) your pages are receiving, where your visitors are coming from and at what time are they visiting. This information will help you evaluate the effectiveness of your Web site. If your Web site is a commercial site, this information will give you insight into

the viability of any advertising campaigns you are running. Enquire if your Web hosting company can provide you with this detailed traffic report.

- **Restrictions on updating your site** This is a very important question. Are you able to update your own Web site? There are some companies that only allow updates by submitting the updates to the hosting company, which then updates the site for a fee. I strongly recommend you to avoid these companies. In Chapter 6 you will realize the advantages of using an e-commerce service provider as opposed to tolerating this constraint that can be placed on you. The information you may wish to update on your site may be time-sensitive or you may even need to publish a price increase, and you could face lengthy delays in getting your information online.
- **Secure credit card authentication** Does the Web hosting company provide secure credit card authentication? You may wish to sell online and need this facility. If they do, what costs will you incur?
- **Catalogue program** A catalogue program or shopping cart software is useful if you intend to sell from your Web site; can you use these programs on your site and, if so, what are the charges?
- **Technical support** Not every Web hosting service offers 24-hour support. No matter what time it is, you should be able to talk to someone if you have problems. It is 1.00 a.m. and you need to update a Web page and you have a problem accessing your site. Always go with a 24-hour 365 days a year service.
- **CGI scripts** These are special programs for user interaction that allow you to create forms on your Web site. These forms allow you to collect data on your visitors for mailing lists etc. They can also be used to receive feedback information. To enable you to use a GCI script to accept these forms you will require your hosting service to accept them. A lot of companies prohibit their clients from using their own scripts, for security reasons, but provide them with their own scripts themselves. They will charge you for this service.

NOTE

Because all these services could involve additional costs, always compare the pricing structures. In Chapter 6 you will see the set costs involved in using an e-commerce service provider and you will realize that this service is the one that many individuals and businesses will adopt.

Travelling user

As the cost of laptops comes down and the introduction of powerful hand-held computers develops, more and more people will start to rely on the eWorld in their daily lives. The technology to have connections from a mobile phone at the same speeds as you have from line technology is just around the corner. You should most certainly look into ISPs that can provide the option for a Travelling User or Roaming. Not all ISPs offer this service. There are many companies that offer this service. AOL at **http://www.aol.com**, CompuServe at **http://www.compuserve.com** and IBM/AT&T Global Services at **http://www.ibm.net** offer access in over 50 countries around the world.

> **Tips, tricks and trivia**
>
> **Around the world on the Web**
>
> Travel.org is a directory of links to sites with a variety of useful information for travellers. Although the site doesn't offer a search engine, it's organized well enough to make locating information fairly easy. From the site's index page, you can click on a continent to begin browsing for travel links to your destination region or city. You find links to tourist bureaus, special attractions and regional guides from Excite and Yahoo! Or you can click the lodging, airlines or travel agents links to find transportation and accommodation for your trip.
>
> **http://www.travel.org**

What If I have to move?

It's not the end of the world. The eWorld is designed for mobility. You take with you your experience, your data and your software tools.

What you leave behind is your address of abc@anywhere. The more important that is, the more care you should take in your initial selection. A good ISP will facilitate your move if you do decide to jump ship and will set up an alias so your email gets forwarded automatically.

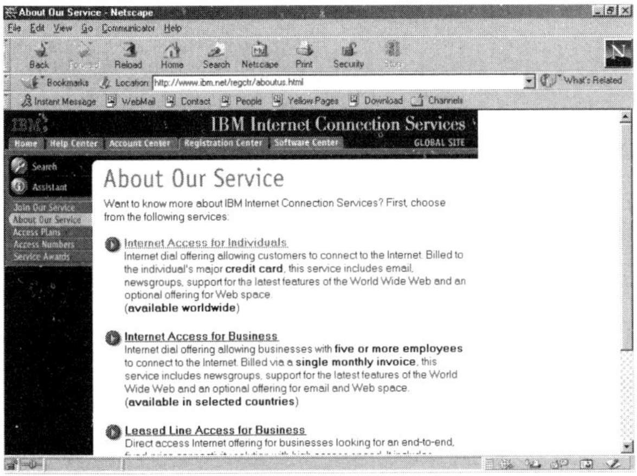

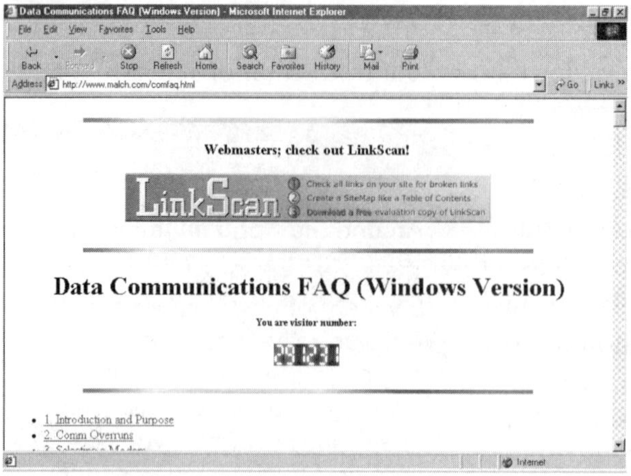

Try to keep a fairly up-to-date address book if you're thinking of a move so that you can send out messages about your move.

Modems

Internal modems have some advantages, especially speed, but they are a little trickier to install. If you need to install your own, and have no technical friends, then the best online guide I have found is at Malcolm Hoar's web site, **http://www.malch.com/comfaq.html**, but yes, you do need to be connected to get it! Another good general source is Yahoo, at **http://www.yahoo.com/Computers/Hardware/Peripherals/Modems/**. If you have a friend that can't get connected, you may want to review these or print them out as tutorials.

Remember that this is almost always the hardest part, getting physically connected. After that, it's all easy and exciting.

A brief history of the Internet

Most summaries of the development of the Internet make the same four somewhat puzzling points: war, anarchy, standards, and cooperation.

War

The 'war' point apportions the role of the American Military in funding ARPANET, a project of the US Department of Defense Advanced

Research Projects Agency (DARPA). Although initial planning started earlier, the generally accepted birth of ARPANET was in 1969, which makes the Internet a little more than 30 years old.

The key purpose of ARPANET was to study ways in which communications over networks could be protected from the dangers of attack. The result of this was a very powerful and surplus network model, without predetermined routing, so that small bundles of information could be sent by whatever routes were functioning and be reassembled as they arrived.

Anarchy

There were some very large firms trying to secure the network market in the 1970s and 80s with their large and proprietary models, but the eWorld just kept growing and growing since it was so easy to connect to and to expand. Some say this is anarchy, since there's no controlling body 'answerable' to one and all who might complain. And, in fact, anarchist group X in Germany could build a network and connect to anarchist group Y in Italy, sending their messages in encrypted form with nobody the wiser.

Nonetheless, most of the traffic on the Internet is very ordinary and definitely non-revolutionary. Almost all of what goes on could also go on via regular mail or fax or the telephone. And, if you have doubts about the degree of anarchy/conformity, an interesting document is at **http://ds.internic.net/rfc/rfc1391.txt** which is a guide to new members of the IETF (Internet Engineering Task Force) which reports to the IAB which is appointed by the ISOC at **http://www.isoc.org**.

The Internet Society is a non-profit, non-governmental, international, professional membership organization. It focuses on standards, education and policy issues. Its more than 150 organizations and 6,000 individual members' worldwide represent a veritable who's who of the Internet community. You could be a member, too.

Standards

The key to the success of the Internet has been the openness of its standards rather than the anarchistic tendencies of its supporters. In order to connect thousands of computers from hundreds of manufacturers in dozens of countries there has to be a great deal of conformity to standards.

These standards are known as RFCs, Request for Comments. Some are much more important than others, but all share the same format. They are almost all available to the public and anyone is entitled to comment on them while they are under development and to prepare code to implement them. To learn more about RFCs visit **http://www.cis.ohio-state.edu/hypertext/information/rfc.html**. There is a lot of detailed information at this site. What is most confusing is that some RFCs serve the role of standards and some are just notes or failed drafts, which nobody has commented on or implemented. To reduce confusion somewhat, those RFCs which are standards are now designated as STD while the others are FYI (for your information).

Three concepts from all these documents are key. Each computer on the Internet has a distinct number for its address. There is no anarchy allowed here, since no two machines may have the same number although any machine may have a number of names.

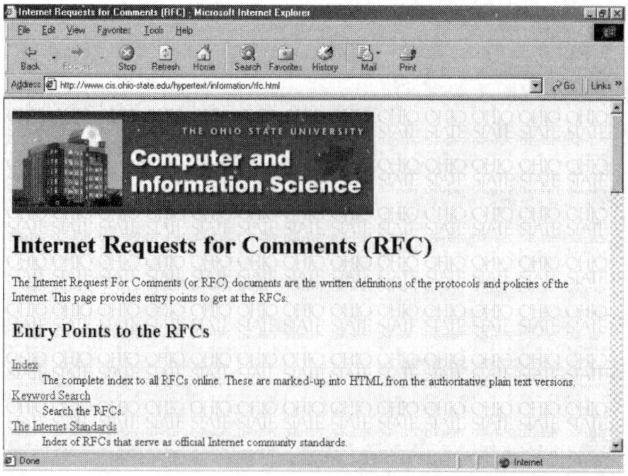

Secondly, communications transmitted on the Internet are broken into packets, each of which is considered an independent entity. These packets can then be individually routed from network to network until they reach their destination. On arrival, they are reassembled and presented to the user or computer process.

Technically, the network consists of a number of layers, from the physical up to the application level. Each layer follows its own standards and thus the hardware of many manufacturers may be involved in any single transmission, but the developers and users can safely ignore all of these brand names and rely on the existence of the standards.

Cooperation

To a large extent, the flexible and robust nature of the technical model is reflected in the organizational model. The original developers wanted a network that would continue to function even if parts of it were destroyed during an enemy attack. The current developers want to expand a model that serves the needs of users without bias; whether or not the users might come to blows if placed in the same physical room, they should be able to coexist in the eWorld.

For a more detailed history of the Internet visit Bruce Sterling's site at **http://www.swifty.com/VB/cone/view/sterling.htm**.

Should I get involved?

The simplest justification is that eWorld tools, such as email and the Web, are quite rapidly becoming indispensable everyday tools, just like the telephone, fax and photocopier. In your personal life you certainly won't fail by not using them, but you are likely to fall behind a little. In business, you will fall behind a great deal.

Eventually, your goal should be to become experienced enough that you can adapt quickly to these new methods of organizing and distributing information.

Only one thing is certain: you can't make an informed decision if you're not informed. The Internet is now well beyond the stage of theory and potential. It's here and it will change to some extent everything we do and how we do it.

Who is the eWorld for?

The eWorld is not just for the select few or those with a unique interest in computers. It is for everybody, you and me.

There is much to learn in the eWorld, and it is truly fascinating. Learning becomes fun and exciting. You can research your hobbies, your profession, life in other countries, other people's thoughts and feelings about everything that you care to mention. Often, you will find summaries about people's experiences, and data that is difficult to get by any other means.

The eWorld gives teachers and students a more stimulating learning environment. You can take a degree while sitting in front of your computer at home. You can join online seminars organized by educational institutes. You can even study at night, when the rest of your family is watching television.

The eWorld lets us communicate with people in other countries at a very low cost. Write a message and send it to someone who has an email address and it will arrive in his/her 'mailbox' within minutes. You can communicate with anyone, anywhere in the world within minutes.

> **Tips, tricks and trivia**
>
> **The Voyeur's search engine**
>
> I am not actually talking about voyeurs in an X-rated sense. Instead, WebCam Central helps you find Web cams covering a range of topics, many of them educational. You can watch elephants in Africa, riders in a taxi cab, or even the ships passing through the Panama Canal. You can browse sites by category (including bridges, animals, beaches, universities, and dozens more) or location (from Antarctica to Yugoslavia).
>
> **http://www.camcentral.com**

How do I use the eWorld to my advantage?

There are millions of online databases out there. These databases are gold mines of information. They contain full-text and reference books, magazines, newspapers, radio and TV shows, reports, and much, much more. In the eWorld, you will find information about almost anything. There are hundreds of thousands of online forums where people call in to read messages and exchange information.

The businessperson sees the eWorld as a new frontier to expand their markets; they recognize it as a means to improve their sales, public relations, customer support, marketing and as a tool to gather market intelligence. In business, it pays to be one step ahead of the competition. Early warnings of customers' needs, competitors' moves, and emerging opportunities can be turned into profitable business advantages. This can reduce potential losses and help develop businesses in more profitable directions.

Tips, tricks and trivia

Internet resources from the ALA

The American Library Association (ALA) has developed ALA Resources for Parents, Teens and Kids, a terrific guide to getting the best the eWorld has to offer for these groups of people. The ALA site is searchable, but this area is mainly a collection of links to other resources. In addition to recommending excellent educational and fun sites, the ALA also helps parents find award-winning children's books. If your kids surf the Web, be sure to scroll down the Families section and click the link to The Librarian's Guide to Cyberspace for Parents and Kids, which offers online safety tips.

http://www.ala.org/parents/

No matter whether your usage of the eWorld is practical, commercial or just a pastime, the eWorld will enable you to have a more fulfilled life in this changing world we are entering.

Some people fear that language might be a problem, in particular if English is not their first language. This is not a problem, as you will learn further on in this book all about using the translation services that are available to you. There are many other languages used in the eWorld.

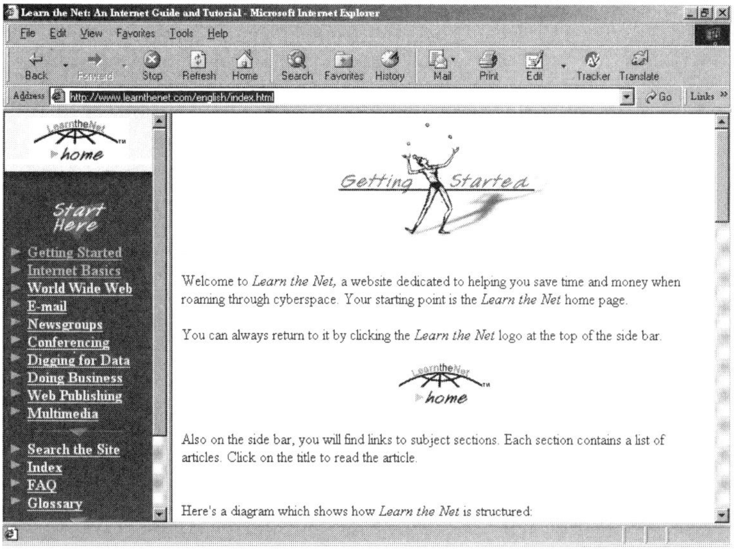

If you have any fears or doubts, think of the words of Albert Einstein: 'A person who never made a mistake, never tried anything new.'

When you first enter the eWorld, an excellent starting point is Learn the Net: **http://www.learnthenet.com/english/index.html**. This site is available in English, French, German, Italian and Spanish.

When you click on Internet Basics you will find helpful information regarding connections, modems, monitor settings, security and privacy, and Netiquette. There is also a Parents Guide and some very useful safety tips on how to protect your children from being exploited in the eWorld.

Why would you want to learn about the eWorld?

What's so remarkable about the eWorld? It seems confusing and complicated and I know nothing about computers or the Internet. Why should I even bother with it? Well, there are lots of reasons.

The eWorld is here to stay

That's right. Like it or not, the eWorld is not going away. From its humble beginnings, the eWorld has exceeded the wildest dreams of all those that even thought they imagined its potential. And what we know as the eWorld today is only the tip of the iceberg. Before long, the eWorld will assume its rightful place in our lives just as the telephone, television and automobile have done, and our grandchildren will be saying, 'You were alive before the eWorld? Gosh you are old!'

> **Tips, tricks and trivia**
>
> **Find historical texts online**
>
> Mississippi State University maintains the Historical Text Archive, a tool that can help you locate historical documents on the Internet. You can browse by region or topic, or you can use the search engine to find specific information. The Webmaster has thoughtfully included tips for using the search engine just below the box you use to enter terms.
>
> **http://www.msstate.edu/Archives/History/**

The eWorld is inexpensive

Even if you're not on an unlimited access plan with your Internet service provider, the eWorld is still the bargain of the twentieth century and will prove to be one of the greatest bargains in the twenty-first century. Imagine how much it would cost to set up an international conference call, so that you could talk to people all over the world, for as long as you wanted to. Without the eWorld the expense would be impractical.

The eWorld is convenient

The Internet is a dream come true for those of us who leave things to the last possible minute. You need to research any subject and the library's closed? Want to plan a romantic weekend for just the two of you, but don't have time to visit the travel agent? You need to shop, bank, and obtain the most competitive quote for any form of insurance? It's instant, convenient, and best of all it's available 24 hours a day.

The eWorld brings the world to you

Do you want to discover new and exciting people, places and things, but feel limited due to your work demands, school schedule, finances, family responsibilities, health, age, etc.? The eWorld is your passport to exploration. You can go to the library and check out books on the topics that interest you, and perhaps join a local club related to your interests. That course of action is certainly preferable to doing nothing. But the eWorld can bring you so much more. The eWorld can bring you an interactive experience that allows you to plan your journey, and you never really know where your journey might take you.

> **Tips, tricks and trivia**
>
> **Intel gives a little something back**
>
> While the eWorld will never replace the experience of seeing traditional art 'live', it does allow for a uniquely personal exploration of, say, the life of an artist, or of a particular social or artistic current, whose details give context and depth as to why a particular work of art is great.
>
> **http://www.artmuseum.net**
>
> This Intel-sponsored site presents exhibits from art museums the world over. Thanks to the biographical and critical information included with each exhibit, you can learn a lot here, maybe more than you can at a real museum.

The eWorld is fun

If you're brand new to the eWorld, you may be thinking there seems a lot of learning for it to be fun. Learning how to use the power and potential of the eWorld is hard work. There's a whole new language to decipher, software to learn, often-rude technical support to overcome, and the panicky feeling that you're way behind in the learning curve. But happily, that's where you're mistaken. By just reading this book you're ahead of the game. The very nature of the eWorld's open exchange between strangers seems to bring out the best in people, a camaraderie that is unsurpassed in any other environment. So relax and enjoy your exploration, and remember, you know more than most, simply by reading this.

Welcome to the eWorld

You're about to start a journey through a unique land without limits, a place that is everywhere at once, even though it exists physically only as a series of electrical impulses. You'll be joining a growing community of millions of people around the world that uses this global resource on a daily basis.

You will be able to use the eWorld to:

- stay in touch with friends, relatives and colleagues around the world, at a fraction of the cost of phone calls or even airmail;
- discuss everything from archaeology to zoology with people in several different languages;
- tap into thousands of information databases and libraries worldwide;
- gather any of thousands of documents, journals, books and computer programs;
- stay up to date with wire-service news and sports and with official weather reports;
- play live, 'real time' games with dozens of other people at once.

And you will have become the newest member of this ever-growing community. If you stay and contribute, the eWorld will be richer for it, and so will you.

Connecting to the eWorld takes something of a sense of adventure, an eagerness to learn and an ability to take a deep breath every so often. Visiting the eWorld today is a lot like journeying to a foreign country. There are so many things to see and do, but everything at first will seem so overwhelming.

When you first arrive, you won't be able to understand the road maps. You'll get lost. If you're unlucky, you may even run into some locals who'd just as soon you went back to where you came from. If this weren't enough, the entire eWorld is constantly under construction; every day, it seems like there's something new for you to try and understand.

Fortunately, most of the locals are very friendly. In fact, the eWorld has a strong tradition of helping out visitors and newcomers. Until very recently, there were few written guides for ordinary people, and the eWorld grew largely by word of mouth in which the old-timers helped the newcomers.

> **Tips, tricks and trivia**
>
> **Locate online libraries**
>
> Vanderbilt Library's Marshall Breeding maintains lib-web-cats, a resource that helps users locate Web sites for more than 4,000 libraries and online catalogues. You can search by name of the institution or by library type and location. The advanced query form lets you specify more conditions in your search, including the automation system used.
>
> **http://staffweb.library.vanderbilt.edu/breeding/libwebcats.html**

Here's where you take a deep breath. As I have said, fortunately most of the natives are actually friendly. With few written guides for ordinary people, the eWorld has grown one person at a time; if somebody helps you understand, it's almost expected you'll repay the favour some day by helping somebody else.

So when you connect, don't be afraid to ask for help. You'll be surprised at how many people will lend a hand!

As you travel in the eWorld, your computer may freeze; your screen may burst into a mass of gibberish. You may think you've just disabled a million-dollar computer somewhere, or even your own personal computer. Sooner or later, this feeling happens to all of us and most likely more than once. But the eWorld and your computer are more robust than you think, so don't worry. You can no more demolish the eWorld than you can the telephone system. If something goes wrong, try again. If nothing at all happens, you can always disconnect. If the worst comes to the worst, you can turn off your computer. Then take a deep breath. And dial right back in. Try it again. Persistence pays, never quit.

Stay and contribute. The eWorld will be richer for it, and so will you.

2

Tips for better searching

For the things we have to learn before we can do them,
We learn by doing them.

ARISTOTLE 384–322 BC

- Effective searching in the eWorld
- Solutions and the future of searching

You are now a citizen of the eWorld. As I wrote in my introduction, 'A world in which the total knowledge, information and ideas possessed by civilization can be shared and made accessible to everyone in the world on their individual computer screens by just accessing the eWorld'. I believe that in the twenty-first century in order to survive you have to learn how to learn, to develop the skill to take any problem or topic, and become accomplished with it as quickly as possible.

That's where the eWorld comes in. I'm convinced that those who learn to control its potential as a research tool will be the real success stories of the next century, particularly as the economy and the world around us become more and more complex.

There are many people who complain that they can never find what they are looking for on the Internet. But they have little right to complain. Ask them about their technique, and they'll admit they spend but a few minutes looking for something before giving up. They'll say they never read the help screens on the search engines they use in order to learn how to do a more 'targeted search'. They have never spent more than a few minutes to learn how to search effectively online and they dismiss the whole matter as a waste of time.

If learning is what many of us will do for a living in the next century, we had better take the time to learn how to learn.

Consider the eWorld as an encyclopaedia: the search engine is the index. In order to facilitate the active nature of the eWorld, search engines are constantly running software called 'robots' or 'crawlers' that read entire Web pages and index all data alphabetically, just like an encyclopaedia's index. You enter your words or phrases and the search engine will provide you with a set of 'result pages', depending on the number of successful 'hits' that your search produces. This is a very brief summary of what a search engine does. In this chapter you will grasp how to achieve far greater success when you are using search engines. Understanding their

Tips, tricks and trivia

By jove, it's Jeeves!

Ask Jeeves provides something more than most conventional search engines. Like some, Ask Jeeves can accept queries in natural language, such as 'How can I treat a sprained ankle?' But Ask Jeeves' edge is that a huge team of editors is constantly working to refine the sources that the service recommends and improve the follow-up questions that it asks to help refine your queries. Ask Jeeves also tracks the most popular questions and lets you look through them. Give Ask Jeeves a try, it might just be worth a bookmark. And parents may want to check out the highly praised Ask Jeeves for Kids service.

http://www.askjeeves.com

operation allows you to take true advantage of the inexhaustible resources of the eWorld. The information is there, but only those who know how to discover and define it will be successful in this changing world.

Effective searching in the eWorld

Looking for that perfect chalet for your ski holiday? Do you need specifications for a particular piece of equipment? Want discussion and commentary on your favorite author? Trying to find out what your competitors are up to? Seeking recent studies on planets in other solar systems? Do you need information on employment for which you might be qualified?

These, and millions of queries covering every conceivable topic, are now being posed daily to the Internet's search engines. With anywhere from 300 million to 400 million or more publicly available documents, an amount doubling every six to 12 months, the eWorld has become a vast, global reservoir of information. The only problem is, how do you find what you're looking for?

You must use a search service to find new information. Search services come in one of two main categories. Each has its place, depending on your information needs.

'Directories' use trained professionals to classify useful Web sites into a hierarchical, subject-based structure. Yahoo! is the best known and most used of these services. Directories are most useful when looking for information in clear categories, such as manufacturers of computers or listings of educational institutions. Each directory uses its own categories and means to screen useful sites and assign them to a single category.

'Search engines' work differently. AltaVista is the best known engine. They 'index' (record by word) each word within all or parts of documents. When you pose a query to a search engine, it matches your query words versus the records it has in its databases to present a listing of possible documents meeting your request. Search engines are best for searches in more difficult topic areas or for those that fall into the areas between the subject classifications used by directories. But search engines are simple, and can only give you what you ask for. You can sometimes get thousands (millions!) of documents matching a query. At best, even the biggest search engines only index one-third to a half of the Internet's public documents.

So, while 75 per cent of users quote finding information as their most important use of the eWorld, that same percentage also quote their inability to find the information they want as their biggest frustration.

Your ability to find the information you request in the eWorld is a question of how precise your queries are and how effectively you use search engines. Poor queries return poor results; good queries return great results. Contrary to the hype surrounding 'intelligent agents' and 'artificial intelligence,' the fact remains that search results are only as good as the query you pose and how you search.

> **Tips, tricks and trivia**
>
> **Wild card**
>
> In a search, a wild card is a character that you use in place of letters to indicate that you'll accept more than one possible result for that particular character. For example, to search a document for all forms of the word 'mean' ('means,' 'meant,' 'meaning,' 'meanings,' and so on), you'd search for 'mean*'. The asterisk is a wild card that indicates you'll accept any word as long as its first four letters are 'mean.' Of course, this particular search also returns the word 'meander,' which is not a form of the word 'mean.' That is the downside of wild cards.

Internet searchers, perhaps including you, tend to use only one or two words in a query. Also, there are very effective ways to 'structure' a query and use special operators to target the results you seek. Omit these techniques and you will spend endless hours looking at useless documents that do not contain the information you want. Or you will give up in frustration after search–click–download–reviewing long lists of documents before you find what you want.

All of us need information. But few of us have studied information or library science, and not everyone has used search services or Internet search engines sufficiently to learn all of the nuances. But, even if you're experienced in these areas, you might find some benefit from glancing through the following topics.

If you do take the time to work through this following material, I guarantee you'll reap tremendous dividends in faster and more accurate results. And, you will be on your way to earning the title of an eWorld 'Power Searcher.'

Searchers' frustrations

Many have likened the eWorld to a huge, global library. While true in some aspects, it has some unusual differences. There is no central 'card catalogue'; the eWorld's growth is outpacing the ability of humans or technology to keep up with it; its sheer size is unknown and perhaps unfathomable; and its content is of uneven quality. One of the challenges of the eWorld is to make its benefit available to the millions of new users who have had no formal training or experience in query formulation or search strategies.

Search engine and directory basics

The major search services in the eWorld are essential starting points for users seeking information. As such, they routinely are some of the most visited locations on the Web.

Search services can be divided into two groups, commercial and non-commercial. Commercial search services go to the effort to catalogue information on the Internet to attract attention and advertising revenues. Non-commercial services exist for many different reasons.

There are more than 1,000 search services presently in the eWorld. There are a dozen or more big, major Internet search services:

- **AltaVista http://www.altavista.com**
- **Excite http://www.excite.com**
- **LookSmart http://www.looksmart.com**
- **HotBot http://www.hotbot.com**
- **Infoseek http://www.infoseek.com**
- **Lycos http://www.lycos.com**
- **Magellan http://www.mckinley.com**
- **Mining Company http://home.miningco.com**
- **AOL http://www.aol.com**
- **Northern Light http://www.nlsearch.com**
- **WebCrawler http://www.WebCrawler.com**
- **Yahoo! http://www.yahoo.com**

There are also 'metasearch' services that provide a central access point to several of these services.

- **Metacrawler http://www.metacrawler.com**
- **Inference FIND http://www.inference.com/infind/**
- **SavvySearch http://guaraldi.cs.colostate.edu:2000**

Search engines use 'spiders' or 'robots' to go out and retrieve individual Web pages or documents, either because they've found them themselves, or because the Web site has asked to be listed. Search engines tend to 'index' (record by word) all of the terms on a given Web document. Or they may index all of the terms within the first few sentences, the Web site title, or the document's metatags. Owing to the ever-changing nature of the eWorld the services must re-sample their sites on a periodic basis. Some of these services re-sample their sites on a weekly or less frequent basis.

Precision, recall and coverage are limiting factors for most search engines. Precision measures how well the retrieved documents match the query; recall measures what fraction of relevant documents are retrieved. Coverage refers to what percentage of the potential nature of relevant documents is catalogued by the engine. Precision is a problem because of the high occurrence of false positives. That is why you get so many seemingly irrelevant documents in your searches. This is due to imprecision in the query, indexing mistakes by the engine, and keywords entered by the Web document developer that do not actually appear in the document. Coverage is a problem for all engines, with the largest ones only covering at most one-third to one-half of publicly available documents.

Search directories operate on a different principle. They require people to view the individual Web site and determine its placement into a subject classification scheme or taxonomy. Once done, certain keywords associated with those sites can be used for searching the directory's data banks to find Web sites of interest.

Tips, tricks and trivia

Dogpile is a metasearch service that submits – and translates, if necessary, your search to 25 search engines. The results are divided into sections by engine. It's interesting to see how search engines vary in their performances on some queries. For example, when you submit a query to the 25 search engines through Dogpile's metasearch and then view the results, you may notice that some services return 10 or more citations, while another returns 0 – all for the same search. The number of results that show up depends on the number and types of pages indexed by the services. The number of sites that show up can also vary depending on the operators you use in your query (whether you use the operators AND or NOT or quote marks or plus signs, for example) because different search engines understand and use different operators.

Dogpile's Help with Syntax section is a great resource when you're having trouble getting the results you want. And if you strongly favour some search engines over others, click the Custom Search option to select the order in which you want your results presented. Dogpile also has options to search FTP sites, yellow pages, white pages, maps, stock quotes, weather, and the Usenet through the same interface.

http://www.dogpile.com

For searches that are easily classified, such as vendors of bicycles, the search directories tend to provide the most consistent and well-clustered results. Yahoo!, for example, has about 1,400 classifications excluding what it calls 'Regional' ones, which are a duplication of the major classification areas by geographic region. When a given classification level reaches 1,000 site listings or so, the Yahoo! staff split the category into one or more subcategories. If a given topic area has not been specifically classified by the search directories, finding related information on that topic is made more difficult. Another disadvantage of directories is their lack of coverage because of the cost and time in individually assigning sites to categories.

Most searches of a research nature tend to be better served by the search engines. That is because there is no classification structure behind the listings; only whether the keywords requested appear in that search engine's index database or not.

The flexibility of indexing every word to give users complete search control, such as provided by AltaVista, is now creating a different kind of problem: too many results. In the worst cases, submitting broad query terms to such engines can result in literally millions of potential documents identified. Since the user is limited to viewing potential sites one by one, clearly too many results can be a greater problem than too few.

Increasingly, the growth of the eWorld is causing the specialization of search services. Lawyers, astronomers or investors, for example, may want information specifically focused on their interest topics. By cataloguing information in only those areas, users interested in those topics are better able to keep their search results limited. Such specialization can also lead to more targeted advertising on those search service sites. Again, though, like the directories, such specialization can limit search results to the boundaries chosen by the service, which may or may not conform to the boundaries sought by the user.

Tips, tricks and trivia

Dealing with professionals

Who would know more about selecting the best resources in the eWorld than a librarian? The Librarians' Index to the Internet is maintained by Carol Leita through the California State Library system. The team of librarians who contribute to the site not only point you to excellent resources on a huge variety of topics, but they also review the sites and sign them with their initials. Whatever you're interested in, be it arts, law or science, you're bound to find great reference sites for your searches.

http://sunsite.berkeley.edu/InternetIndex/

Search services rank documents

A Web page, or document, can contain various kinds of content, some of which is not shown when you view the document in your browser.

- **Title** – an embedded description provided by the document designer; viewable in the titlebar (it is also used as the description of a newly created bookmark by most browsers).
- **Description** – a type of metatag which provides a short, summary description provided by the document designer; not viewable on the actual page; this is frequently the description of the document shown on the documents listings by the search engines that use metatags.
- **Keywords** – another type of metatag consisting of a listing of keywords that the document designer wants search engines to use to identify the document. These too are not viewable on the actual page.
- **Body** – the actual, viewable content of the document.

Search engines may index all or some of these content fields when storing a document on their databases. Over time, engines have tended to index fewer words and fields. Then, using proprietary algorithms that differ substantially from engine to engine, when a search query is evaluated by that engine its listing of document results is presented in order of 'relevance'. Because of these differences in degree of indexing and algorithms used, the same document listed on different search engines can appear at a much higher or lower ranking than on other engines.

Though not hard and fast, and highly variable from engine to engine, four factors tend to influence greatly the ranking of a document in a given query:

- **Order a keyword term appears** – keyword terms that appear sooner in the document's listing or index tend to be ranked higher.
- **Frequency of keyword term** – keywords that appear multiple times in a document's index tend to be ranked higher.
- **Occurrence of keyword in the title** – keywords that appear in the document's title, or perhaps metatag description or keyword description fields, can be given more weight than terms only in the document body.
- **Rare, or less frequent, keywords** – rare or unusual keywords that do not appear as frequently in the engine's index database are often ranked more highly than common terms or keywords.

Some engines, notably Excite, attempt to 'infer' what you mean in a query based on its context. Thus, the meaning of **heart** can differ if the context of your search is cardiac disease as opposed to Valentine's Day. The methods by which these inferences are made are statistically based on the occurrence of some words in conjunction with others. Though useful for simpler queries, such inference techniques tend to break down when the subject of the query or its modifiers do not fit expected query relationships. For commonly searched topics, this is generally not a problem; for difficult queries, it is a disadvantage to standard full-text indexing.

Cottage industries have emerged to help Web site developers place themselves higher in the search engines' listings; it is clearly more valuable to be within the first few listings sent to a user than to be buried hundreds, or thousands, of documents lower. A constant battle is being waged between the engines and those desiring high listings from adjusting the system to 'unfair' advantage.

Crude, early attempts to 'spam' search engines to get higher listings included adding hidden terms like 'sex' that were searched frequently but not the real subject of the document. Other techniques were to use certain keywords repeatedly, such as 'cars cars cars cars cars' to get a higher frequency rating. Another was to cram the page with high-interest terms using the same colour as the overall Web page, thus 'hiding' the added keywords. The leading search engines have caught on to these and now have automated ways to prevent the worst of these spamming techniques.

More subtle techniques, however, are hard to prevent. For example, a listing for ski resorts in France could also add hidden tags for 'Caribbean' or 'beach resort' knowing that wealthy Caribbean travellers may also be looking to take ski holidays. If you as the searcher asked for Caribbean vacations you may wonder why you've got a listing for French ski resorts. It is because of such techniques that you can sometimes get document listings from a search that seems to have nothing to do with your query.

So, differences in how search services rank documents, how developers themselves choose to characterize their Web documents, and simple errors in how computers process and index these pages can all lead to highly variable ranking results from different search services.

Characteristics of searchers

Professional information searchers do not have a single style. There is no 'correct' way to search on the Internet. Search styles have been described as ranging from 'ants', the carefully planned, methodical search hoping to get exact results on the first try, to 'grasshoppers' jumping from one topic to another, refining results as more is learned. Only you can determine what is your style.

There is only one important measure of a successful search: getting the results you desire. And within that context, there is only one important basis for judging whether one search strategy or another is superior: whether those results are obtained faster.

Surfing and browsing in the eWorld are seductive. One begins with an objective in mind, finds new sources of interest, and hours later can wonder where the time has gone. It is often difficult to discover whether the original search interest was obtained, or whether the whole process was productive or not.

> **Tips, tricks and trivia**
>
> **Finding sites quickly with Navigator 4.5**
>
> Netscape Navigator 4.5 can make finding an organization's Web site easier than ever. When you type a company name into the Netsite box, Navigator looks for a matching URL. For example, if you type 'Compaq' in the Netsite box and press Enter, Netscape automatically takes you to:
>
> **http://www.compaq.com**

Recently, information professionals using the Web to do searches in comparison with traditional online search found it took on average 2.4 minutes per document to get acceptable results.
The actual 'average' search time does not really matter. The point is that certain aspects of searching can add delays to getting desired results and increase frustration:

- No matter how precise or accurate the query, a large percentage of results returned by search services will not be what you're looking for.
- Actual search time in getting listings from services is relatively fast; the one-by-one document download and review is the most time-consuming part of the process.
- Larger listings of documents from the services require more evaluation time.
- Often too little time is spent on search and query formulation; any improvements you can make toward more precise and accurate queries will lead to fewer documents to review and faster overall times to the results you want.

The conclusion is that time is well spent in understanding how to pose a proper query and how to take advantage of the way that search services work.

Keywords – the essence of the search

Despite all the gobbledygook about things like 'Boolean' and query operators, the most difficult and fundamental aspect of a search is the keywords used in your query.

A search is essentially looking for information about a topic.

Query concepts: what, where, when and how

Mastering the concepts behind a search is not as complicated as it may seem at first. The first few searches are perhaps difficult, but as your technique improves your searches will become faster. Like riding a bike for the first time, it does take some practice.

One of the biggest mistakes you can make in preparing a query is not providing enough keywords. Statistics show that most users submit 1.5 keywords per query. This number is insufficient to accurately find the information you are seeking. A primary task in query making is for you to identify a sufficient number of appropriate keywords.

If you are new to searching, the first task when making a search is writing down what information you are looking for. Before doing a search, it is important to define your subject matter as completely as possible. After experience is gained, you can skip writing things down and plunge right into it.

Formulating a query is similar to solving a mystery. Some pieces of information are available, but if sufficient information were available the answer would be known and there would be no need to seek more. This is the nature of a query: missing information. It is up to you, the searcher, to define your query sufficiently to discover that missing information and solve the mystery.

Focus on nouns and objects

Almost without exception, the central keywords in your queries will be nouns. Though sometimes adverbs and adjectives can help refine your search, the key point is a noun, or series of nouns. Why is this?

The most precise terms we have in language are for tangible, concrete 'things' or objects. Actions and modifiers are very diverse, easily substitutable, and generally not universally applied in any given description. For example, take the concept of 'fast'. A thesaurus will give 75 or more different words for fast.

Boolean basics

Despite its intimidating name, Boolean search techniques are really quite simple to learn and can add tremendous effectiveness to your searching.

Boolean searching draws its name from George Boole, a mathematician and logician from the nineteenth century. He developed Boolean algebra, which is the basis for this form of structured search technique. Boolean algebra is also of prime importance to the design of modern computers.

Most information in the eWorld is unstructured. Boolean techniques, while not supported by all Internet search services, provide a way for you to bring structure to this unstructured environment.

Without Boolean techniques, you are stuck with doing a lot of free-text searching, looking for documents that contain words you think will be in the document you are seeking. Sheer document volume makes free-text searching difficult and most likely to fail. Boolean techniques give you the power to narrow your search to a reasonable number of potentially useful documents, thereby increasing your likelihood of success.

Boolean overview

Boolean logic is used to construct search statements using logical **operators** and specified **syntax.** These are combined into **Boolean expressions,** which always are either true or false when evaluated.

Operators are the rules or specific instructions used for composing a query in a keyword search. While each search engine has its own operators, some operators are used in common by a number of search engines. The following are among the most used operators.

Boolean

Employs AND, OR, NEAR and NOT to connect words and phrases [i.e. terms] in the query where:

AND requires that both terms are present somewhere within the document being sought.

NEAR requires that one term must be found within a specified number of words.

OR requires that at least one term is present.

NOT excludes a term from a query.

When using these operators, remember to capitalize them as shown above.

Query example: Clinton AND Starr

Plus/minus signs

Employs [+] before a term to retrieve only the documents containing that term. It is similar to the Boolean AND.
Employs [-] before a term to exclude that term from the search. It is similar to the Boolean NOT.

Do not leave a space between the operator and the term that follows.

Query example: Clinton+Starr

Quote marks

Indicate that the words within the quote marks are to be treated as an exact phrase, or reasonably close to it. It is similar to the Boolean NEAR.

Query example: "Clinton and Starr"

Stemming [truncation]

The ability of a search to include the stem or the main part of a word [e.g. sing is the stem for sings, singer, singing and singalong]. Stemming can be automatic, or it may require use of a wild card, symbolized by an asterisk [*] to initiate.

Query Example: sing*

Case sensitive

Adjacent capitalized words are treated as a single proper name, e.g. Clinton. Commas separate proper names from each other.

Query example: Clinton, Starr

Operators may seem complex to the beginner at first, but they become familiar with use. For more detailed information on the use of operators, go to the Help sections of the search engines. AltaVista provides the most detailed operator help section.

■ Summary AND conclusion

The + and the – keys: these two characters on your keyboard can do so much when you are searching. Let us take, for example, keying in the word Clinton. The search engine results would give you what is called information overload, millions of pages of information on Clinton. If you want to find out about Clinton and Starr, you enter Clinton+Starr and you get pages relevant to these two names. Now you enter Clinton+Starr-Lewinsky and it really is surprising how few pages appear.

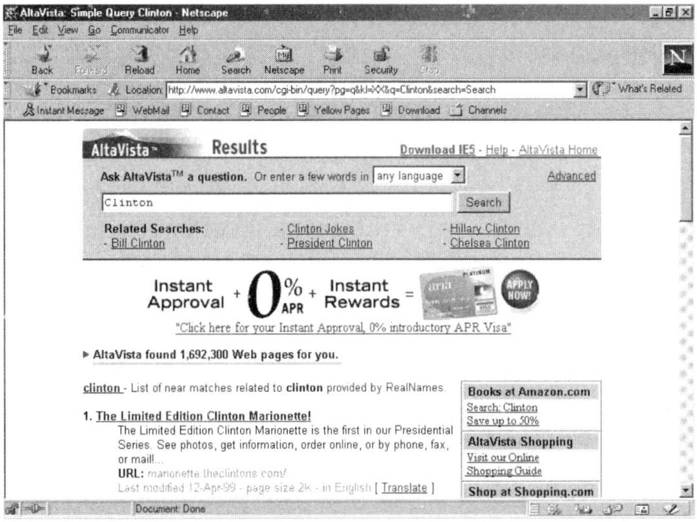

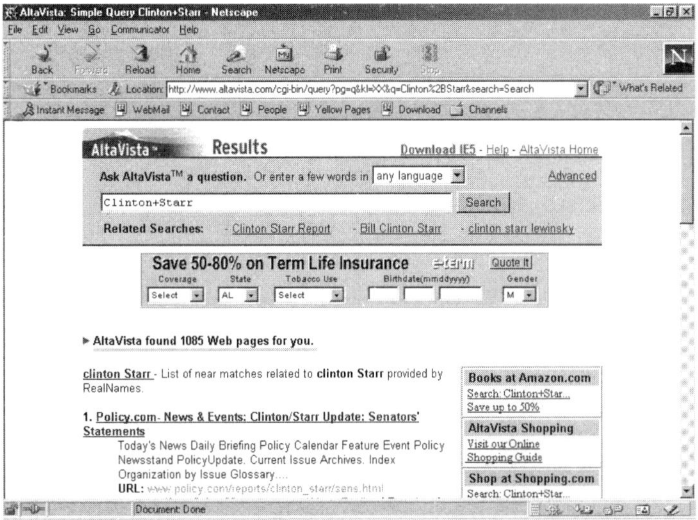

Tips, tricks and trivia

Exploring AltaVista's advanced options

If you're frustrated by the number of irrelevant hits returned by an AltaVista search, try clicking the Advanced link on the right side of the search box. You can easily set date ranges by filling in the boxes on the right. You also have plenty of room in the search box to enter Boolean operators such as AND, OR, NOT, and NEAR. (Note, however, that the + and - operators don't work in the Advanced search.) NEAR can be especially handy because it tells AltaVista to look for your search terms occurring within ten words of each other.

http://www.altavista.com

In our first search, using just the word Clinton, we have 1,692,300 Web pages found. This is information overload. In our second search, using Clinton+Starr, we have 1,085 web pages found for us. In our third search, using the words Clinton+ Starr-Lewinsky, we find we have 39 Web pages found.

The + and - characters will be all that 90 per cent of search engine users will require, but it really is worthwhile to spend time on the search engine's help screens. Understanding their operation allows you to take true advantage of the inexhaustible resources of the Internet. The information is there, but only those who know how to discover and define it will be successful in this changing world.

TIP

+ and – should be your most frequently used operators.

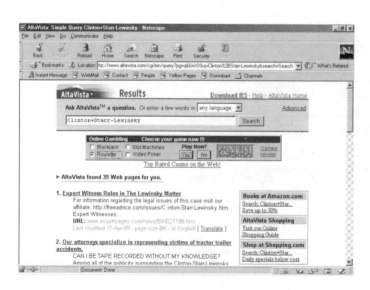

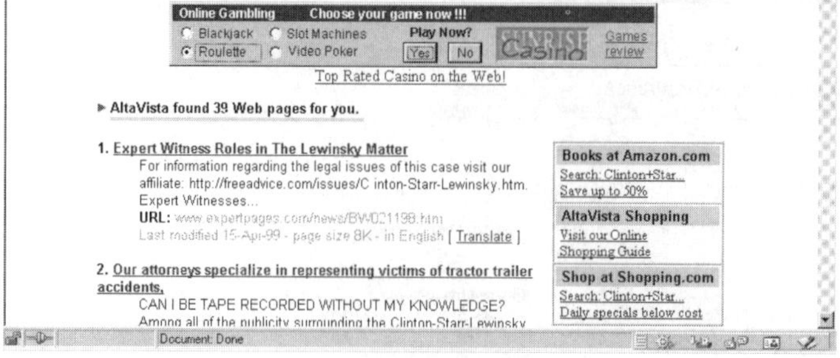

Pitfalls to avoid

Here we describe many of the common mistakes made by eWorld searchers. Some are within the control of you, the searcher. Others are due to the rapid growth of the eWorld and the limitations to the search services of the eWorld.

Avoid misspellings

You know, it's so obvious that it is most often not mentioned: searchers in the eWorld are dreadful spellers! In your query and searching, if you misspell your keywords, you are immediately penalized. Web developers also misspell words in their own documents. If the Web developer misspells a word, it is entered as such on the database. If the searcher issues a misspelled query term, that is what is searched for. So, recognize that computers are stupid and guard against these mistakes yourself. Sloppy entry of query terms will cost you time and cause you frustration.

Unnecessary terms

Think of constructing a query as being in a card game. You have only so many cards (terms) to play to get a winning hand or successful results from your query. Using unnecessary terms loses one of your cards, and lowers your prospects for success.

TIP

Limit your keywords to six. Check to make sure you're not duplicating 'levels' in your terms.

You can generally spot unnecessary terms by asking the question, 'Is this term already covered by another term?' If the answer is yes, pick the term at the appropriate level and discard the other one.

Ignored terms

There is an emerging class of words that are becoming like stop list terms – often ignored by the search engines because of their prevalence in the eWorld. Examples include: computer, Internet, Web, sex and software. These words, and others like them, are not always ignored. It appears that at high-demand search times some of the engines choose to ignore processing them.

Should you experience such a response, one solution is to make sure that you place these words in quotes or make them part of a phrase. The ignored behaviour appears to be limited to use of such terms as individual words in queries, and then only at some times of the day.

Alternative spellings

English has become the standard language for Internet communications. However, some of the largest user domains on the Internet come from a background of traditional public school (UK) English. There are perhaps 50 countries around the world whose English is traditional, and not based on usage and spelling as in the United States, and all the major search engines are based in the United States.

As a searcher, you should be aware that many common terms – colour/color, organise/organize, behaviour/behavior – might differ in spelling between these two forms.

Too many terms, synonyms

There are two overall guidelines for the size of your queries:

- Limit the key concepts (e.g. Boolean expressions) to three or fewer; on rare occasions this guideline can increase to four.
- Keep the actual terms in your queries to no more than six.

These guidelines are not just an effort to refine query construction, content and syntax. They are given by experience that indicates that at high numbers of term counts, search engine behaviour can become erratic and unpredictable.

It is difficult to judge the latter point, since each search service closely guards how it indexes, retrieves and scores queries. Many are competing to gain advantage in where they are listed on search engine results; and there are real technical demands to serve all search requesters in real time at peak demand periods.

The fact that search service rules are today unclear is unlikely to change any time soon. As users, we are left with observing engine behaviour, reading the public help documents, and gleaning insights from others in the eWorld who have been looking at these problems. This is not really an attractive state of affairs. Without any definitive and public disclosure by the search services of how they handle these matters, there is a lot of room for misinterpretation and misunderstanding.

Such disclosure is unlikely to happen in the foreseeable future. Searching has become big business in the eWorld, and as the starting point for most users and most searches, will likely remain so. In this competitive, market-share- and revenue-driven environment, the incentives for major search services to disclose more than they already are doing is minimal, and will possibly even diminish.

Finding people

Here are some tips on finding people on the Internet:

- Use speciality engines.
- Use search services that support mixed upper and lower case.
- Be careful, first names are often not reliable; many individuals use initials or diminutive forms for first names ('Joe' vs. 'Joseph' vs. 'J.'), or may be cited by others in different ways.

Tips, tricks and trivia

Cher's official Web site, supervised if not created by the star herself, is surprisingly low key. Here you can see lots of pictures, many of which she obviously captioned herself and many of which feature her departed ex-mate, Sonny; listen to some of her music, including the recent hit 'Believe', but none of the old hits, such as 'Half Breed' or 'Gypsies, Tramps and Thieves'; watch a lengthy trailer for her latest movie, *Tea with Mussolini*; or read what turns out to be a very interesting biography. It is a well laid out Web site.

http://www.cher.com

Finding email addresses

One of the most common requirements for eWorld users wanting to correspond with others is for information on email addresses. Here are some suggestions for finding the email address of a would-be correspondent:

1. Ask them! Use the phone if necessary.
2. Ask them to email you first, then use your email program's 'Reply' function. Then just add the email address to your address book.

Tips, tricks and trivia

Sounding off to world leaders

I am not recommending that you create any international incidents by writing letters to world leaders. But I do know where you can find mailing and email addresses for most prime ministers and presidents, as well as the heads of environmental and foreign affairs ministries. You can even find out how to write to some monarchs. The free site, called Address Directory for the Politicians of the World, is maintained by Donald Vermithrax. So if you'd like to send a fan letter to King Albert II of Belgium or an invitation to Fiji's President Ratu Kamisese, be sure to bookmark this site.

http://www.trytel.com/~aberdeen/index.html

3. Search an online directory service. Here are some which have substantial databases of names:

   - *Four11*
     http://www.four11.com/
     More than seven million unique email addresses.
   - *Whowhere*
     http://www.whowhere.com/
     Online white pages service comprising several databases including email addresses, US phone numbers and postal addresses, home pages, Internet Phone directory, company Web sites, and others.
   - *Internet Address Finder*
     http://www.iaf.net/
     Searching by personal name or domain name.
     Available in English, Dutch, French, German, Italian, Portuguese.
   - *Bigfoot*
     http://www.bigfoot.com/
     If a search is unsuccessful, Bigfoot will provide a list of suggestions. Also offers tips on searching.
     Available in English, German, French, Italian, Spanish, Japanese.
   - *World Email Directory*
     http://worldemail.com/
     Provides access to millions of email, business and phone addresses worldwide. Uses WebCrawler to collect data and provides a powerful search engine with flexible search capability.
   - *X.500 directory services*
     X.500 is a standard for directory services, enabling a user with an X.500 client to access the global net of X.500 directory services via any X.500 server. You can search for a person's contact details within an organization or country or, if you have no information to start with, conduct a global search. X.500 directories of staff details are maintained by many organizations throughout the world, and national directories are available in many countries such as Austria, Belgium, Denmark, Germany, Hungary, Italy, Luxembourg, the Netherlands, Norway, Poland, Slovakia, Slovenia, Spain, Sweden, Switzerland, the UK and the USA.
     See this page from Dante for details:
     http://www.dante.net/np/pdi.html

A UK Web gateway, the Worldwide Directory Service, is at: **http://www.cse.bris.ac.uk/comms/ccrjh/search-form-world.html.** In the US, the InterNIC also provides a country listing for X.500 searching: **http://ds1.internic.net:8888/**

Finding places

Here are some tips for finding information about geographical locations on the Internet:

- Try limiting your searches by country domains.
- Use regional Yahoos.
- Used mixed case when searching for proper place names.
- Consider using the geo-graphic-speciality search engines.
- Try using the location options in HotBot's SuperSearch mode.

> **Tips, tricks and trivia**
>
> **How Far Is It?**
>
> How Far Is It? is a bookmark-worthy site. Enter two cities – ANY TWO CITIES – and this site returns 1) the distance between the cities, as the crow flies; 2) the direction you need to go to head from the first city to the second; 3) maps and driving directions! It's easy, fast and comprehensive.
>
> **http://www.indo.com/distance/**

Finding documents

Here are some tips for finding documents:

- There is a tremendous storehouse of information not actually catalogued by search engines because the documents are not distributed as Web pages. When looking for such information, consider using meaningful document title names plus common extensions for such files (e.g. .PDF for Adobe Acrobat, .DOC for MS Word documents, etc.) in your queries.
- Use the Anchor option in AltaVista, matched with an appropriate query dealing with your topic of interest.

Summary

1. Before you begin, learn how to assemble your topic and formulate your query.
2. As a first choice, use a metasearcher using phrases and a relatively simple query formulation.

3. As a second choice, pick the specific search engines with the specific features that best support your current query.
4. As a third choice, consider directories that might contain references to comprehensive sites in your specific topic area.
5. As a fourth choice, consider specialized search engines.
6. Finally, use major search engines with full-Boolean logic applying the rules and lessons we've offered in this tutorial.

> **Tips, tricks and trivia**
>
> **Power search on Deja.com**
>
> Deja.com (formerly DejaNews) offers a Power Search feature. Instead of navigating through the site to find the area you want to search, you can use one form to enter your search terms and choose the type of information you want to find: discussions, ratings, communities, or Deja classic. The form also lets you choose the scope of the archive you want to search, and you can even specify particular forums or authors.
>
> **http://www.deja.com/home_ps.shtml**

As you gain experience, you can begin cutting out the middle steps. By the time you're doing serious searching using your queries, you really only need spend some time first getting your query right and then with a full Boolean search using phrases and three or so concepts linked through the + operator and multiple search engines.

- Spend time BEFORE your search to **assess carefully what** it is **you're looking for.**
- **Use nouns** in your queries – the who/what, when, where, how and why; avoid conjunctions, verbs, adverbs and adjectives.
- Use **keywords at** the **right 'level'** of specificity: precise, but not overly restrictive.
- **Use phrases** where natural; they are your most powerful weapon.
- **Use** structured ('**Boolean**') syntax, especially the '**+**' **operator.**
- Constrain your search by using **two** or **three** related, but narrowing, **concepts** in your query.
- BUT, generally, keep overall query length limited to **six keywords** maximum.
- **Use advanced** search **options** and speciality features when appropriate.
- **Use multiple search engines** for your most **important queries** – research shows accuracy improves many-fold.
- For **difficult searches, use** only search engines that support **Boolean syntax,** or tools or metasearchers that do.

- For specific topic searches, consider search engines tailored to those topics.
- Save time by **learn**ing your **search engines** and advanced, 'power searching' techniques.

Solutions and the future of searching

You have spent considerable time on all aspects related to how to search in the eWorld and the search services available. What does the current state of eWorld searching suggest for the future? And, are there easier ways than needing to learn all of the subtleties of various search services?

My thoughts on the future of eWorld searching

Major search engines will continue to be one of the most important first access points to the eWorld. The sheer growth and chaos of the eWorld secures this. But there will also be two different forces: towards consolidation on the one hand and speciality on the other.

We see the continued specialization of search engines on two levels. The first level, involving the major search services, will see consolidation and specialization at very different ends of a spectrum according to the needs of various user communities.

At consumer level, the push will be to provide more 'intelligence' to respond to simple query needs. This will enable natural language querying. Services that emphasize this strategy will attempt to become 'one-stop' destinations, offering much more than searching, as a means to keep visitors longer. Virtually all of the directory services now fit in this category. One might call this the McDonald's or Burger King approach to

> **Tips, tricks and trivia**
>
> Google's silly name and bare-bones opening page belie its capabilities: it's one of the fastest and most comprehensive search engines on the Web, and it's still in beta. (The service is in fact named after 'googol', or 10 to the 100th power.) The creators' goal is to 'make huge quantities of information available to everyone.' While I would be the last to guarantee the performance of beta anything, I recommend you try out Google the next time you need to *just search*, and can do without all the categories, news, special features, and what have you.
>
> **http://www.google.com**

Tips, tricks and trivia

Increase your search options

InFoPeople's Best Search Tools gives you quick access to 10 search engines, directories and meta-search services. Just choose the tool you want and enter your search words. Some sites, such as Meta Crawler and Infoseek, also have click or drop-down options to narrow your search. The site is definitely worth a visit for difficult searches or to help you compare search services for topics you frequently research.

http://www.infopeople.org/src/srctools.html

establishing a broad, branded consumer service. Absolute coverage of the eWorld's content will be less of a force; listing positions will be based on payments, popularity and advertising support. Query simplicity will be emphasized over user control and elaborate syntax.

At the other end of the major search service spectrum will be full-text engines, with full Boolean support and many filter options, to serve the information-intensive user community. Great emphasis will be placed on expanding the eWorld's coverage by these services. The revenue model here may be advertising revenues from firms targeting this area or providing demonstrations of advanced technology. Some are now experimenting with the provision of 'special' information on a subscription basis, which may work well for business users; but I have doubts whether this is a sustainable revenue model for teachers, students and others with strong information needs.

The second level, an opening created by today's inability for the major services to cover the eWorld, will likely be the fastest growing category. This level is the specialization of engines by major topic area – law, science, medicine, business, etc. – to serve those specific communities. We are seeing much consolidation occurring in each of these niches.

3

Using the eWorld to translate

Things used as language are inexhaustibly attractive.

RALPH WALDO EMERSON 1803–82

- AltaVista translation
- Translation from the information provider
- Language learning

The eWorld is a global communications network; but, until now, its language barriers have limited its spread as a global business and personal medium.

In its infancy English was the universal language. Many of its users were technical people, who, regardless of their native language, had grown up in the habit of reading their computer manuals in English.

Then, with the commercial expansion of the eWorld, tens of millions of ordinary people from all walks of life went online. Many of these people do not understand English or are uneasy using English. As a result, businesses of all kinds are attempting to serve the needs of these growing users, providing local language, along with selling services and products online. This means that an increasing ratio of the content on the eWorld is difficult for English-speaking people to understand. It also means that an increasing number of non-English-speaking Web users cannot understand the content of Web pages written in English. As a result, the eWorld has been splitting into local language sections, and the costs have been escalating for those companies that want to reach a global market in having their Web pages translated into multiple languages and then having to make changes to those translated versions every time they update the content of a page.

The AltaVista Search site **http://www.altavista. com** has adapted to this multilingual environment by partnering with companies around the world to set up mirror sites, like Telia in Sweden and Telefonica in Spain, which provide instructions and help in nearly all European languages. AltaVista also provides users with the ability to limit their searches to pages in a particular country with the command domain: followed by the country identifier, e.g. domain:de for Germany, and to limit a search to pages in a particular language using 'language tags'. This approach will help global companies with multilingual capabilities to navigate through the language section of the eWorld, but everyday users and small companies have found themselves trapped in their own different language regions.

> **Tips, tricks and trivia**
>
> **'Morph'**
>
> In nerdspeak, a 'morph' is a digital picture that someone has altered with a software program. The eWorld is full of celebrity morphs; you can see some examples at Morph Me, at
>
> **http://www.everwonder.com/david/morph.html**

Using the 'language tag' function at AltaVista, picking a particular language in Advanced Search, selecting 'give me only a precise count of matches', and performing a search for *?, you can see that the AltaVista

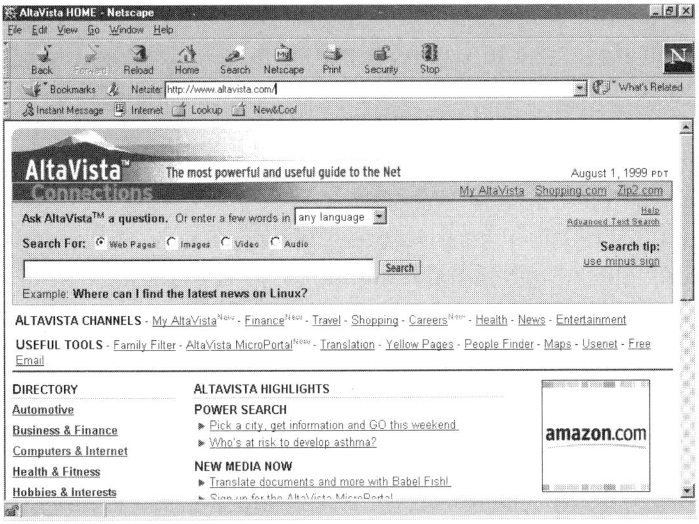

index includes over 7 million pages in Japanese, 6 million in German, nearly 4 million in French, 2 million in Spanish, and nearly 2 million in Italian. English still predominates – the total in the index today is about 350 million pages, but thousands of non-English pages are added every day, including pages with information that could be valuable to you if you could both find it and make sense of it.

Automatic translation software is available for some languages, but it can be awkward cutting-and-pasting Web page text into the software and then bouncing back to the Web to follow links and search further. You lose the usefulness and speed of information access that makes the eWorld so powerful.

For business communications, automatic translation can provide a good first introduction, and is very helpful. But it is not good enough for Web site owners to rely on it as a means of providing their content in multiple languages. If the translation sits on their site, it reflects on their brand; and they need to go out of their way to avoid the visible

Tips, tricks and trivia

Towards more trite, less original speech

Why struggle to say something in your own words when you can use a cliché instead? The Cliché Finder, at

http://www.westegg.com/cliche/

makes finding any often used phrase easy: just type in the word or words you need your cliche to address, and it returns all the matches it can find from its database of 3,300-plus overused phrases and aphorisms. The Cliché Finder is also a great way to double-check your clichés as nothing is more embarrassing then getting them wrong. It can even help you expand your cliché literacy, by displaying 10 random cliches or letting you peruse the entire database, line by stale line.

embarrassing mistakes and cultural errors that automation so often generates. That means that they have to pay high prices and struggle with long delay times for human experts to refine and correct the automated translation. They also have to accommodate the added disk space required for the translated text and improve their internal operations to support the increased difficulty of a multilingual Web site.

Even if individual users had their own translation software and even if many businesses could afford to maintain multilingual sites, language would still be a barrier to search. With all the millions of pages out there, how could you find those pages that have information that is potentially valuable to you but that are only available in non-English languages? And how could non-English-speaking people find pages at English-language sites?

A free service recently added at the AltaVista Search site goes a long way toward providing practical solutions for all these problems, helping to make the eWorld truly global. This is one of those developments, like the initial launch of AltaVista, that change the direction of the eWorld. The availability of free instantaneous translation helps break down language barriers, opening new markets and business opportunities and encouraging international awareness.

AltaVista translation

Have you tried the translation service at AltaVista? Go to **http://www.altavista.com** and submit any query, then click on 'translate' next to any of the items in the results list. Or go straight to the translation page by clicking on the 'Translations' tab above the query box or by going to **http://babelfish.altavista.com.**

You can enter a URL, or type or cut-and-paste any text into the box and you can translate from English to French, German, Italian, Spanish or Portuguese; or from any of those languages to English. Unless the server is extraordinarily busy, you get the results almost immediately, and you are likely to get remarkably good translations.

This service uses automated translation software from Systran (**http://www.systransoft.com**). It has the strengths and the limitations of automated translation. Do not expect perfection or expect it to understand and correct spelling mistakes or grammar. You will find it will give you quick and useful translations of information.

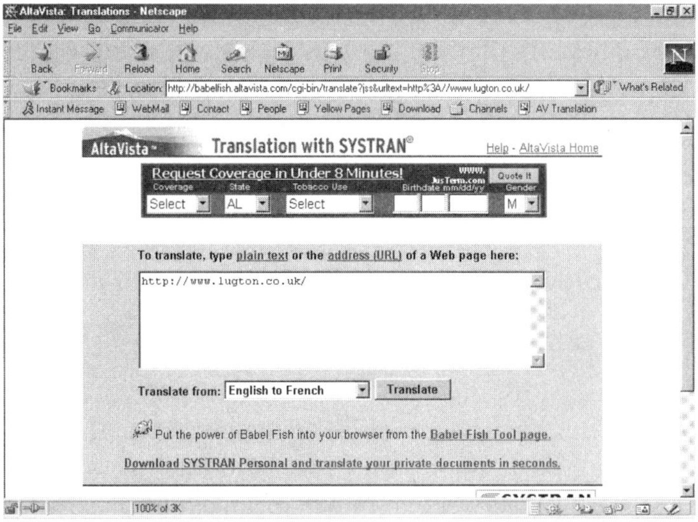

You can get some laughs from checking how it handles tricky figures of speech that would challenge an experienced interpreter. Or you can use this as an aid to help you smoothly navigate through foreign pages.

Because the software runs on Compaq's powerful Alpha computer systems at the AltaVista site, you get very fast results, though response-time may slow somewhat when tens of thousands of users make requests at the same time.

And the translation service is linked into the AltaVista search service, making translation part of your normal Web-navigating experience. Whenever you do a search, matches in your results list that are in any of the six languages now covered come with a 'translate' link. Clicking on that takes you to a page where you select the language you want to translate it to. Then clicking on 'translate' again provides you with the page itself, with its entire graphic look and feel, including all its hyperlinks, with the text in the language of your choice. From there you can continue to explore as you normally do in the Web environment.

This development seems natural for AltaVista, which is based on

Tips, tricks and trivia

To Wit

Aphorisms Galore! encourages you to 'feed your wit'. The site is more than just an index of witty sayings by famous people. It's also quite readable on its own, with especially interesting quotations posted on its home page. You can enter words in the Search box or browse by author or category (Love & Hate, for example). The site also offers customization features that allow you to place quotations from favourite categories or authors at your fingertips.

http://www.aphorismsgalore.com

a massive, language-independent index. Search engines that are built around the syntax of any particular language lock themselves out of the rest of the world. But AltaVista understands nothing about any language. It just captures all the text it finds and treats it all the same.

Constraints of the system

Today the service only provides translations between English and five European languages, not between those European languages (e.g. French to German) and not any of the other major languages of the world such as Arabic, Japanese, Chinese or Russian.

Also, because of performance issues, the size of the text it will translate is limited, normally about 5–10 Kbytes, which is about one to two times the size of the text of the average Web page. If a document is longer than about half a dozen paragraphs, only the beginning will be translated; then you will encounter the words 'TRANSLATION ENDS HERE' and the balance of the target Web page will appear in the original language. If the balance of such a large document is important to you, you can cut-and-paste additional pieces of text from the original into the form at AltaVista's translation page, one piece at a time, by hand. Admittedly, that's cumbersome, but it will solve your immediate problem.

Keep in mind that this service only translates plain text. Words embedded in graphics remain unchanged. And words that appear in Java applets or inside frames or inside databases do not get translated when you submit a URL for translation. And if you submit for translation a URL that is behind a firewall or on the other side of a password-protected registration page, AltaVista won't be able to fetch and translate the text. But you can cut-and-paste text from an applet or from a database query or from inside a frame. You can cut-and-paste text from any source at all from newsgroups or forums or chat sessions or your email or your own personal files that reside on your personal computer. Or you can simply type in whatever text you like.

Things it can do for you

Multilingual email correspondence Type your messages in the form at the AltaVista translation page. Then cut-and-paste the translated text into the email you are sending. And when you receive messages in a language that you don't understand but that AltaVista can handle, cut-and-paste the email into that same form.

Newsgroup, forum and chat participation Read and submit to newsgroups, forums, and even chat in foreign languages, once again by cutting-and-pasting text into the translation form. For convenience, you might want to keep the AltaVista translation page open in a separate window.

Travel Check local-language Web pages from places where you intend to travel, learning about accommodation and entertainment and events.

News Read local-language news stories on the Web, getting a foreign perspective on events, and perhaps greater detail than that offered by global news sources.

Games Play online strategy games (like Diplomacy), with participants all over the world, who do not have a common language, but who can use the translation capability at AltaVista to go beyond that barrier.

Research If you suspect that information that you need is available in another language, enter your query words in the translation form; then cut-and-paste the translated text into the query box. The translated words will have the appropriate accent marks, even if you are unable to generate those accents with your keyboard and software. In addition, you could limit your search to the target language using language tags.

Tips, tricks and trivia

What's Poot?

Just one of the most popular Web-only computer games in the world. Like the best games, it's simple. All you have to do is place your mouse over a grid and find the hidden, yellow word 'Poot' in less than 10 seconds. Like all the best games, it's nearly impossible to win at its highest degree of difficulty. And like all the best games, it's pointlessly addictive and has fostered a cult of players who spend their non-playing time chatting about Poot, buying Poot merchandise, and drawing Poot-inspired art.

http://pootpoot.com/?927856970play

Language study If you are reading a book in a foreign language, you might want to keep the AltaVista translation form online as you do so and type in unfamiliar words, as an alternative to looking them up in a dictionary. You might also benefit from experimenting with automatic translation back and forth to and from the language you are studying, investigating the limitations, where human knowledge and experience is essential for understanding. Those are the aspects of language that you should focus your efforts on. Automatic translation will gradually transform language study, just as the ready availability of calculators transformed the study of mathematics.

Distance education Today, over 7 million people a year take courses at a distance, and many of those are delivered over the eWorld. Many of these people reside outside the US and are taking courses at US institutions. The ability to rapidly and readily translate messages for email and forums should make it easier for students who are not fluent in English to participate actively in courses delivered in English, and for English-speaking students to participate in courses delivered in foreign languages.

K-12 education Arrange partnerships with schools and classes in other countries, using the AltaVista translation capability to break through language barriers, so children with no language in common can carry on dialogues with one another through email and forums. This could be part of social studies programmes intended to foster international understanding. This service could prove important to non-English-speaking students in predominantly English-speaking schools and to the teachers who administer them.

Translation from the information provider

Today, some Web sites are required by law or by the charters of their organizations to provide all their content in more than one language. For instance, this is true of European Union government sites and in many instances the vast and complex realm of the United Nations. In other cases, while not officially required, multilingual capability is highly desirable both from a practical standpoint, potentially opening new markets for businesses, and also as a matter of respect for the culture and heritage of people in the target audience.

So how can companies and organizations take advantage of the AltaVista translation capability, getting maximum benefit at minimum expense?

First, make sure that your pages are in a format that can be translated. If much of your content is plain text, then you are in good shape. But if you are using sophisticated techniques that create pages dynamically or are using frames or the text is generated from databases or appears in Java applets, then you have locked yourself out from taking full advantage of this new capability. Perhaps you should consider creating a plain text version of your pages that will be translatable and also be indexed by search engines like AltaVista.

If your pages do have translatable text, you could use AltaVista to translate them and save the resulting pages, even large pages created by cutting-and-pasting chunks, at your site; then offer visitors the choice of which language they would like to see. But in that case, you are vulnerable to the vagaries of automatic translation, and an horrendous blunder caused by the inability of the software to understand a colloquial phrase might damage your company's reputation among the very people to whom you are trying to open your site.

Tips, tricks and trivia

Tale of two nations

Your Nation provides access to statistics from around the world in novel ways. For example, the Compare option lets you choose two countries from drop-down boxes and then choose a category, everything from paved airports to life expectancy. When you click the Generate button, Your Nation presents the data with a graphic and note summarizing the difference between the two nations in that particular category. The Rank feature allows you to view the top five or bottom five in a selected category. Summary provides a quick snapshot of a nation's data, including population, gross domestic product, literacy, and life expectancy. If you use the site for frequent research on a particular region or data category, you can choose settings to limit all your searches to those areas of interest.

http://www.your-nation.com

Also, in that case, you take on a significant maintenance burden – having to change your translated pages every time you change the originals; and additional overhead in terms of disk space and Web site complexity.

But the underlying technology of AltaVista makes possible a very interesting alternative. Every search at AltaVista generates a unique URL, which a user can bookmark and an information provider can cut-and-paste into Web pages, making hyperlinks that automatically generate particular AltaVista searches, providing up-to-date results whenever you want them. That same capability applies to the translation service.

When you do an AltaVista search which yields a particular page in the match list and then click on the word 'translate' next to that match, you arrive at the AltaVista translation page with the URL of the target page already in the form. Check the 'location' of that translation page, it is not **http://babelfish.altavista.com**. Rather you see that a unique URL, which the contents of the translation form with the URL you are interested in, has already been entered. You can bookmark that page and get back to it whenever you want. And you can cut-and-paste that massive, complex URL and make a hyperlink from your own Web page to there.

In other words, if you have a Web page with about 5–10 Kbytes of text, small enough so you can feel confident that in most circumstances AltaVista will translate the whole thing, you can make a hyperlink from that page that will take a visitor to AltaVista's translation page with the URL of your page already in the box. So you could have a link at the top of your page that tells visitors, even in more than one language, 'for a rough translation of this page, click here'. Once at the AltaVista translation page, the visitor then chooses the target language and gets the translation, at no cost to you. A simple explanation at your site can inform your visitors that you are not responsible for the quality of the translation and you are providing this link as a convenience to your visitors.

> **Tips, tricks and trivia**
>
> **A Prediction From 1949**
>
> 'Computers in future will weigh no more than 1.5 tons' *Popular Mechanics*

If your pages were in English, this technique would open your site to visitors who do not understand English, but do read French, German, Spanish, Italian or Portuguese.

The following frames show how Scotland's Craft Brewers Co-operative site **http://www.lugton.co.uk** can be translated into French using this free service:

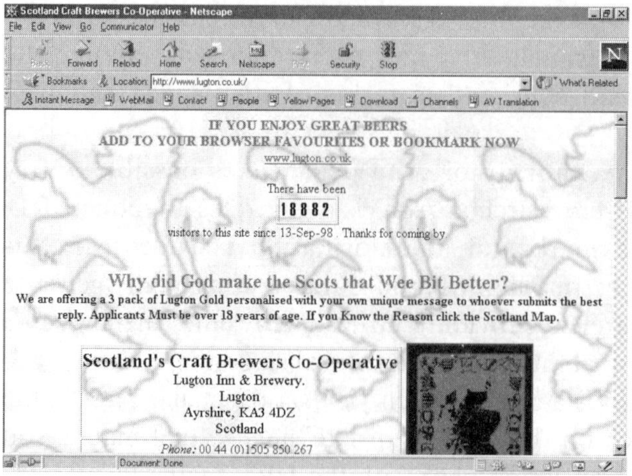

And now selecting French:

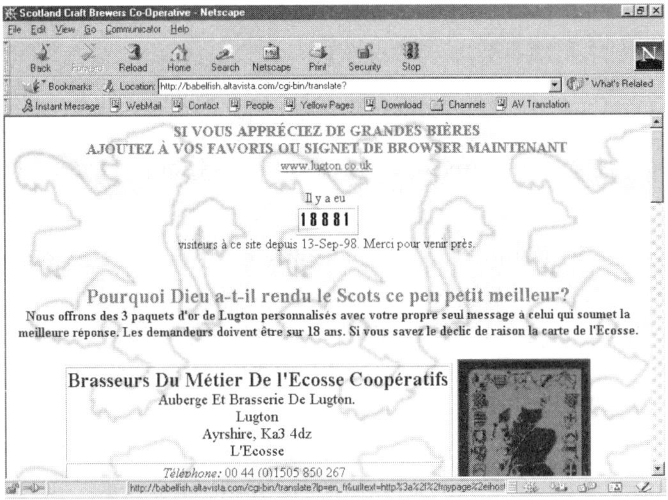

It really is amazing!

Getting people to find you

But how will people find you in the first place? They'll never translate your pages if they don't know you exist.

A practical solution is readily available. AltaVista recognizes 'key word' metatags. If you really want to open your site to foreign visitors, make those keywords foreign words. Use keyword metatags on all your pages to provide translations of the words and phrases that potential visitors to your site are likely to search for.

First decide what words and phrases are most important. Then use AltaVista to translate them into the target languages and cut-and-paste the translation results into your keyword metatag. Then once you have completed your page, go to AltaVista, click on ADD/REMOVE URL and enter the URL of that particular page. Then the new text for that page, including the foreign words that you have just entered in your keyword metatag, should be in the AltaVista index in a day or two. When someone is searching for those foreign words they will be able to find your pages, and then, using your translation link to AltaVista, will be able to read the complete text in their native language. So with the minimum of effort, you can make your Web site and your eWorld business really global.

Language learning

These are some special language conferences and services that are available through the eWorld:

- **Spanish** The Vocabulary Builder at **http://home.earthlink.net/mikcar** will help you to increase your Spanish vocabulary. Select a group. Click at each picture to hear the Spanish word. All sound files are in the WAVE format. Categories include: Food, Transportation, Sports, Animals, Verbs, Days, Months, Clothing, Weather, Numbers, and Telling Time.
- **French** Subscribe by email to **listserv@inrs-urb.uquebec.ca**.
For more in French, visit this North African link:
The Algerian Scientific and Technical Information Research Centre (CERIST) at **http://www.cerist.dz/esrs/cerist/home.htm**.
- **LEARN-CHINESE** Email to **listproc@ucdavis.edu**.
- **Irish, Scottish, and Manx Gaelic** Subscribe by email to **listserv@listserv.hea.ie**.
- **Students of Japanese** Subscribe by email to **listproc@hawaii.edu**.
- **Japanese** Subscribe by email to **listserv@utkvm1.utk.edu**.
- **Italian** Subscribe by email to **listserv@icineca.cineca.it**.
- **Italian** Subscribe by email to **majordomo@inet.it**. This is a 'distribution-only' mailing-list for ByTheWIRE, a biweekly newsletter written entirely in Italian that covers topics related to the global Internet. You can also read it on the Web address **http://www.inet.it/btw/home.html**.
- **Italian** UN INDICE suddiviso per soggetto dello spazio Web italiano. On **http://www.mi.cnr.it/IGST**.
- **Spanish** The Spanish Language Page at **http://www.elcastellano.com** contains information on dictionaries, grammar, translation, forums, literature, conferences, etc.
- **Welsh (also Breton, Cornish)** Subscribe by email to **listserv@listserv.hea.ie**.

If English is a foreign language to you, reading interesting things online is in itself a great master. Learning how to write the language is not very easy. Often, you may find yourself trying to find a word that properly expresses your meaning. The English as a Second Language page

http://www.usd.edu/engl/ESL.html is an interesting place well worth a visit. It has links to help on grammar, idioms, dictionaries, online conversation practice, listening training, and more. For more on English grammar, see **http://www.edunet.com/english/grammar/index.html**.

Casey's Snow Day Reverse Dictionary may not be able to help in such cases, but it is worth a try. The service tries to determine matches between a query (the definition that you type in) and definitions in the dictionary. At **http://www.c3.lanl.gov:8064**.

Tips, tricks and trivia

There has to be a better word

In real English, a 'geek' is an especially perverse performer; a circus geek, for example, is usually some side-show tent dweller who bites the heads off live chickens. So I am not exactly crazy about the name of GirlGeeks?, a site devoted to telling the stories of the computer industry's leading female players. Read biographies, listen to interviews, and learn about these high-tech priestesses.

http://www.girlgeeks.com

For a starting point for resources of foreign languages to English, try: **http://central.itp.berkeley.edu/~thorne/HumanResources.html http://central.itp.berkeley.edu/thorne/HumanResources.html**.

Languages covered include Arabic, Chinese, Czech, French, German, Hebrew, Italian, Latin, Middle English, Portuguese, Russian, Scandinavian Languages, South Asian Languages, Spanish, Swahili, Tagalog, Turkish and Yiddish, and there are also links to other 'foreign' language learning resources and home pages.

MeanBiz.HispanoNet is a Spanish language mailing list where issues related to the eWorld and how it can influence the life and businesses of Hispanics from all over the world are discussed. Subscribe by email to Lista-MeanBiz.HispanoNet at **vallejor@gate.net**.

For lists of Spanish language Web servers and Internet resources, try these pages: **http://mel.lib.mi.us/humanities/language/LANG-spanish.html http://www2.mmlc.nwu.edu/mmlc/language/spanish**

ITINET en Espanol is a commercial Spanish language online service offering news, conferences, fax. Free demo at **telnet://itinet.net**. At the prompt Usuario: answer ITINET.

The WWW Human-Languages Page is a wonderful resource for anyone interested in foreign languages. Their database contains links to over 1,700 Internet resources about more than 100 different languages (1998). It lists regional databases across the world where information about foreign language Web pages, mailing lists and newsgroups is stored. It has links to Schools and Institutions, Linguistics Resources, Text & Book

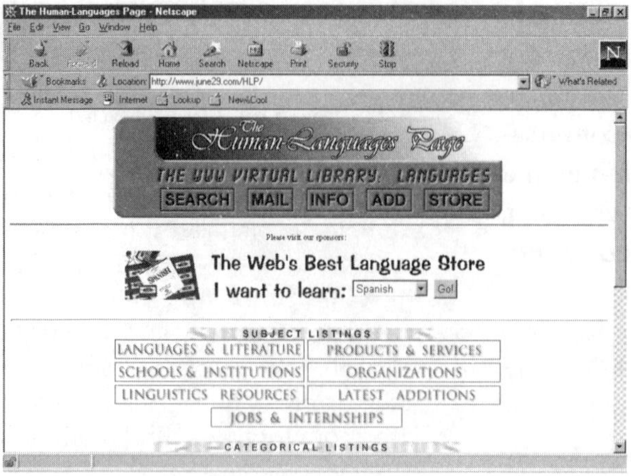

Archives, Languages and Literature, Commercial Resources. Web address: **http://www.june29.com/HLP**.

Offerings include dictionaries like 'English–German Dictionary', tutorials like 'Let's Learn Arabic', and 'Travellers' Japanese Tutorial', literature, other references and resources.

Languages covered include Aboriginal languages, Afrikaans, African, Arabic, Bulgarian, Catalan, Chinese, Croatian, Danish, Dutch, English, Esperanto, Estonian, French, Gaelic, German, Greek, Hawaiian, Hebrew, Indonesian, Hindi, Italian, Japanese, Klingon, Kurdish, Latin, Lojban, Mongolian, Maori, Native American languages, Nepali, Persian, Philippine, Polish, Portuguese, Rasta/patois, Romanian, Russian/eastern European, Sardinian, Scandinavian, Serbian, Slovak, Slovene, Spanish, Swahili, Swedish, Tagalog, Tamil, Thai, Tibetan, Turkish, Urdu, Viennese, Vietnamese and Welsh.

Check the Language and Translation links at **http://www.geocities.com/Athens/Acropolis/3137**. You may also find the world's largest free dictionary interesting at **http://www.logos.it**.

Try **the Ethnologue** at **http://www.sil.org/ethnologue** for the languages of the world. This is a catalogue of more than 6,700 languages spoken in 228 countries. Its Name Index lists over 39,000 language names dialect names and alternative names.

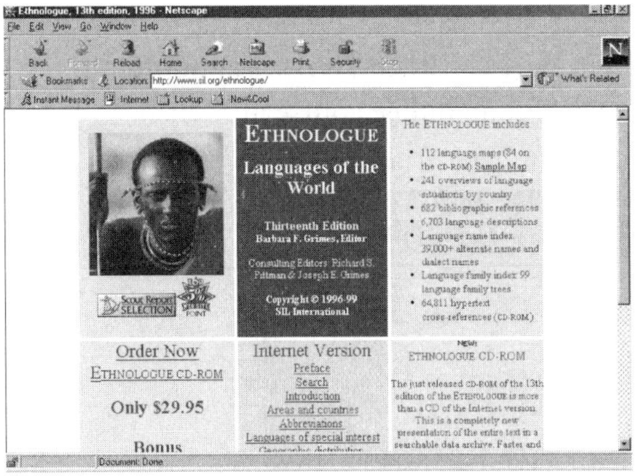

These Chinese language-related information pages:

http://www.webcom.com/~bamboo/chinese/chinese.html

http://www.webcom.com/bamboo/chinese/chinese.html

http://www.cnd.org:8022/WWW-HZ/WWWChinese.html

point to Chinese-language-related resources, and have links to viewing and listening to Chinese on the eWorld, language study courses, educational and viewer software, FTP sites, and more. If you really want to go there to learn the Chinese language, China business taught in English, and martial arts, visit **http://www.worldlinkedu.com**.

There's a Teach Yourself Russian Web page (requires installation of KOI-8 fonts) at **http://www.bucknell.edu/departments/russian/language**.

The Russian Dictionary with sounds and images pages has pictures of animals and food paired with Cyrillic text and recordings of a native speaker pronouncing the words. Its World Wide Web address is: **http://www.wavefront.com/~swithee/dictionary/welcome.html**.

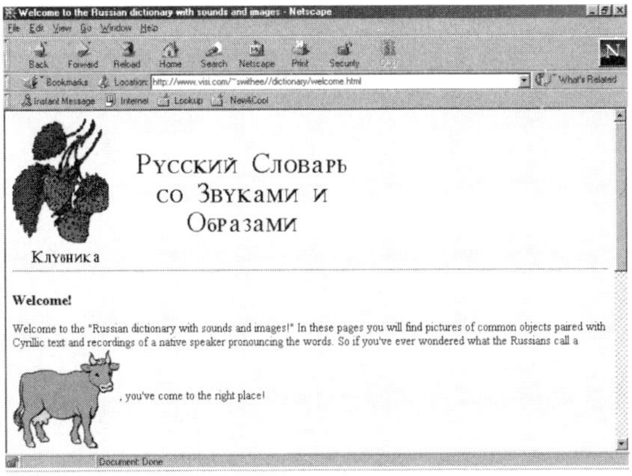

If you understand French, visit the Web pages of l'Agence de Coopération Culturelle et Technique (ACCT) in Paris, at **http://www.francophonie.org**. Try **http://stp.ling.uu.se/call/french/** for an online course in French.

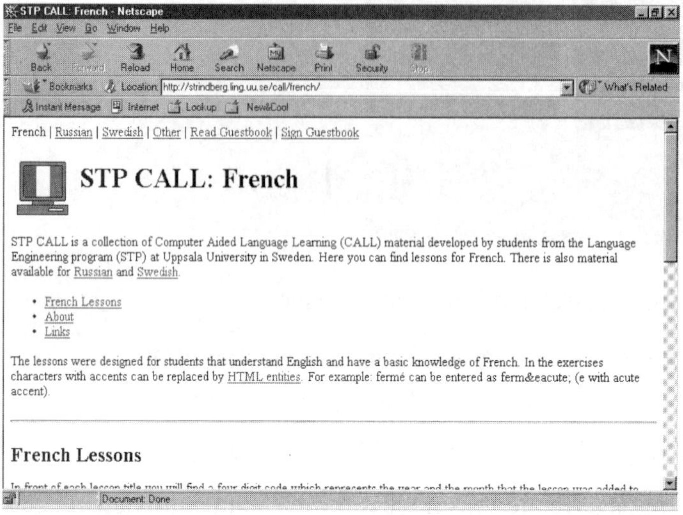

The above site was developed by students from the Language Engineering programme (STP) at Uppsala University in Sweden. There is also material available for Russian and Swedish.

4

Dealing with email

No arts; no letters; no society.

THOMAS HOBBES
1588–1679

Introduction

Email saves you money

I have many friends all over the world and it is surprising how our method of communication has changed as email has grown. It is definitely the most inexpensive means of communication in the world today. Sending a letter to Australia that will take at least a week to get there will cost you €1. Send an email to Australia and your message is there in minutes, and costs less than a penny. There is a very strong economic argument for using email.

Choose your ISP *cautiously*!

Your email address will possibly become as important to you as your phone number. When you set up with your ISP they will give you your email address. It is so important to make the correct selection when you are choosing your ISP. It will not be long before you begin to rely on your email. You may not be happy, for many reasons, with the service your ISP is giving you. You decide to change. Then you have the hassle of informing all your friends and business contacts of your new email address. You may also have had stationery, business cards, advertisements and letterheads printed. Because you have made an error in judging your ISP all this must be changed. Choose wisely!

IBM/AT&T Global network publishes Inverse statistics, which serve as a benchmark of how their service rates against the industry average. These positive ratings show why I for one use their network:

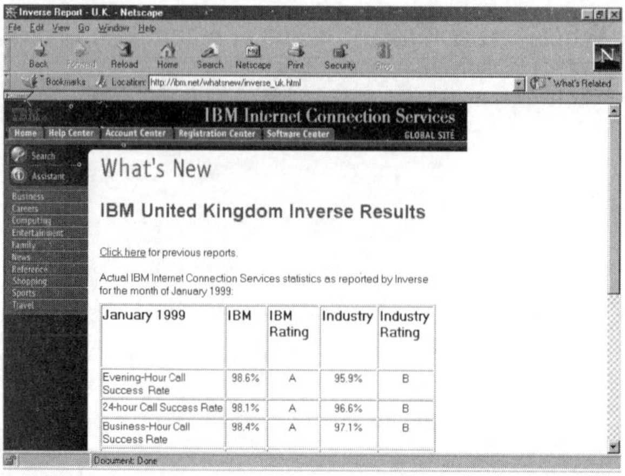

Email

It would be impossible to attempt to tell you all you need to know about email in this book. There are so many different types of email software programs and they all have their little differences that make it impractical to cover them all. But in this section I will describe the basics of using email and some of the things to be aware of.

More people use the Internet to communicate via email than for any other purpose. One reason is that it is so simple and straightforward. Everyone is familiar with sending and receiving paper mail, often referred to in the eWorld as 'snail mail' in reference to its relative speed. The same functions occur in email: you compose and send messages, you receive and read messages, but this way it's all done by computer, you don't need stamps, and messages are transmitted anywhere in the world in a matter of seconds.

> **Tips, tricks and trivia**
>
> **'Morf'**
>
> Morf, with an 'f', is a chat/newsgroup/email acronym for 'male or female'. You've been morfed when someone in cyberspace crosses the line and asks you what gender you are. The term is usually derogatory; in the eWorld, nobody's even supposed to know you're a dog, never mind a male or female.

Receiving mail

Your Internet service provider is the usual source of your email. One of the services you get from them is a mailbox on their email server. That mailbox is available 24 hours a day for others to send you messages. When you wish to check your mail, you connect to the Internet provider using your email program to download and read any messages that have come in for you.

Sending mail

When you wish to send a message, you compose it in your email program, address it either by typing in an address or choosing from a list of your regular correspondents, and the email program uploads the message to your provider's email server, which immediately routes it to the addressee.

Tips, tricks and trivia

A resource for all experts

Allexperts.com can help you hook up with one of more than 3,100 volunteer experts and ask them a question via email. You can settle those sports or movie trivia contentions, find out about a medical condition, or even get advice on improving your life. The site also contains sections on religion, law and business. So don't hesitate to ask!

http://www.allexperts.com

NOTE

If you are charged by the hour for your Internet connection either through a service provider or online service, you should try to compose email messages before you go online so that you are not charged for the time spent writing the message.

Some etiquette of email and some tips

- Always use an explicit subject line that is relevant.
- Never use all-capitals in your emails as this is called SHOUTING.
- Check email daily.
- Delete unwanted messages immediately since they take up a lot of disk storage.
- Keep messages remaining in your mailbox to a minimum.
- Mail messages can be downloaded or transferred to files then to disks for future reference.
- Never assume that your email can be read by no one except yourself; *others may be able to read or access your mail.*
- Keep files to a minimum. Files should be downloaded to your personal computer's hard drive or to diskettes.
- Routinely and frequently virus-scan your system, especially when receiving or downloading files from other systems, to prevent the spread of a virus.

Email in practice

The following frames are of my mailbox and will give you an example of how it works. In the inbox we see I have received several messages which are listed by who the message is from, the subject of the message and at what time and date the message was received.

I can view any of the messages simply by clicking on the message with my mouse. Depending on the email software this set-up may change. You may be using different software from me and the message could be very different.

To create a message is very easy; this is one in progress.

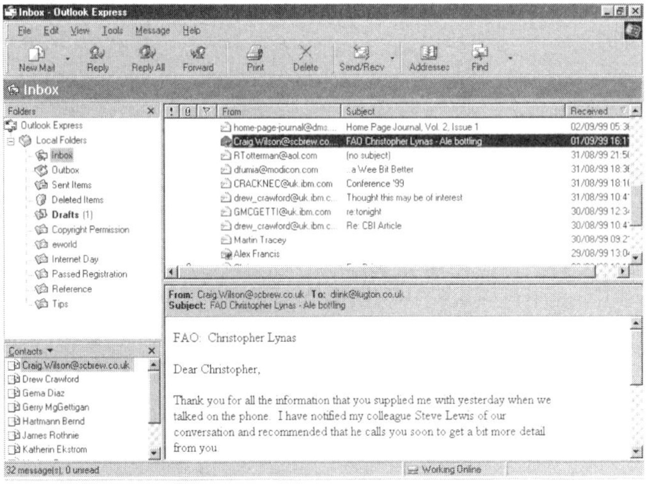

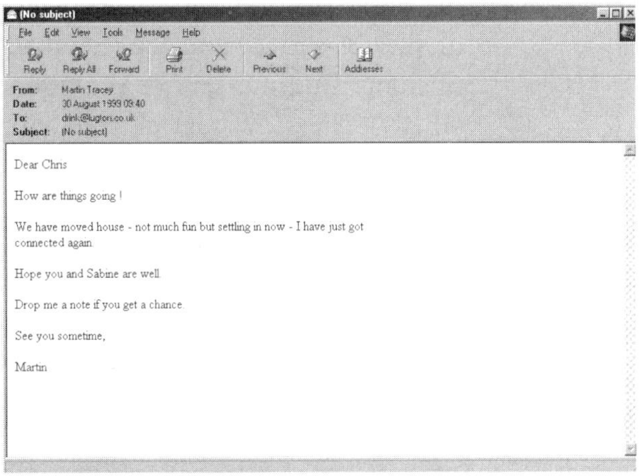

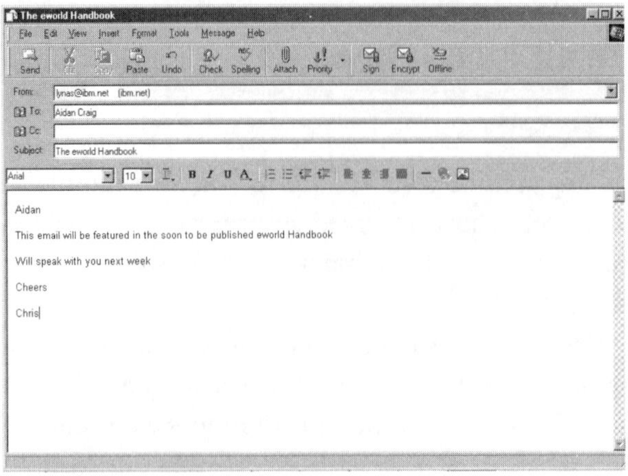

When the send button is clicked the message is sent to the recipient. The cost-effectiveness, capabilities and scope of email make it one of the most useful tools in the eWorld.

Junk email/spam

One of the greatest problems that the eWorld is facing is how to confront the growing problem of junk email/spam. For direct marketers it is a dream come true; for everyone else it is a nightmare. The growth of junk email offering unsolicited and unwanted goods and services which in the main are non-existent or illegal is increasing at an alarming rate. Junk email is causing serious problems for the eWorld and does affect the quality of service and the resources of many Internet service providers (ISPs). The slow service that you can encounter could be down to your ISP trying to cope with the torrent of junk mail that is hitting their servers. Much of this is caused by despicable junk emailers, who send wave after wave of junk email to the millions of eWorld users around the globe.

Tips, tricks and trivia

Pain.com

Bills itself as 'a world of information on pain' and seems to live up to the billing. Use the Pain Expo section to find painkillers by brand name, generic name, or specific pain relieved; search the Pain Library for articles on pain; or read Pain News. Or find a chat room where you can discuss your type of pain with others afflicted.

http://www.pain.com

When is it email, and when is it email abuse?

Email is a tremendously powerful communications tool, used by millions of people in thousands of positive ways. Unfortunately, such a powerful tool has the potential to be used in other less productive ways.

Someone sending email incurs no incremental cost; sending one message costs about the same as sending 100 messages. Some people, who in my view are guilty of theft and fraudulent business practices, use email to send messages to thousands, even millions, of people at once. These are usually advertisements, appeals for financial assistance or scams intended to defraud the unaware. Almost all of these messages go to people who did not ask to receive them. Also, some people use email in 'denial of service' attacks, using various methods to flood someone's emailbox with so many messages that their email becomes unusable.

> **Tips, tricks and trivia**
>
> **Allergy help**
>
> AllAllergy is a gateway site to Internet resources for people with allergies and asthma. The Articles area includes special sections for children and teens, and features links to allergy tips, glossaries, pollen counts, and even chest sounds produced by allergic reactions and asthma! Browsing though the Publications area takes you to online sites or ordering information for print journals and newsletters; it also provides direct links to journal articles available online. The gateway can hook you up with allergy-related events, organizations, and products.
>
> **http://www.allallergy.net/allallergy/**

Notable exceptions to bulk email abuse are legitimate mailing lists, where people subscribe to receive messages pertaining to a particular subject. These lists can be large, and they can account for large numbers of messages being sent, but they are not an abuse of the email system. Quite the opposite, in fact; they are a perfect example of the productive power of the eWorld.

What is 'unsolicited email'?

Unsolicited email is any email message received where the recipient did not specifically ask to receive it.

Taken by itself, unsolicited email does not constitute abuse; not all unsolicited email is also undesired email. For example, receiving 'unsolicited' email from a long-lost friend or relative is certainly not abuse. The reason that it is defined separately is that email abuse takes several forms, all of which begin with the fact that the email received is unsolicited.

NOTE

Usenet convention holds that, by posting to a newsgroup, you are soliciting individual replies via email.

The following are examples of soliciting email:

- posting to Usenet or saying in a chat group: 'please send me email about this particular subject';
- sending email to an advertised auto-reply address: 'for more information, send email to info@someinfo.com';
- filling out a Web form which explicitly mentions email: 'fill this out to get email about whatever'; 'fill this out to get on the mailing list about whatever'; 'check this box to get on the 'whatever' mailing list'.

The following actions DO NOT constitute 'soliciting' email:

- just posting a message to a Usenet newsgroup or any other public forum;
- chatting in IRC or other chat groups;
- simply visiting a Web site;
- filling out a survey form at a Web site that does not explicitly say it is for mailings;
- putting one's email address on any other form, such as product registrations or magazine subscriptions;
- posting one's email address on a Web page. Web page authors should clearly specify the reason an email address appears on the page;
- entering into a business relationship or conducting a business transaction; for example, purchasing a product or service from a company, or downloading a free trial version of a software product from a Web site.

What is 'bulk email'?

Bulk email is any group of messages sent via email, with substantially identical content, to a large number of addresses at once. Many ISPs specify a threshold for bulk email: 35 or more recipients within a 24-hour period.

Once again, taken by itself, bulk email is not necessarily abuse of the email system. For example, there are legitimate mailing lists, some with hundreds or thousands of willing recipients.

What is 'commercial email'?

Commercial email is any email message sent for the purposes of distributing information about a for-profit institution, soliciting purchase of products or services, or soliciting any transfer of funds. It also includes commercial activities by not-for-profit institutions.

UBE, UCE, MMF, MLM. What do they all mean?

The term 'spam' covers all of the above but I shall detail below what each means. Spam is used to describe many kinds of contemptible activities, including some email-related events. It is technically incorrect to use 'spam' to describe email abuse. For more on 'where did the term "spam" come from?', see **http://www.cybernothing.org/faqs/net-abuse-faq.html**.

UBE: Unsolicited Bulk Email

Email with substantially identical content sent to many recipients who did not ask to receive it. Almost all UBE is also UCE, see next. UBE is undoubtedly the single largest form of email abuse today. There are automated email sending programs that can send millions of messages a day; the bandwidth, storage space, and time consumed by such massive mailing are incredible. One month's worth of mailings from one of the most contemptible bulk email companies was estimated at over 134 gigabytes. Each message was sent over the email, consuming bandwidth. Then, each message was either stored locally or 'bounced' back to the sender, taking up storage space and even more bandwidth. Finally, each recipient was forced to spend time dealing with the message. These are all legitimate,

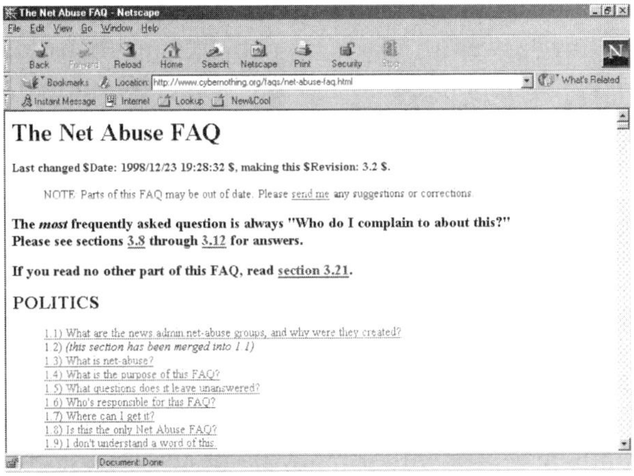

measurable costs, and they are not borne by the sender of the messages. UBE is, at best, exploitation of email for profit; at worst, theft. There are currently few regulations regarding UBE; the potential for growth is open-ended. All by itself, UBE could render the email system virtually useless for legitimate messages. Some would argue that there is such a thing as 'responsible' UBE; those who honour 'remove' requests and use the lists on 'Remove Me' or 'No Spam' Web sites would fit their description of 'responsible'. However, due to the types of messages contained in most UBE, and the historic lack of responsibility on the part of the sending organizations, UBE and UCE have earned a reputation as being distasteful and widely unpopular methods of spreading information.

UCE: Unsolicited Commercial Email

Email containing commercial information that has been sent to a recipient who did not ask to receive it. This is widely used, and confused with UBE (see above). UCE must be commercial in nature but does not imply massive numbers. Several ISPs specify a threshold for unsolicited commercial email: **sending one UCE is a violation.** In a specific case, individuals took offence at having been sent commercial messages regarding their Web sites. Their addresses were posted for the purpose of comments and suggestions about the site; the messages received were commercial offerings to buy ad space on the site or sell something to the site maintainer.

MMF: Make Money Fast

Messages that 'guarantee immediate, incredible profits!' including such schemes as chain letters. Originally a problem in 'snail mail' and on fax and on Usenet, these messages are now expanding into email. Chain letters and most MMF schemes are illegal. They should be reported to the proper authorities. Also, chain letters and MMFs don't work! No one sends the 5 dollars, and claims of unlimited wealth made by people who then ask you for money should be taken with a large pinch of salt. Clueless students send many chain letters and MMFs; usually a note to the webmaster of their system is sufficient to cure them.

MLM: Multi-Level Marketing

Messages that 'guarantee incredible profits!' right after you send them an 'initial investment' and recruit others. Some of the MMF senders will say, 'This isn't one of those illegal get-rich-quick schemes. No, this is multi-level marketing, and perfectly legal.' However, many MLM schemes are little more than illegal pyramid schemes with a fancy name to confuse the unwitting. Particularly popular recently are 'Work at Home!' schemes. Whether or not the offer is legal is not important. MLM is commercial email, so go ahead and complain.

What is a mailbomb?

Delivery of enough email to a mailbox to overload the mailbox or perhaps even the system that the mailbox is hosted on. Mailbombs generally take one of two forms. A mailbox might be targeted to receive hundreds or thousands of messages; this makes it difficult or impossible for the victim to use their own mailbox, possibly subjects them to additional charges for storage space, and might cause them to miss messages entirely due to overflow. This is seen as a 'denial of service attack', perhaps also harassment, and is not tolerated by any known service providers. Alternatively, a message will be bulk-emailed, with the intended victim's address forged in the From: and/or Reply-To: lines of the headers. The victim is then deluged with responses, mostly angry. There is a third, particularly nasty, form of mailbomb. This one forges subscription requests to many mailing lists, all for one recipient. The result is a huge barrage of email arriving in the victim's email box, all of it unwanted, but 'legitimate'. Many mailing list administrators are countering this form of abuse by sending a confirmation email to each subscription request, which must be returned in order to be subscribed to the list.

I've been mailbombed – what should I do?

Contact your ISP immediately. They can help stop the inflow, and also help track down the source of the mailbomb.

What is email harassment?

Any message or series of messages sent via email that meets the legal definition of harassment.

I've received spam in my mailbox – what should I do?

By responding in some kind of abusive fashion, you lower yourself to the level of the person who sent you the offending message. You might also lose Net access through your ISP. You could:

- ask the sender not to send you any more;
- complain to the appropriate people;
- just ignore it and delete it.

Ask to be 'removed' from their list

Some spam contains instructions on how to be 'removed' from the sender's mailing list. Usually this means sending a specifically formatted message to a particular address. While this is a relatively trivial task, it is not particularly effective; I asked to be 'removed' and I got another spam; I asked to be 'removed' and the message 'bounced'.

Complain to the appropriate people

If you send a complaint, be polite, or at least civil. Most times the person receiving your complaint is **not** responsible for the spam; if you expect their help, a little civility goes a long way. Be sure to include full headers when sending a complaint.

Decipher the headers and complain to the spammer's ISP. Some service providers also have abuse addresses; e.g. abuse@ Internet service provider. If you are on a service which uses filtering, forward to the appropriate address on your system so that they can see where new sources of spam are coming from, and possibly add them to the list. If the message originated in Europe, the European contact is at **http://www.ripe.net**.

Just ignore it and delete it

If you only ever get one or two spam messages, this is a logical and reasonable course of action. When the numbers increase, come back to this section and read about other actions.

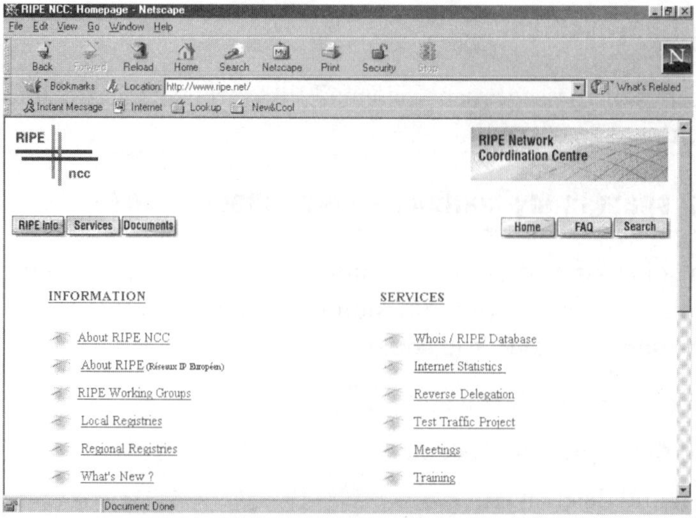

Where do these people get my email address?

- Run programs that collect email addresses out of Usenet posting headers and collect them from subscriber lists.
- Use Web-crawling programs that look for mailto: codes in HTML and documents that retrieve them from online directories.
- Buy a list from someone who already has one.
- Take them from you without your knowledge when you visit their Web site.
- Use a finger on a host computer to find online users' addresses.
- Collect member names from online 'chat rooms'.

For the latest on Web browser security issues, see http://www.cert.org/.

How do I keep my address off the lists?

If you do a lot of Web browsing, be careful about filling out forms. There are also those who sell addresses collected in this manner. Don't assume that because you are visiting the site of a 'reputable company' this will not happen to you.

I did all that and I still get spam!

Your options are few; your address is probably on one of the lists that gets swapped/bought/sold among the bulk email 'community'. There have been several reports of spam dropping off considerably as soon as someone has stopped posting to Usenet; this may indicate that the spam companies are constantly creating new lists, and not reusing old lists.

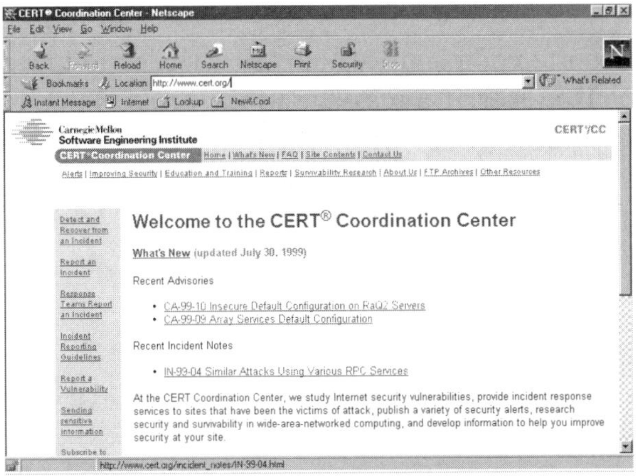

I asked to be 'removed' and I got another spam

Not surprisingly, many spam companies treat a 'remove' request as evidence that the address is 'live'; a 'remove' request to some bulk emailers will actually guarantee that they will send more to you. For many others, the remove procedure does not work, either by chance or design. At this point perhaps you're starting to get a feel for the type of people with whom you are dealing. Also, getting removed doesn't keep you from being added the next time they harvest addresses, nor will it get you off other copies of the list that have been sold or traded to others. In summary, there is no evidence of 'remove' requests being an effective way to stop spam.

I asked to be 'removed' and the message bounced

Probably the remove procedure was false. The bulk emailers are an unpopular lot; they forge headers, inject messages into open SMTP ports, use temporary accounts, and pull other stunts to avoid the avalanche of complaints that follow every mailing.

What about 'Remove Me' Web sites and other global 'Remove' Lists?

They depend on the goodwill of the spam-sending agencies to work. That is, the senders must use and honour the lists for them to be effective. There is no evidence that they do so. There is nothing to stop them from *adding* all those addresses to their lists! Also, because UCE and UBE are sent postage-due, such sites are effectively attempting to legitimize a form of recipient-paid advertising; you'll have to decide for yourself whether you want to support such an effort by placing your address there.

List of basic administrative contacts

The search for the best person to complain to at any site has led to much speculation and argument. However, if a message to the original poster doesn't get you anywhere, somebody at one of the following addresses might be able to help. Be aware, though, that some of the more experienced and well-financed junketeers have their own domains. Moving upstream may be your only choice.

Abuse

A lot of ISPs and network operators have created 'abuse' addresses for complaints about net-abuse. That's usually the best place to start.

Postmaster

RFC 822, the document that set most of the current standards for Internet email back in 1982, makes it mandatory for all sites that pass email to have a postmaster address so that problems can be reported. The purpose of postmaster has expanded at many sites to include net-abuse, both email and otherwise.

Administrative or technical contacts

If you have access to the whois command, you can type (for example) whois example.com to find out who the administrative and technical contacts are for a domain. This will list their email address, and often their phone and fax numbers. Whois for InterNIC is available via the Web at: **http://www.internic.net/cgi-bin/whois**. Its European counterpart is at: **http://www.ripe.net**. The bulk emailers are aware of this resource as well, and InterNIC does very little to check the integrity or authenticity of the supplied information. So don't be surprised to find contact addresses such as 'nobody@nowhere.com', and phone numbers that don't work.

Upstream providers

Determining who's upstream using email headers can often be confusing – many people get it wrong, due to their own inexperience or forgery on the part of the sender. U*E is worthless unless it contains some legitimate contact information, though. If you've been around the block *vis-à-vis* headers, and you're familiar with the whois and traceroute tools, you can probably find the upstream provider.

http://www.abuse.net

Now you can send mail to domain.name@abuse.net, and it will (probably) be sent to the appropriate contact for that domain. Be advised that this is a wholly experimental service. Be sure to visit the Web site before sending email to this service; it will explain what the service does, and how to subscribe to it. You can find it at: **http://www.abuse.net**.

I've contacted everyone involved – heard nothing back!

Not all ISPs respond to every complaint. With some, this is because the bulk emailer is his own ISP. With others, it is due to the volume of complaints received. Many of the larger ISPs and backbone providers will send

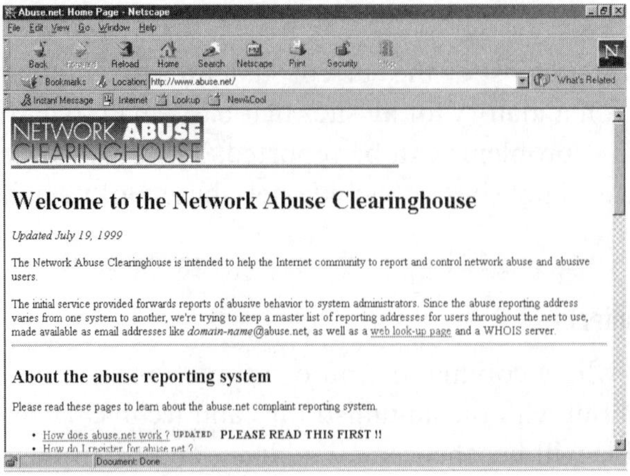

an automated response. Don't be offended by this; they are probably deluged with complaints. The more they get, the sooner they'll find a permanent solution, so keep sending them. Also, although the responses are automated, they may still contain specific information; UUNet's replies contain a unique ID number, intended for use in any further communications regarding that particular incident.

I've contacted everyone involved – they told me to go away!

Complain to the next step up the chain. If they, too, brush you off, keep complaining anyway. Some of the upstream providers claim no responsibility for the actions of their customers; in lieu of a 'short, sharp shock', the best thing to do is to keep badgering them. Still other ISPs will tell you there is nothing they can do about such activities; that is pure poppycock. If they happen to be **your** provider, you might consider letting them know what you think of their incompetence/laziness/irresponsibility by finding another ISP. Be sure to tell all your friends.

They told me they cancelled the account, but I got another spam!

Some sites have been created for no other purpose than sending spam. Some of these will do their best to spread confusion about their operation by misleading and outright lying to those who complain. This has included 'removing' offending accounts, only to give the user another account to start over again. Also, some UBE 'operators' use a 'hit-and-run' strategy, getting free trial or 'throwaway' accounts at other ISPs to actually send the mail.

In addition to that, forging headers is **extremely** common. At least one UBE'r has been kicked off an account, forged his next barrage with the no longer valid address from the ISP that kicked him off, **and** bounced the mail off that provider's mail server.

In UBE, appearances are often deceiving.

I sent a complaint – they said they had nothing to do with it!

They had nothing to do with it. The headers were misread or forged. They're a bunch of lying, no-good such-and-so's. If you're pretty certain that's the case, send as much evidence as you have to their postmaster and their upstream provider.

I sent a complaint – they responded with threats!

Sometimes, threats come from newbies, so simply sending evidence to their postmaster is enough to get them removed. Also, depending on the nature of the threat, other legal measures may be available to you.

I never want to see another message from UBEs-Our-Biz.com again!

Some ISPs maintain server-level junk filters. If your ISP does not do this, ask them to consider it. They may also subscribe to the Real Time Blacklist, which is a list of sites deemed to be sources of net abuse. More on the RBL can be found at **http://maps.vix.com/rbl**.

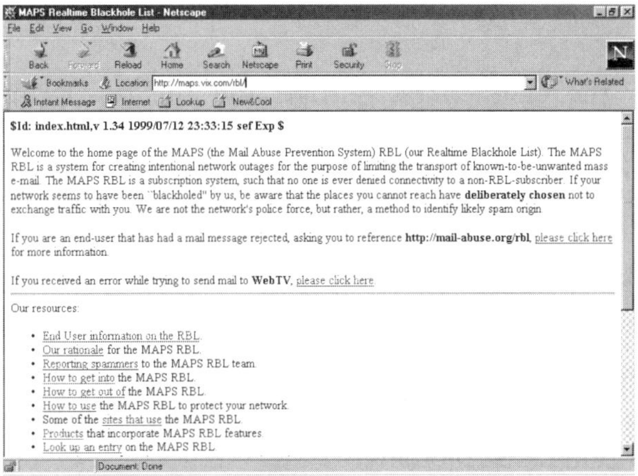

Some email client programs are equipped with filters, which will dump, bounce, or auto-reply to email based on user-defined criteria. Note that this does not prevent the U*E from being received and stored on your mail server until you deal with it. Some email programs will download and act on just the headers; others require the entire message to be downloaded before acting on it.

Consider getting a procmail filter set up if your connection method and ISP will allow it. Procmail is a subject in and of itself; some good starting points can be found in the email Abuse Resource List, found at **http://members.aol.com/emailfaq/resource-list.html**.

Also, **n.a.n-a.email <news://news.admin.net-abuse.email>**, **.misc <news://news.admin.net-abuse.misc>**, and **.Usenet <news://news.admin.net-abuse.usenet>** often have threads on the latest procmail tricks and stunts. In addition, there is a newsgroup, **news://comp.mail.misc**, that discusses procmail among other things.

Who cares about it? Just delete it

The waste of resources, not to mention your time, has already taken place. Besides, if UBE goes unchecked, you might be looking for a keyboard with multiple DEL keys, and a few extra fingers with which to push them.

How can we stop it?

What about freedom of expression, freedom of speech, and so on?

A founding principle of the Council of Europe and the European Community is freedom of conscience and freedom of expression. However, the 'freedom to be left alone' is another cornerstone of European liberty and democracy. From Germany's Basic Law:

> **§1 (1) Human dignity is inviolable. To respect and protect it is the duty of all state authority.**
>
> **§2 (1) Everyone has the right to free development of his personality insofar as he does not violate the rights of others or offend against the constitutional order or against morality.**

Principles such as these are equally enshrined in the European Convention for Human Rights, as mentioned in these points taken from paragraph (17) of the preamble to the 'Distance Contracts' Directive:

- the principles set out in Articles 8 and 10 of the European Convention for the Protection of Human Rights and Fundamental Freedoms of 4 November 1950 apply;
- the consumer's right to privacy, particularly as regards freedom from certain particularly intrusive means of communication, should be recognised;
- specific limits on the use of such means should therefore be stipulated;
- Member States should take appropriate measures to protect effectively those consumers, who do not wish to be contacted through certain means of communication, against such contacts, without prejudice to the particular safeguards available to the consumer under Community legislation concerning the protection of personal data and privacy;

In a similar vein, Germany's Law on Unfair Competition starts off with:

§1 Whoever in the course of business competition institutes practices which offend against good manners can be enjoined to cease and desist or to pay damages.

EuroCAUCE are working hard in attempting to maintain and further acceptable business practice with regard to the use of email.

If you are European, visit EuroCAUCE **http://www.euro.cauce.org**; this site is dedicated to outlawing spam throughout all of Europe.

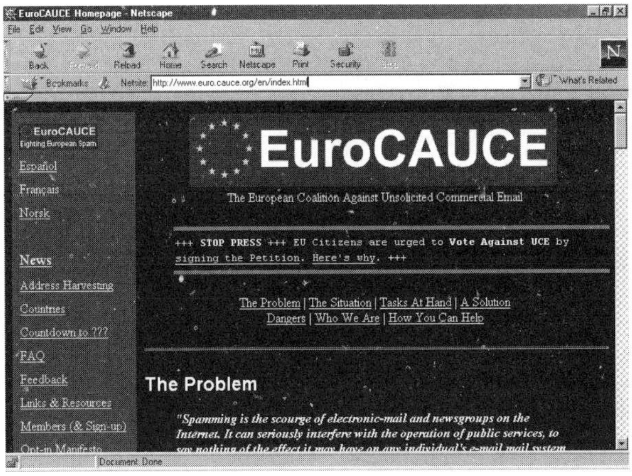

■ Privacy analysis of your Internet connection

To get some idea of the information that is collected about you when visiting a Web site, go to the following site: **http://Privacy.net**.

By selecting either 1, 2 or 3, which will depend on your browser, you will be astounded by the information that is collected by just visiting a Web site. Listed below is a list of some of the data that is collected:

Your IP address: This is your Internet 'identity' and is similar to a telephone number. Everyone must have an IP address to communicate on the Internet. It is possible to block IPs from accessing a site or provide custom content to specific IPs. Your IP could be the same each time you log on (static) or your provider or company may provide a different one (from a pool that they own) each time you log on (dynamic).

Your computer name (if it has one): This is optional.

What cookies are on your system: A cookie is a text file placed on your system. According to the specification, only the site that placed the cookie can retrieve it when visiting a Web site (of course, it is available to anyone who has access to your hard drive). A persistent cookie stays on the system until the expiration date. This system allowed the cookie to expire no later than 2038. A session cookie expires in a short time interval or 'session' which is set by the Web site. In this case it expires in 20 minutes. This type of cookie is often used when 'shopping' at a Web site since it allows the system to keep track of an order while the customer browses different pages. It is also often used to provide custom content on repeat visits.

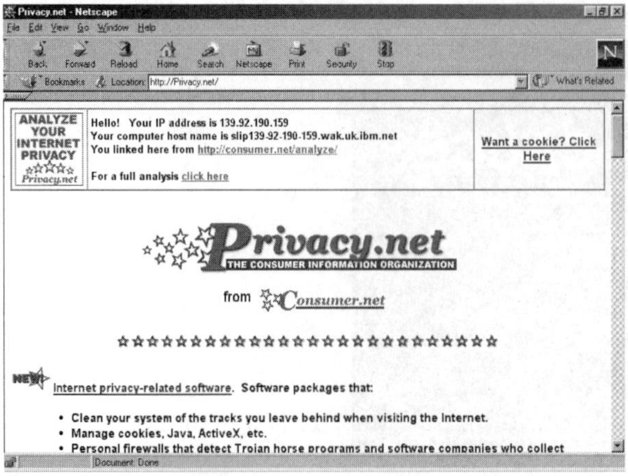

You linked from here: This is the 'referrer' information. Most browsers send this information to the Web site when a link is clicked.

Your browser type, operating system, and browser capabilities: Again, most browsers send this information when a request is made. Browser capabilities are based on a database of information about browsers. The screen resolution and viewable window are detected from the browser and is done in a slightly different way for various browsers.

Does your browser give out your email address? Very old browsers will send out your email address in response to a 'HTTP_FROM' request. This is rare today. Many browsers also provide email information as a password for File Transfer Protocol or FTP. In the past it was common for FTP sites to allow anonymous log-on and ask for the user's email address as a password. Some browsers (3.0 or before) provide the email address as the password for anonymous log-on. The line of stars image near the top of the page is loaded via FTP instead of HTTP. The username and password supplied by the browser are collected in the log files. This was a common trick used by junk mailers to collect addresses in the past. About 10 per cent of users have their email addresses captured this way.

Trace route (traces your signal through the Internet to Consumer. Net just outside Washington, DC): This is a program that documents each 'hop' your signal takes going through the Internet. Usually, this goes from the user to their Internet provider then to the user's 'backbone' provider (a 'backbone' provider is a major provider that can exchange data with most of the other major providers). This 'backbone' provider transfers the signal to the Consumer.Net 'backbone' provider (which is Cable & Wireless) and eventually the signal gets to the Consumer.Net server.

Who registered your domain? (if computer name has a 'fully qualified' Internet name ending in .com, .net, .org, .gov, .mil or .edu): This looks at the computer name, truncates the beginning, and looks at just the domain name (such as Consumer.Net, AOL.com, etc.) A lookup is performed to the domain registration database (which is publicly available) and the results are displayed. This could time out if the Internet registration computer is busy. Domains other than the ones listed must be looked up using different registration sites.

How is your domain configured? When a domain is registered on the Internet certain information must be made available, such as where to send email, in order for the domain to function on the Internet. An 'nslookup' is performed on your domain name. This downloads the domain name configuration file for your domain.

Who owns your network? This also uses the Internet registration database. A 'WHOIS' command is performed on the user's IP address, except that the last field is changed to zero, i.e. 206.156.18.0. This looks up who owns that block of IP addresses anywhere in the world (Consumer.Net links the Americas, Asia-Pacific and European databases).

Are you running a Web server on your machine? The Consumer.Net server makes an HTTP request to your computer. If your computer responds, the header information is displayed.

How to get off the lists

> **Tips, tricks and trivia**
>
> **Get past the anger**
>
> If the members of your family suddenly find themselves at odds, you may find this site useful. This page features links to articles on conflict topics (caring for two generations at once, staying friendly with your ex-spouse, and so on), reading lists, chat rooms, and other potentially helpful sites. For all its interpersonal shortcomings, the eWorld is one of the fastest ways to learn, or remind yourself, that you're not alone, which is a great comfort in difficult times. Suite101's Family Conflict Resolution page, at
>
> **http://www.suite101.com/welcome.cfm/family_conflict_resolution**

These are URLs for pages that contain information about **YOU**, where you live, your phone number, your email address, etc. Maybe that's okay with you, maybe you would like to be easily found by old friends and the like. However, be advised that this information is easily 'mined' by Internet junk emailers.

Visit each Web site and look for yourself. If you find your name and want your information removed, send mail to the contact address below, requesting that they remove you from their database and refrain from including you in the future.

> NOTE
>
> **Note the mail you send must contain enough information for the services to know which record to delete. It's best to send the information that the service tracks. Also, be aware that, unfortunately, there is no legal obligation for the companies to remove your name.**

http://www.four11.com

Information they have about you: email/phone

support@four11.com

http://www.whowhere.com

Information they have about you: email/phone/address

delete-entry@whowhere.com

http://www.switchboard.com

Information they have about you: email/phone/address

webmaster@switchboard.com (DELETE in the subject line)

http://bigfoot.com

Information they have about you: email/phone/address/map

overexposure@bigfoot.com

http://www.searchamerica.com

This service requires a subscription to view information. Their information page claims that they track names, addresses, and telephone numbers.

webmaster@searchamerica.com

http://www.abii.com/lookupusa/adp/peopsrch.htm

Information they have about you: phone/address/map

consumerupdate@abii.com

EuroISPA is the pan-European association of the Internet services providers' associations of the countries of the European Union. The association was established when a number of such ISP associations signed the

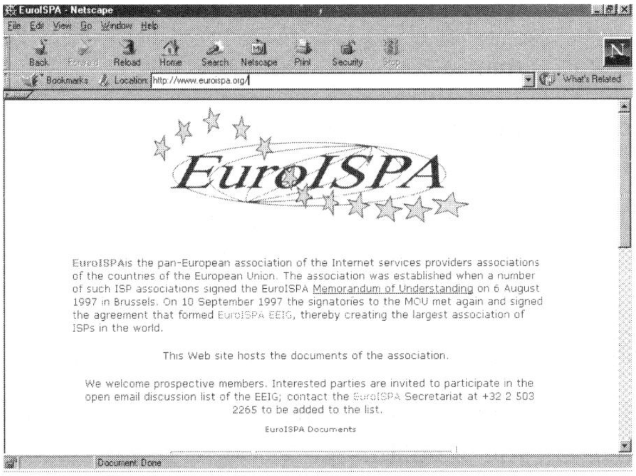

EuroISPA Memorandum of Understanding on 6 August 1997 in Brussels. On 10 September 1997 the signatories to the MOU met again and signed the agreement that formed EuroISPA EEIG, thereby creating the largest association of ISPs in the world. Visit their Web site on **http://www.euroispa.org/** and there is a fund of information there.

What is happening in Europe about it?

Consumers hate junk email

- 22,000 people from around Europe have signed an online petition to call for unsolicited email to be prohibited.
- 10 per cent of unsolicited email is pornographic (source: Computing Services and Software Association). Pornographic email is often misdirected to minors and people at the workplace who have done nothing to indicate a desire to receive it.
- 68 per cent of US Internet users say that they find unsolicited email useless and bothersom (source: *idem*).
- Two-thirds of US Internet users support legislation to prevent the widespread use of unsolicited email as a marketing tool (source: *idem*).

Industry hates junk email

'The "free" distribution of unwelcome or misleading messages to thousands of people is an annoying and sometimes destructive use of the Internet's unprecedented efficiency' – Bill Gates

The Internet Direct Marketing Bureau **http://www.idmb.org** has endorsed an opt-in policy that is designed to give users greater control over the flow of pitches that pour into email boxes.

- Unsolicited commercial communications cost UK business £5,000,000,000 per year (source: Novell).
- It is unacceptable to legitimize a practice that permits advertisers to invite themselves to use Internet provider infrastructure and consumer phone bills to pay for their marketing.
- **Unsolicited email is already banned in the Netherlands and Germany.**

Opt-out has been shown to be unworkable in the USA, proven by the large amount of unsolicited email still circulating.

Opt-out will not work

- Direct marketing associations cannot produce reliable industry self-regulation because the costs of sending commercial email are so low that most junk mailers will not need to be association members.
- 90 per cent of commercial email in the USA is unsolicited, producing a huge burden on Internet networks (source: Computing Services and Software Association).
- The cost structure of junk email is fundamentally different from physical junk mail, which is why junk email must be legislated for differently.
- Email marketing is a trans-national issue; it cannot be dealt with effectively on a nation-state level.
- Email address 'harvesting' programs are cheap and can produce mailing lists of hundreds of thousands of addresses at almost no cost.
- Article 7A of the Data Protection Directive states that 'Member States shall provide that personal data may be processed only if the data subject has unambiguously given his consent'.
- 'Tagging' of email (like #/# in the subject heading) does nothing to resolve the issue of costs imposed on Internet providers and disadvantages new Internet users who are not aware of how to set up a filter on their email client.

Under a simple opt-out system, the ease with which new lists are created means that new lists would be created more quickly than consumers could remove themselves from the lists.

Opt-in will work

- Opt-in gives consumers control over where they are sent emails from, thereby increasing the likelihood of their opening the commercial emails they receive.
- Opt-in provides marketers with clear information on how many consumers are interested in their product.
- **Opt-in gives consumers the opportunity to request marketing information they require, marketers the possibility to target their messages to those who wish to receive them, and Internet providers the possibility to continue to provide fast, effective and safe electronic mail for consumers.**

Proposed amendments to Article 7

Original text from Commission draft:
http://www.ispo.cec.be/Ecommerce/legal.htm:

Unsolicited commercial communication
Member States shall lay down in their legislation that unsolicited commercial communication by electronic mail must be clearly and unequivocally identifiable as such as soon as the recipient receives it.
Amendment from the Committee on Economic and Monetary Affairs and Industrial Policy **http://www.europarl.eu.int/committees/en/default.htm**:

a) Member States shall lay down in their legislation that unsolicited commercial communication by electronic mail must contain at the beginning of its subject line the following text string:
#/#
So as to be immediately and unequivocally identifiable as such as soon as it is received by the recipient, whatever the language or mail software used.

b) Member States shall provide for an opt-out system for consumers to have their electronic addresses removed from mailing lists.

Amendment from the Committee on the Environment, Public Health and Consumer Protection **http://www.europarl.eu.int/committees/en/default.htm**:

Member States shall lay down in their legislation that unsolicited commercial communication by email must be clearly and unequivocally identifiable as such as soon as it is received by the recipient. Member States shall lay down in their legislation that providers of electronic commercial communications shall provide the means for the recipient to discontinue receiving unsolicited electronic commercial communications. Member States shall also lay down in their legislation that Information Society service provider render accessible to their recipients information about their privacy policy according to the Directives on the protection of personal data (95/45/EEC and 97/66/EEC).

Support is needed for this growing and significant problem in our eWorld. All responsible Europeans should support the legislative efforts in their home countries and within the European Community, but also be aware of the efforts for self-regulation.

■ Keep up to date

Visit the many anti-spam sites that can be found in the eWorld and be kept informed of the latest methods of dealing with this disagreeable problem.

Part II

Small businesses and the Internet

5

Making sense of the eWorld

For I dipped into the Future, as far as human eye could see,
Saw the vision of the world, and all the wonders that would be;
Saw the heavens fill with commerce.

ALFRED, LORD TENNYSON
1809–92

When everyone is moving in one direction, common sense says it's time to check things out. This is the way it is with the eWorld. It is impossible to pick up a business publication without a major story detailing the promises of the eWorld's possibilities. It all points in one direction: there are no limits to the potential of the eWorld. At the same time, there is reason to be somewhat cautious. While the eWorld offers business an enormous new marketplace, many of those fuelling the current frenzy, the countless eWorld vendors, are also the ones who have the most to gain. Not wanting to be left out, it appears that many know little more than their customers do. The eWorld is still a learn-by-doing enterprise. If nothing else, the eWorld has established a new pecking order. Companies without a home page are looked down upon by those who have a home page; and they view those with simple Web sites with disdain for not having one with glittery graphics. While company directors often take excessive interest in their company's advertising and marketing, it's doubtful that many have seen a home page. Even with the current eWorld elitism, only a small number of companies with 100 or fewer employees have access and the majority have no plans to get it in the near future.

> **Tips, tricks and trivia**
>
> **Let them talk**
>
> 'What happens when AI (artificial intelligence) programs start conversing with each other?' That's the question The Forbin Project asks. Unfortunately, the answer is 'not exactly the most stimulating conversation you'll ever read'. Still, it's enlightening to read spontaneous dialogue between two "chat bots" and fascinating, on some level, to think that they conducted the conversations, no matter how boring, by actually responding to each other's words. And those with a phobia about computers can leave this site knowing that even though a computer can beat you at chess, it won't be replacing you as a conversational partner in the near future.
>
> **http://birch.eecs.lehigh.edu/alice/forbin.html**

Clearly, email is the major reason for getting on the Internet for most businesses. In fact, this is the one reason why every company, large or small, should have it. It is *the* way to communicate effectively today. While there will continue to be a place for overnight services, so-called 'snail mail', the telephone and even the fax, these are useful only under special circumstances when it comes to normal business communications. In 1999, more data messages were sent by telephone than there were voice messages. The move to transform fax machines into combination photocopy, answering fax, and scanning devices is evidence of the decline of the one-use fax. If there is a warning in all this praise for email, it is the extremely limited writing ability of so many people. The telephone remains popular simply because most people in business have difficulty expressing themselves in writing, while others shudder at the prospect of having their words come back to harm them.

Without question, email is the most powerful, flexible and convenient business tool to be introduced since the arrival of the telephone itself. Email aside, the rush to having Web sites and 'being on the Web' deserves some serious thought. Whether it's making plans for a Web site, reviewing an existing one or simply taking time to decide the most appropriate strategy, there is no valid reason for taking uninformed action. What is needed is a checklist for thinking through eWorld issues:

Be prepared to make a continuing investment. A Web site isn't just a non-hard copy of a brochure, document or newsletter. It is more similar to television than it is to print. While it's relatively easy getting a site up and running, keeping it fresh is demanding, frustrating and time-consuming. Because a Web site is out of sight, it can easily be ignored, even forgotten.

Get ready for upgrading your Web site. There was a time when only really big companies issued full-colour brochures. Not so today. Colour is everywhere. Competition keeps pushing the development. It's the same with Web sites. First it was plain copy. It didn't take long for graphics and photos to be added. Now it's sound and movement. First it was enough to include a telephone number and an email address. Now the site visitor expects to find an interactive environment.

Develop a plan to gain high visibility. High visibility has long been the core of successful marketing. Nothing has changed when it comes to a Web site. Obscurity is a curse for most businesses. Even though they may be excellent at what they do, if they are unknown, they have trouble being taken seriously by the marketplace. A Web site budget must include a carefully crafted programme for directing visitors to the location. While being listed with the major search engines is essential, it is a company's responsibility to promote its Web site continuously.

Make information the primary Internet product. Using the eWorld to make sales is possible. Customers are buying insurance products, airline reservations are being made, banking is taking place and used cars are being sold on the Web. There are virtual catalogues ready to replace their hard-copy counterparts. There's no better example of using the eWorld to make sales than Amazon.com. While bookstores will survive, the ability to research books, read reviews and then order books is here. Will it be long before the physical book disappears and the file is simply downloaded, eliminating the need for bookshelves? The eWorld's primary role, however, is making it possible for anyone to access information quickly and efficiently. This is the way estate agents make their catalogue accessible. Those who provide comprehensive, helpful information capture the customers. The key to making a Web site 'attractive' is not just graphics, but the quality of the information available. Just as the customer, whether consumer or business-to-business, demands solid data, the Web site visitor may be even more critical, a situation that is certain to have an impact on the quality of information on Web sites. Wasting time is not tolerated today. When the visitor arrives at a Web site, his or her expectations are very high. Being disappointed can only taint a company's image. Today's young adults will continue to view the eWorld as a social and communications medium as they get older, but as they reach their time-pressed middle years early in the next century, the eWorld's informational value will supersede its entertainment value. For millions around the world, the 'time-pressed' years have arrived, and there is intense, unrelenting pressure to do more in less time.

The essential issue is ease of access. The eWorld is changing the way we do business. The small retailer in Norway can be doing business in Australia and around the world using a Web site and the competitor down the street won't even know it. Just as important, customers have total freedom since they can decide when and where they want to do business. This is perhaps why more companies and customers are reaching the conclusion that a Web site can offer the best customer service. Saving money by having customers get information without involving a live person is obvious. But it isn't just the financial savings that are significant. It's the fact that the customer is in control, rather than being dependent upon others. This is a crucial element in Web site thinking. In the eWorld business is undergoing a transition to a direct age, where the customer is in charge of the process. This reinforces the need for companies to provide both sound information and interactive capabilities on their Web sites. Instead of wasting time making uninformed assumptions, the information is available online. It's a perfect example of making better decisions, faster.

The eWorld is one more element in an overall marketing and selling strategy. A web site is one more tool available to companies to communicate their message and to draw prospective customers to their 'door'. There are those, of course, who continue to take a wait-and-see attitude, perhaps much the same way they responded when personal computers made their appearance. Some waited for PC prices to come down; others waited for the products to improve. Still others waited until their competitors passed them by. Getting started with a Web site is crucial, at least the initial planning. Building the Internet into a company's marketing mix is essential today. It cannot be avoided. The first step may be as basic as reserving a domain name. But the danger is thinking in either/or terms. Abandoning all other forms of marketing in favour of a 'big splash' on the Net is nonsense. Even with the computer and the eWorld playing a crucial role in marketing and sales, the task is to maintain perspective by getting ready to be an effective eWorld player, while maintaining a well-rounded and compelling overall marketing mix. The major mistake is to misinterpret what the eWorld means. People fall into the trap when they say, I don't really see the opportunity to make sales over the eWorld at this time. They miss the point. The eWorld issue isn't making sales. The opportunity it offers is one of creating customers, people who want to do business with your business no matter where they may be, simply because they have connected with you. The operative word with the eWorld is 'connected'. When there is a connection, there is also a sale, whether it is next door or 2,000 miles away. Anyone who still thinks of the eWorld as just fun and games just isn't aware. Linking with others, providing support and communications and researching competitors are the real motives for using the eWorld.

6

Creating a Web site

ECommerce is not optional – it's a competitive necessity.

- The way to the Web
- What does this all mean?
- Setting up an eWorld store is easy with eCommerce service providers
- SunCommerce
- Yahoo! Store
- Points to consider

We are now seeing emerging what are called 'eCommerce service providers'. This is the cutting edge of new technology and it makes it easy for anyone to set up an 'eWorld' shop. This service is, without any shadow of a doubt, the NO RISK option for anyone contemplating setting up shop on the Internet. They require very little technical knowledge and it is the most economic means of trading in the 'eWorld'. In this chapter you will learn of the types of service and flexibility available to you in creating your own Web site. We will take a look at three available services, but not in an attempt to supply you with complete coverage of the players in the market place. Many more will be appearing, as this service is destined for enormous growth in the twenty-first century. We will also look at how to plan the strategic elements of your Web site and on how to get the most from your site.

> **Tips, tricks and trivia**
>
> **Help for comparison shopping**
>
> Productopia was founded a year ago with the mission 'to be the essential online resource for consumers deciding what to buy and where to buy'. The site is indeed building a content base that consumers will find useful. Although only a few dozen product categories are currently available, reports include not only data on individual products but also pointers for shopping and links to relevant Web sites. For example, the Women's Running Shoes category includes tips on finding a good fit, a link to the American Orthopedic Foot and Ankle Society, plus Productopia's top three picks for quality, style and value. Many of the products have global names.
>
> **http://www.productopia.com**

The way to the Web

In the growing world of eCommerce, online trading is fast becoming the competitive necessity of the supply chain for small and medium-sized companies. These companies are making the best headway in eCommerce. Non on-line companies are being left behind. The problem is being compounded for many middle-market companies as they feel they cannot afford to take the risk. The real question they should be asking is 'Can we afford not to be involved?' Companies that ignore the importance of eCommerce will lose a growing proportion of the market they serve. They also restrict their position to meet rapidly changing customer needs.

A lot of small businesses are being left out of the online retail explosion that is happening on the Internet. We hear every day of the successes of Amazon.com and Dell Computer with their millions in daily sales.

The reason the majority of businesses have not acted on this is the enormity of such an undertaking. You would require an expensive full-time direct connection to the Internet, a big-time computer server, and a complicated catalogue program. Once all that is assembled, you now require expert advice, not to mention someone from Mensa to install real-time secure credit card processing. The cost to establish such a scheme would be uneconomic for the bulk of small businesses, but also in the daily operation of such a project; they would have to engage expensive third-party support or employ highly technical staff to maintain and update it. Having been involved in such a venture I compare it to sailing on the west coast of Scotland, and that is similar to standing under a cold shower ripping up €50 notes!

What would a small to medium-sized business or even an individual give to have the ability to implement a system that will handle real-time credit card authentication, shipping charges, tax calculations and all the other functions of a professional Web site, but also allow you the facility to edit, change and update your Web site on a real-time basis with no technical knowledge required and no expensive third parties involved?

The eWorld is adapting to this and eCommerce service providers are now emerging. These services allow anyone the facility to create online stores in hours. These companies are in the main offering 30 days' free trial, which allows you to create an online store for a trial period, and then cancel without penalty. This surely is the NO RISK option.

What does all this mean?

To give you some insight into the mechanics of these services and using IBM's HomePage Creator as an example, the services work on the following principles:

- IBM hosts your Web site, like any other Web hosting company.
- IBM has incorporated advanced software into this Web site, enabling you to create an online store.
- IBM operates in conjunction with a company called NetBanx (**www.netbanx.com**), which specializes in online transactions, to create the ability to process secure credit card transactions.
- Netbanx requires you to obtain a merchant account for each credit card you plan to accept, i.e. Visa, MasterCard etc. If you already

have these accounts, you provide Netbanx with this information. If you do not have accounts you must arrange these separately.

- When you have set up, anyone with access to the Web and a credit card can go to your Web site and order a product. The complete transaction is processed through IBM and Netbanx's computers, which notify you of the certified order. The complete transaction is clear to your customer but the coupling of the IBM and Netbanx systems is invisible.

All of the major European banks have information on their merchant services and point of sale equipment. Just visit your bank's Web site and you will find some useful information.

You will find you will incur some costs in setting up an account with each credit card company in terms of set-up, transaction charge and a percentage of the value of the sale. We are sure to find, in Europe, major changes in these services as the competition of the eWorld takes effect. The next two frames illustrate two of the many services offered in the American marketplace. You can check these pages out on

- **http://www.acceptvisamastercard.com/index.html**
- **http://www.1stmerchantcardservice.com/**

You should note the commission rates that these companies are charging. In Europe you would need to be a national airline to get these rates at entry level. The competition of the eWorld is taking effect.

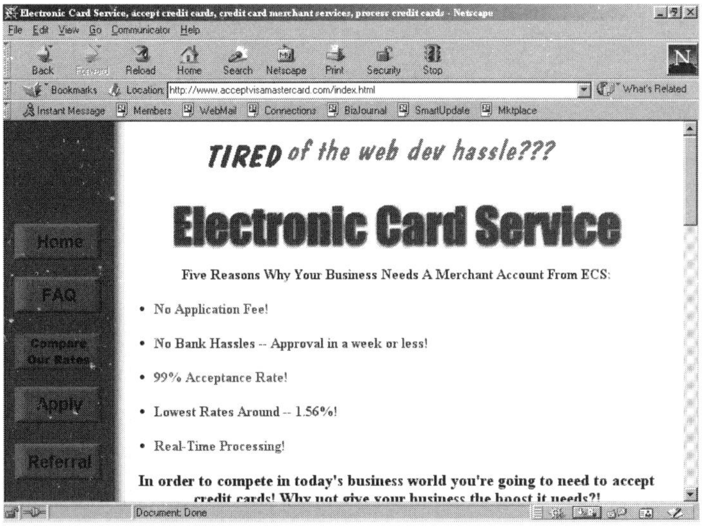

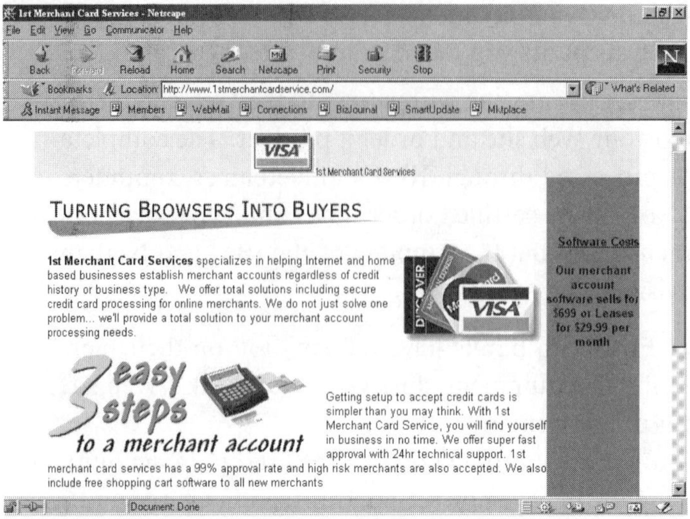

Netbanx's, which is soon to become EuroNetbanx, aim is to help business attain eCommerce objectives. The company provides a secure system that Web sites can connect to and use for credit and debit card transactions. Starting with Barclays Merchant Services, NetBanx progressed quickly in establishing both a customer base and strategic partnerships. Designed for the business-to-consumer environment, the services are commercially robust, reliable, available and supported around the clock.

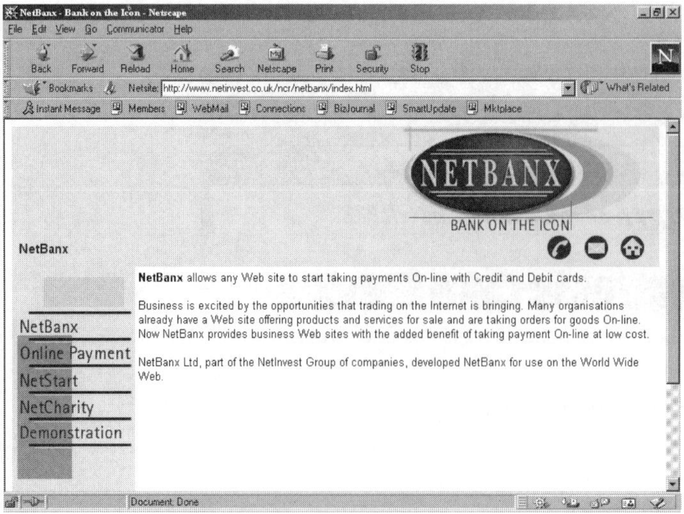

Setting up an eWorld store is easy with eCommerce service providers

Take, for example, the IBM HomePage Creator. You sign up online and for €22 per month you are in business. That is for the basic system. If you require the credit card authorization service you sign up for the 'bronze' service for a monthly fee of €34.5 and with that you get your own Web site with real-time secure credit card authentication, multiple shipping rates, product descriptions and images. Included in the package is free registration with all the major search engines, the facility to register with NetNames your own personal domain name, i.e. www.yourname.co.uk, and within hours you are on a level playing field with the big boys. IBM is offering a free 30-day trial.

IBM set up their service to make it easy for people without much technical skill to establish a Web site, which can gain global (and local) exposure very quickly and inexpensively. The HomePage Creator really excels as the answer for individuals and businesses which are looking for an online eStore, and with prices starting at €22 per month it is the most economic eCommerce service available.

Once you have signed up online, you are supplied with all the online help you will ever need. You are given an administration account that you use to create your store. The system takes you through every procedure, even down to registering your 'domain' name through NetNames. You will see in Chapter 7 how to check with NetNames the availability of any names you may be considering.

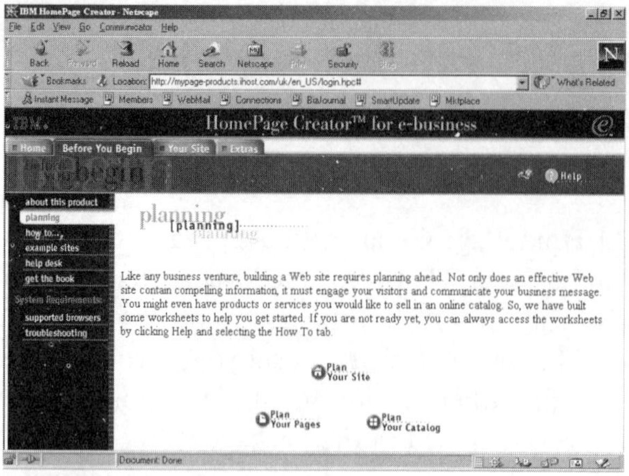

The Planning page on IBM's HomePage Creator is the best place to start. There you will receive helpful information on how to proceed with the building and the planning of your site.

In my working week I wear many hats. In addition to my writing, speaking and consultancy businesses, I am also Chairman of Scotland's Craft Brewers Co-operative. The Co-operative is a wonderful example of what a small organization, with a limited budget, can achieve through the eWorld. The following frame shows the Control Panel that details the components (i.e. graphics and other content) that you have applied to your Web site.

Tips, tricks and trivia

Forrester Research (**www.forrester.com**) predicts online retailing will generate $17 billion in sales by 2001.

The following frame shows the edit facility in which you can upload your own photographs:

The next frame shows the catalogue feature:

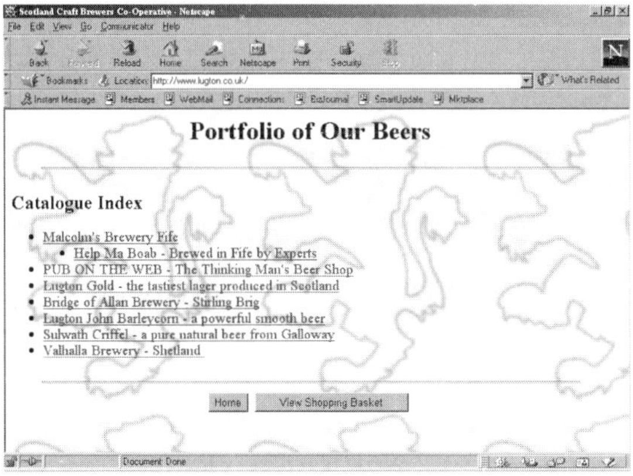

In setting up your catalogue you include the price, weight, tax status, description and any other relevant information. Part of this information is used on the Web page and part is used by the transaction system when an order is processed.

Once all credit card accounts are established, you provide the details to NetBanx through the IBM Merchant Services Section on the HomePage Creator Web site.

This in turn takes you to the IBM–Netbanx Web site where you can obtain all relevant information associated with the merchant services facility.

When a sale is made on your Web site you are notified by email and a credit is applied to your account. You can also access the Web site to receive detailed information about orders placed on your site.

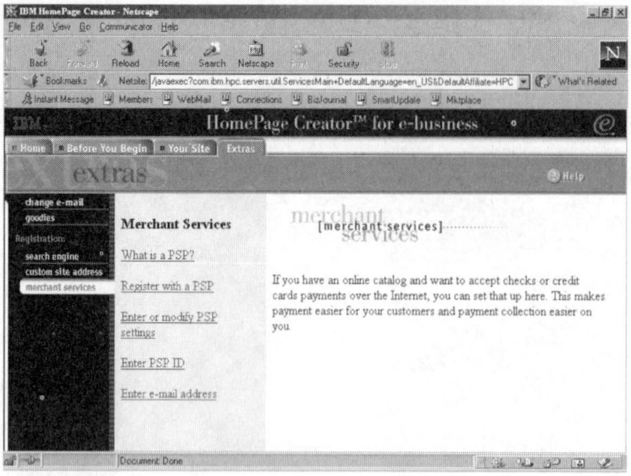

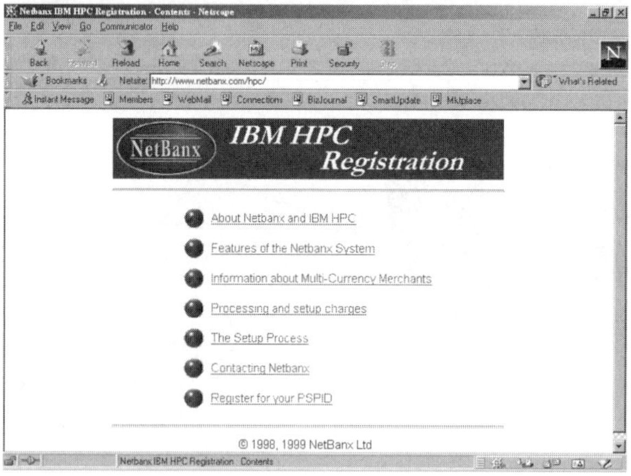

When you consider you are receiving all these facilities for €8.5 per week, it is definitely a no-risk option and well worth investigating.

SunCommerce

SunCommerce is a Canadian company that offers a similar program, that promises to give you an online store in five minutes and believe it or not they do! They offer two services:

- Secure Merchant Lite
- Secure Merchant Pro

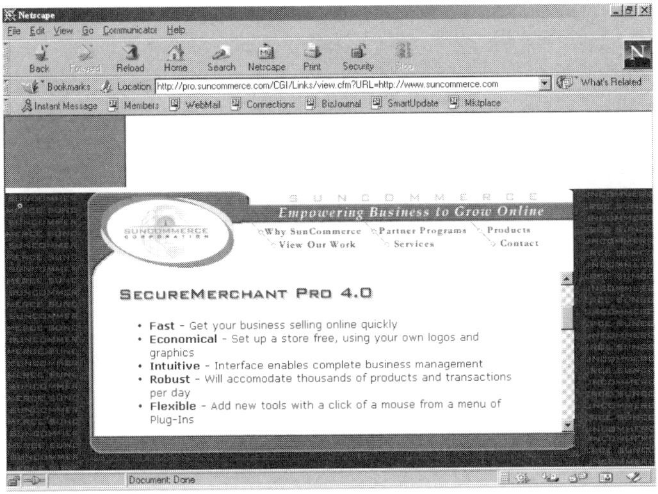

These services have different levels of features, i.e. the number of products you can list and allowing suppliers to link into the system. They do offer you a trial period. The cost is $99 per month. To try it simply visit their Web site and select to create a new store. Then just set up an administration account.

They also have a demo site where you can familiarize yourself with the features.

Most people look at the front-end of a program, that which appears on the screen, as opposed to the back-end, where there is so much information and buying trends recorded. SunCommerce Corp. have included access to a fund of effective information in their program which is most beneficial to any business.

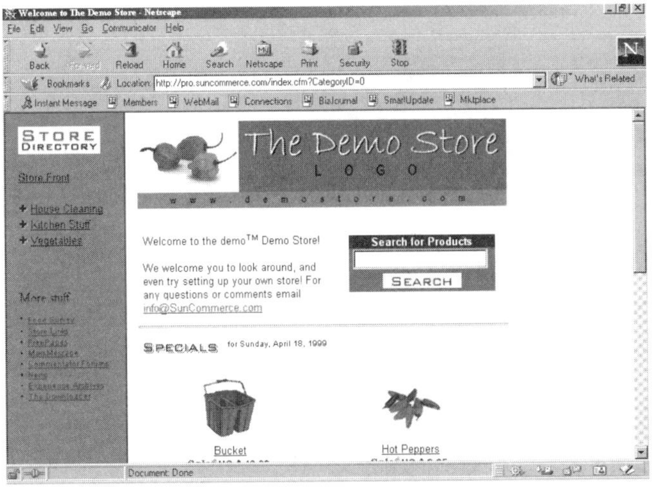

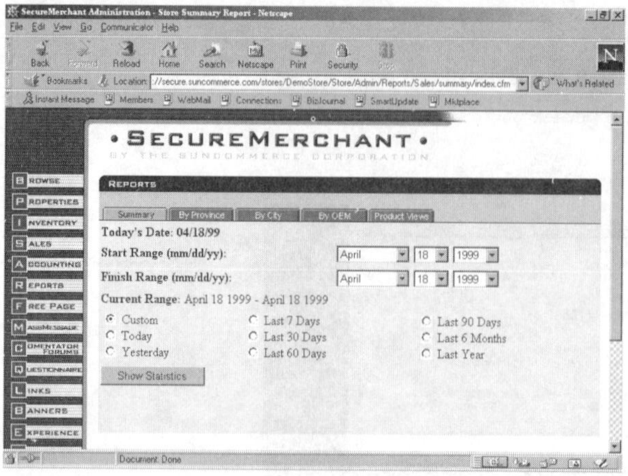

The management at SunCommerce has vast experience in eCommerce. They created the technology that supports MegaDepot (www.megadepot.com), one of the largest online computer stores in Canada. They have given this knowledge and experience to their service and you can get the benefit of it for only $99 per month.

Yahoo! Store

Our third example is Yahoo! Store; it is run by the same people that operate the popular Yahoo! search engine service. Yahoo! Store allows you to set up an 'eWorld' store quickly and easily at prices starting from $100 per month; their features are similar to the two other services you have read about.

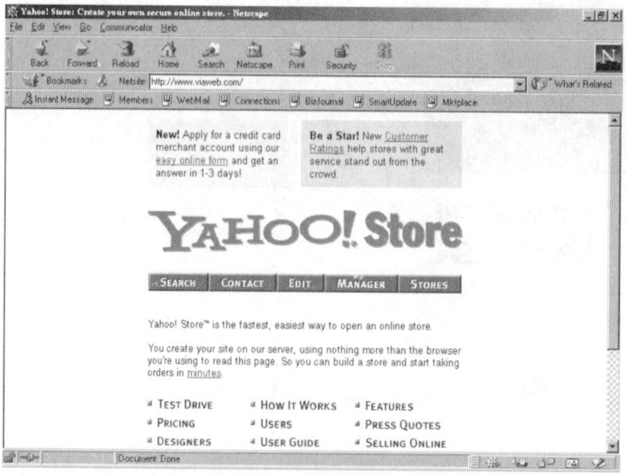

Points to consider

It can be quite complicated setting up an eWorld store, not from the technology but from the taxation, customs and shipping issues, which you must factor into your prices. In regard to the courier service you use, always insist they provide you with a 'trackback' system which you can put on your Web site. This allows you to interact with your online customers. It is part of the essence of good online trading. Send an email when the product is dispatched, informing your customer of the dispatch date and 'trackback' number. By doing this you enable the customer to monitor, in the eWorld, the progress of his goods as they travel to him. It also creates confidence in your business.

> **Tips, tricks and trivia**
>
> **All Things Automotive**
>
> All Things Automotive bills itself as 'the best automotive directory on the Web' and, with links to 3,000 sites, it may be. You can browse for links by category, including car museums, parts sources, racing, even finance and insurance. And if you're a fan of a particular make of car or motorcycle, you can find links to plenty of specific resources.
>
> **http://www.autodirectory.com**

Always pay attention to the charges that are levied to your online business:

- credit card transaction fees and the discount rates that will be applied;
- the cost of your monthly Internet Service Provider;
- the cost of your Web site host provider, though if you use IBM Home Page Creator or SunCommerce then this hosting fee is included in their price.

Calculate a breakeven point on how much you need to sell in order to recoup your set-up and monthly fees. This will encourage you to make your site work for you, which you will learn about later in this part.

In conclusion, regarding creating a Web site, you should *first and foremost* define a strategy on what you wish your Web site to achieve. Set yourself goals for your Web site. These goals should be measurable, so you can determine whether you are meeting them or not. Set goals for your site's profitability. Even if your Web site does not generate a profit in itself, it needs to contribute to your business's overall bottom line and its position in the global marketplace. By setting solid goals you will have realistic expectations for your site and they will help you determine your strategic plan. Unless your business has a large budget to spend, go initially for an 'eCommerce service provider'. Start with a simple site; as your Web business evolves, your knowledge and experience will evolve with it. With you having built it, you will understand all the parts of your business and what it will take for your business to succeed. This is most certainly the no-risk option for any business to test the waters. It also allows you the benefit to update, modify and improve your site without sustaining the expense of a third-party contractor.

For more information on IBM HomePage Creator, SunCommerce, and Yahoo! Store visit:

http://www.ibm.com/hpc

http://www.suncommerce.com

http://www.store.yahoo.com

7

Domain names

- What is a domain name?
- What are the different kinds of domains?
- Who can register a domain name?
- How do I register a domain name?

What is a domain name?

A domain name is an easy-to-remember way of identifying a single computer connected to the Internet. Every computer connected to the Internet has its own unique numerical address (an IP address, for example 155.40.151.0) that looks like a phone number. A domain name is an easy-to-remember series of words or letters that is set up to 'point at' the actual numerical Internet address of a computer. When you type a URL (for example, **http://www.eurohandbook.com**) into your browser, the browser makes a request to a special Internet computer, a Nameserver, to find out the numerical Internet address of the computer whose URL you typed into your browser.

Why should I register a domain name?

Your domain name is your identity in the eWorld. If you want people to find you in the eWorld, either to access your Web site or to send you email, you should have a memorable domain name to help them find your location. You should also consider registering your domain on the Internet to stop other persons using it.

> **Tips, tricks and trivia**
>
> **A secret identity you don't want**
>
> Yes, the eWorld is a great way to heighten your company's visibility. Unfortunately, there are people out there who might try to heighten it in ways that may be detrimental to your business, like having searches for your company turn up other less savoury sites as well. Find out what I am talking about, and what you can do to prevent it, at CyVeillance:
>
> **http://www.cyveillance.com**

What can I do with my name?

Your domain name is your passport to business around the world. You can market your company, your products and your services to a worldwide audience by creating an Internet site. You can project a larger picture of your organization through this site, creating a 'shop window' in markets that you would traditionally find difficult to target. You can be contacted cheaply, efficiently and internationally via email.

What are the different kinds of domains?

Generic top-level domains (gTLDs)

Generic top-level domains are not linked to any territory. Generic top-level domains include the familiar .com, .org, and .net, with plans for further names to be added in the future.

Country top-level domains

Each country and territory in the world has its own top-level domains. The United Kingdom, for instance, uses .uk, France uses .fr, Denmark .dk, and so on. Each country domain has its own rules and regulations about who can register. There are, however, 80 countries where anyone can register a domain name without requiring a local presence. These are called the 'high risk' countries.

Who can register a domain name?

In a generic TLD anyone can register any name, assuming that it's not taken already. That's not to say that if you register someone else's name (and they can prove it's theirs), you won't have it taken away. In a country TLD, there are often restrictions about who can register a domain name. Common restrictions include having to be a registered company or having to produce a trademark.

What is an NIC?

NIC stands for Network Information Centre. A Network Information Centre is responsible for administering every domain name record registered under its particular top-level domain. Each top-level domain has its own NIC. More than one top-level domain can be administered by the same NIC. For example, the .com, .org and .net top-level domains are run by InterNIC. Each NIC is responsible for setting the fees for registering a name under their top-level domain.

What characters are allowed?

Domain names are always lower case (a to z instead of A to Z). Numbers (0 to 9) and dashes (-) are also allowed. The dash cannot be the first or last character. .com names can be 2–22 characters and .uk names can be from 3–80 characters.

How do I register a domain name?

There are several companies offering this service. I have used NetNames in all my domain name registration activities bar one which turned out to be a nightmare. The quality of service and pricing from NetNames is first class and they are a global company. The following frames will show how I registered the domain eworldhandbook.com:

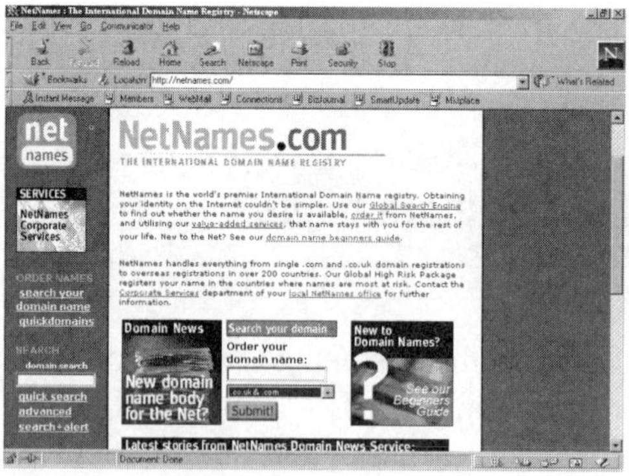

Once at **http://www.netnames.co.uk** which is linked from this page and covers Europe, the Middle East and Africa, I came to this Domain Search facility:

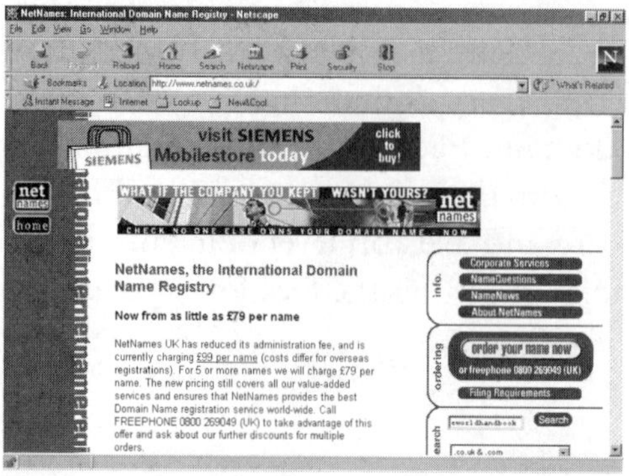

I entered eworldhandbook into search frame and it responded with this screen:

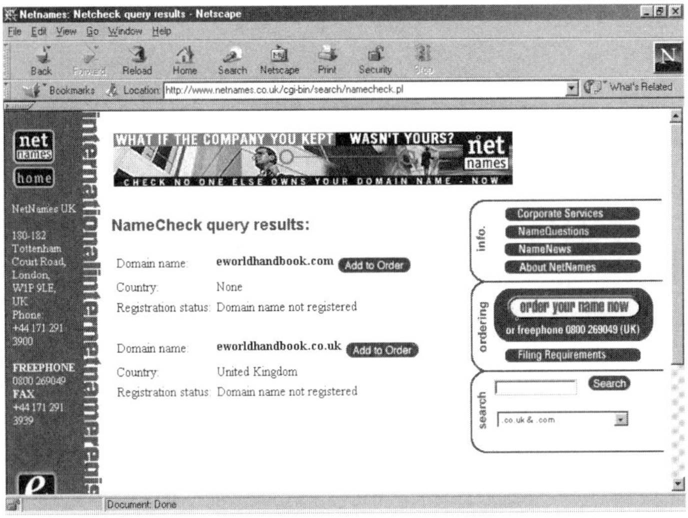

After registering my details and using my credit card to pay for it. I had completed this transaction in less than five minutes. Now you know how the eWorld Handbook registered its domain name and how it was so easily done.

8

Strategy = profit

A man ought to read just as inclination leads him; for what he reads as a task will do him little good.

SAMUEL JOHNSON
1709–84

- Introduction
- The commercial reality
- The importance of strategy
- The perfect mixture of terrestrial and online strategies

Introduction

The best piece of advice I can give you regarding strategy is basically what strategy is all about. At the start of your strategic planning, focus your thinking with the end in mind.

With the rapid growth of the eWorld, most people have had little time to try to find out what it really is all about. But they are aware something important is happening. They are crying out for information. They see the potential for setting up a business in the eWorld and the hordes of people trying to sell them something to get them on their way. This is not what they need; they need a strategy.

There are many strategic impacts of the eWorld

The eWorld will become a tool by which individuals and companies can start to market their goods and services to the other companies and individuals with whom they do business. It will provide a platform by which they can provide support and feedback to their business counterparts. In the short term, it will be the means by which they can make their services available to the eWorld population of consumers and businesses.

The most important trend that we are seeing in the eWorld today

The eWorld is linking corporate information systems, which are establishing a strategic link to their customers. The real impact of the eWorld will come when people discover that by providing the customer the ability to interact directly with their information, they can establish a strong link to the customer that will make the customer less likely to do business elsewhere. They will discover that the real strategic value to be found in the eWorld is not simply marketing activities, but is in using it as a tool to build a strategic and enduring information link to the customer. This is the real impact of the eWorld for every business enterprise in the world.

The commercial reality

The commercial reality of the eWorld isn't with the exciting technology gimmicks that are so much in vogue. Instead, it is the discovery that the eWorld is a technology that permits businesses to network and develop inter-company business applications, a change so vast that it promises to reshape the entire corporate world. For the last 20 years companies around the world have invested huge sums of capital and human resources into computerizing their operations: financial and accounting systems; production control systems; word processing and document management systems. They have learned how to use the power of computers for internal purposes. Yet few business organizations have learned how to 'network business'. Yet the eWorld changes all that. The future belongs to those who discover how to computerize their client relationships.

The eWorld is the foundation of a new business world in which there will be a need for networked links to customers, business associates, suppliers, in fact to everyone. Doing business via computer networks is going to be very different from business via phone and fax. What are the benefits of customer support via email? How can we link the data in our computer to the eWorld so that our suppliers can automatically monitor stock volume? Can we really build this custom data module so that our industry associates can pull custom market data from us through the Internet? What can we do strategically with the eWorld that gives us an advantage?

I believe people in business, management and information technology professionals are going to have to rethink what business is all about. Networked business is the cutting edge of this new technology, and things will change at an alarming rate. The age of networking is upon us, and you will have to stay informed.

Businesses and governments around the globe are set to adopt the eWorld with a vengeance. It will become the backbone of their future procurement networks, and small businesses will find it necessary to participate in order to win any type of contract or tender. As the world's banking systems become integrated to the eWorld, small business will find it necessary to get online in order to pay bills, receive invoices and undertake all of the other day-to-day activities. All entrepreneurs, regardless of the type of business, will have to be online, whether they like it or not.

The eWorld is littered with Web sites that are really pathetic. Many suffer from a worthless design that is guaranteed to chase visitors away as soon as they arrive.

There is a site that features some of the worst of the eWorld, Web Pages That Suck: **http:/www.webpagesthatsuck.com**. Despite its vulgar name, the site does an exceptional job in describing why so many Web page designs just don't do their job and are a complete waste of space.

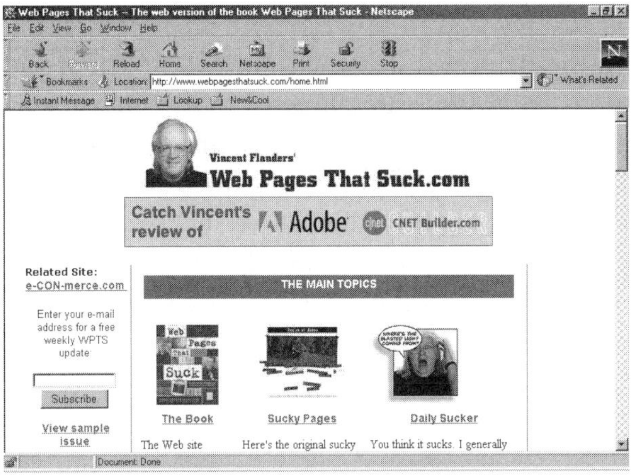

Beyond appearances, many small business sites fail because the entrepreneur hasn't defined the purpose of the site before creating it. There are far too many Web sites that lack a strategic purpose, and as a result accomplish no business goals.

There are many managers who create a Web site without first establishing its objective. The result is something that not only looks displeasing, but damages the character of the business as well. It is not only small businesses that are making these mistakes; many large and even global companies create Web sites with no thought on what they want to achieve from them.

To avoid such costly mistakes, make sure that you understand the range of strategic opportunities available to you using the Internet. These can involve marketing, online sales, cost reduction, public relations and customer support. Then determine your online strategy. What are the main objectives you would like to accomplish? Do you want to build awareness of your company, or reduce customer support costs? Once you have done this, decide how the eWorld can help you achieve those goals.

One of the best ways to do this is by researching some 'best practices'. Scour the Web to find sites of companies in your industry, and study what they have done. There is a list of best practice sites in Europe, which are detailed in Part 4.

Determine what you like and don't like within a range of comparable Web sites. Consider adapting the best of what you see for your site.

Examine what appear to be the company's online strategies, as well as how the site's design helps to achieve them.

Outline your site on paper. Set out the aims and the objectives of the site prior to design, so that you and your Web designer know exactly what needs to be done. Your efforts will also help to set the site's strategic purpose.

At this point, you should be prepared to proceed with creating the site, either on your own or with the help of a designer. Never think that the strategic purpose of your site is set in stone. Be prepared to experiment and adapt, as you will be constantly learning from other sites in the eWorld.

Having the ability to communicate the information and knowledge we have is going to be the key deciding factor in whether we succeed. Keeping the information to ourselves is of no use to customers. They want it all and they want it now. They want it in a way that is easy to find and does not require a lot of effort on their part.

The importance of strategy

From a business development outlook, the eWorld is the most significant thing to happen since the invention of the telephone. It is changing the way we do business and those that do not prepare for this change are going to be left behind by those that do.

Consider the importance of the telephone for corporate strategies. By making the world a smaller place, opportunities became more and more global. Business became faster as communications became faster. In the same way that the telephone has changed business strategy, so too will the eWorld.

> **Tips, tricks and trivia**
>
> **Are you a Godfather fan?**
>
> Want to kill an hour before you realize it? Visit J. Geoff Malta's Godfather Trilogy and start reading the quotes from each film:
>
> **http://www.jgeoff.com/godfathr.html**

Strategy = profit

With all the excitement and hype of the Internet it is easy to forget that it is simply a means to an end. It is a tool to be used in order to achieve the strategic aims of the company. To simply publish a Web page without first reviewing your strategy will be damaging to your company.

When you start with strategy, you start with the end in mind. The eWorld will change where that end is and change the way we can achieve it. Your eWorld business strategy will include a large section on marketing and this can be subdivided into the following, commonly known as the six Ps;

Product
Price
Promotion
Place
People
Process

Product

They simply have to be products in demand, require a minimal amount of human interaction, and appeal directly to consumers who already have a good idea of what they want before they purchase. Not all products are perfect for the eWorld. In fact, some products are extremely difficult to try to promote on the Web and your money and efforts might be better placed elsewhere. Even the most basic product carries an aspect of service and customer support. The eWorld is in a position to affect that level of support. If your business is more heavily information based, i.e. software, then you will totally change how you get the product to the marketplace.

Price

The eWorld can considerably reduce processing costs and consequently affect the price. If you are supplying direct from the factory to the end user, you may be cutting out two or three layers of the supply chain, which will have a dramatic effect on the cost of goods.

Promotion

This is the obvious area where most people look for the eWorld to perform: taking existing products and procedures and simply trying to sell more of them. There is no doubt that in most cases it works, but it could work so much better if the entire strategy was thought through first. New customers, new challenges, new needs, new products.

Place

In the eWorld, there are no physical stores, only 'virtual' locations that provide selling points for the consumer. These locations are actually electronic Web pages which are housed on large servers all over the world and their 'place' does not matter. The next chapter goes into this aspect in some detail.

People

Your people are your most important asset. Change your business and you need to change your skills base. If you decide to change from a high street bicycle shop to an online shopping cart system, then it would be wise to invest in training. If suddenly you find you have to export, then you may require training on how to satisfy customs and deal with the paperwork. If you see ongoing participation in newsgroups being a vital part of your promotional strategy, then you may need to contract the services of a good copywriter, who can sustain interest and not be seen to be blatantly advertising. Language skills will also be useful.

Process

What information your company has and how it can access it is very important to its strategy. A good example of this is DHL **http://www.dhl.com**, where a customer can interrogate their system directly and progress deliveries. This simple service has had huge implications on the company infrastructure, affecting every aspect of the business. This was not something that could have been implemented without thinking through all the ramifications.

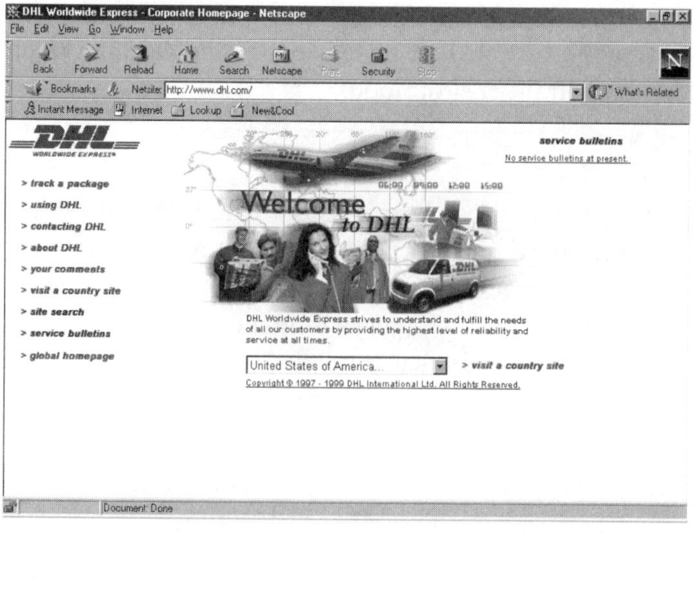

Other aspects of strategy

Financial structures, location, the number of employees, office space required, warehousing requirements, skills base, pay scales, legal obligations, your supply chain, copyright protection – the list goes on. All of these are strategic issues directly affected, in varying degrees, by the implementation of an Internet policy.

The perfect mixture of terrestrial and online strategies

If you are new to the Internet then perhaps you are still 95 per cent terrestrial and only 5 per cent virtual. Other businesses which have developed their virtual shop may have made the transition to 95 per cent virtual and only 5 per cent terrestrial. This is a strategic issue and it is in your interests to redefine your corporate objectives and integrate your virtual and terrestrial aspects into a single business strategy.

By looking at the big picture from the customer's point of view, you will start to see what it is you are trying to achieve. Nearly all existing systems are geared around the companies' needs, not the customers'. The eWorld has started to change this.

Your online and terrestrial marketing should be coordinated and working towards the same objectives. It is vital that your marketing and sales functions are aware of your Web site activity. Simple things such as including your Web site address on your letterhead and business cards are still rarely done.

As you look at the possibilities the eWorld is opening up to you, make sure you are implementing the most basic rule of strategy – start with the end in mind.

9

Where you are located does not matter

Introduction

In the eWorld the location of where we conduct our business does not matter; this fact distinctly illustrates the far-reaching impact of the eWorld on every business. This elimination of the importance of location is the major cause of downsizing and helps explain why companies can only grow by getting smaller. The removal of location as a factor in doing business is going to change commerce for ever.

A bank confidently recruits customers far beyond its farthest branch. It searches for new customers who have never heard its name with a simple, but dramatic message: 'Wherever you are, we're there; however you want to do business, we'll do it; whatever you need, we have it.' These customers will never see a bank building, meet a teller or talk face-to-face with a manager. It's quite possible that this new customer will never speak directly to a human being at the bank. The principal of another bank laments the number of ATMs dotting the landscape, fearing that fewer customers will want to visit his bank's counter. He is right. They won't. His place is in history. Another bank executive reflects on the changes and reveals more than he may realize. 'You just have to keep your fingers crossed.'

> **Tips, tricks and trivia**
>
> **How to know what time it is in Greenwich**
>
> You can find out, if you have access to Time Zone Converter at
>
> **http://www.timezoneconverter.com**
>
> Just choose a location from the scores listed, and you get the current time there, plus the current Greenwich Meridian Time (GMT). You can also use the site to answer questions like 'If it's noon in Moscow, what time is it in Sydney?'

We now see major developments at first-e, the Internet bank, a bank with no branches and serving a global market. It promises free banking, top interest rates and 24-hour access to your accounts. Check it out on **http://www.first-e.com**.

But the future will not be a matter of luck. The insurance agent speaks of the value of a personal relationship with customers as a badge of pride, something that makes his business enduring. But it is almost as if he is trying to convince himself that 'personal service' still holds the old magic. It doesn't. Whether it's banking, retailing, insurance or any other business, the issues are the same. Some see the challenge as a race to retirement, hoping they can last long enough to hand the problems to someone else. In reality, there is only one problem, one issue, and for some, one opportunity. It's the challenge of the eWorld's dramatic changes to the business environment.

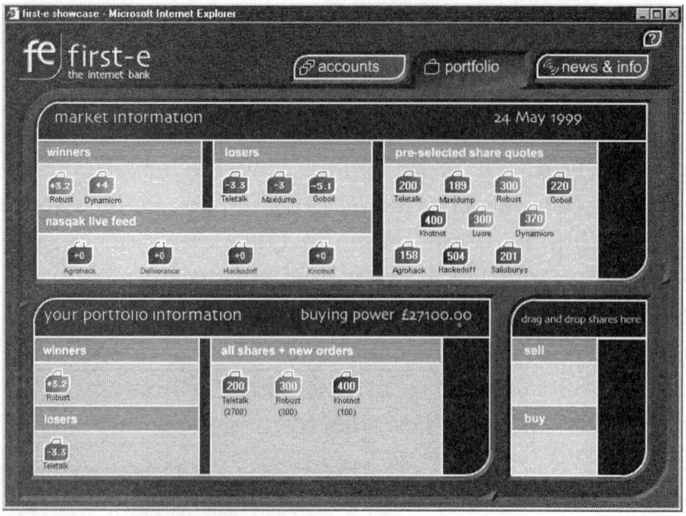

Every consequence of the business model is changed, including those that offered an advantage. The traditional distributor had a place, a 'protected territory'. The same is true for just about every local business that carved out a geographical niche. All this is changing. Whether it is the local bank or the local optician, location has now become non-existent or a meaningless proposition. The eWorld is creating an age of 'everything–everywhere' where near and far have no meaning, 'a world without location'. In effect, location has become irrelevant, and the difference is inspiring.

When most of us were in school, information was somewhere, in a book, a laboratory, or a library. Today, information and knowledge is your computer connected to the eWorld. How to access it has replaced where it is located. There's no better example of such change than Amazon.com. The old question would be 'Where are they?' The new question is 'How do I get to them?' The issue is access, in this and a growing number of cases, through the eWorld. Amazon.com has access to 1.2 million books.

Even FedEx means location, moving something from here to there and there to somewhere else. Not so with email. There is no location, either here or there. Face-to-face meetings survived recession, downsizing and even stringent cost controls. Pressing the flesh is persuasive. The handshake lingers as a symbol of relationship. But it's all about to change. Videoconferencing where everyone is together in a virtual room is here. And it's affordable and it reduces cost. It heralds the influence of position and the irrelevance of location. In our old society, even thinking globally and acting locally is out of date. When it comes to marketing and sales, what is relevant today? What operates? What makes sense? Here are several ideas for moving into the eWorld's business environment.

Think customer

Geography continues as nothing more than a meaningless mental barrier. 'We want customers we can service easily, not more than 100 miles from the office.' Why draw the line? Why erect such a barrier? Without boundaries, the emphasis changes to defining the customer, not the customer's location.

> **Tips, tricks and trivia**
>
> **Something to think about**
>
> The term: User
>
> You probably know that 'user' is the term the computer industry uses for 'customer'. I would just like to take this opportunity to point out that only one other industry calls its customers users: the illegal narcotics industry. I don't mean to suggest anything by this, I just couldn't help but notice the coincidence as I think the eWorld does become addictive.

Think communication

The salesperson's traditional business area is a waiting room, an office, a conference room, a car, an aeroplane, a hotel and a restaurant. But today it's the salesperson's presence that's the problem. What the customer wants is careful, continuous, useful communication, not a smiling salesperson. Communication is the necessary interaction. While the telephone is still significant, it is quickly fading from a priority position in the process of communication. Talking on the phone takes too much valuable time and this is why voice mail is seen for what it is, a barrier designed to stop time abuse. Today's salesperson is a gatekeeper, a manager of communication. The laptop, cell phone and modem are the tools. Using some program for information management, the sales rep is armed for the day's work. The number of calls no longer counts; it's the flow of information that has value.

> **Tips, tricks and trivia**
>
> **Speak at your own risk**
>
> Ah, nothing makes callers happier to find you 'not in' than a not terribly tactful but creative answering machine message. Creative Answering Machine Messages, at.
>
> **http://albrecht.ecn.purdue.edu/~taylor/humor/answering.html**
>
> has a long list of these and a few harmlessly clever ones, too. Use them as is or adapt them into your own recorded works of comic genius.

Think access

Fax machines are still here, but their importance is declining. The only significant issue is speed of service. Customers are worried about delayed, inconvenient, inefficient service more than they are about the quality of products and services. Amazon Books understands the problem, as do the airlines. The issue is no longer 'where', it is only 'when'. It has to be all there when the customer wants it.

Think differently

Businesses thrive on action; they avoid concepts. We all want the quick, foolproof answer. But today, gimmick thinking is expensive. Wasting resources by making one change after another is self-defeating. Unlike the past, there is no right time to make a move. Those that wait will fall behind.

Think seamless

Business thinking tends to be linear. The planning charts move from one stage to the next and then to a conclusion. Start and end; design and build. But for many firms, sales and manufacturing are now one process. There are no more 'steps' as in the past. Ordering, processing, manufacturing and shipping are all part of a single process. When it comes to marketing and sales, only seamless is successful. The new model comes from the software industry where the emphasis is on 'upgrades,' a continuous refinement and improvement of products.

> **Tips, tricks and trivia**
>
> **Resources on death and dying**
>
> Growth House organizes information on death and dying issues. The site has its own search engine, as well as a directory of other Web sites, which are reviewed by medical experts in the field. Professionals can also exchange information on hospice-related topics, including palliative care and pain management.
>
> **http://www.growthhouse.org**

The sales force pleading for something new to sell remains, but it, too, is a relic of the past. The primary selling thought is a continuous process of assisting customers to stay ahead of the competition. It is no longer having something to sell that's new; it's knowing what the customer needs to accomplish. Marketing becomes continuous in this environment, consistently creating customer interest by focusing on customer issues. When Amazon Books emails a message to the customer who has placed an order that 'you will be pleased to know your books have been shipped', the message is marketing. Quality communication matched with a positive message creates the environment for the next sale. Marketing and sales are seamless.

Thinking from within

Contradictory as it may seem, whatever your geographical location the eWorld leads to increased connectivity. This is the message of a recent Intel study on how those born in 1971, the year the computer chip was invented, see themselves getting the news by the year 2000: 59 per cent indicate that they expect the eWorld to be their source, while 31 per cent think they will depend on TV and radio. Only 10 per cent see themselves relying on the print media.

In the past, most change has been a response to changes driven from outside the organization. As something new becomes available, a decision is made about if and when to adopt it. The source of learning has tended to come from the outside. With rapid change, this means that companies must try to run faster and faster to keep up with the competition. More often than not, keeping up drifts into falling behind.

The power of the eWorld rests in its ability to give individuals access to information so that ideas, concepts and knowledge flow up through the organization instead of from the outside in. The promise of the eWorld rests in its ability to make us all teachers. The impact of these ideas on marketing and sales can be nothing less than revolutionary. There is always a tendency to ignore change and continue on the same path. While this may have been possible in the past, it will lead to a dead-end in today's eWorld business environment.

Conclusion

Location

Location will no longer determine a company's area of operation. Companies will organize certain types of work in three shifts according to the world's three main time zones: the Americas, East Asia/Australia and Europe. No longer will location be key to most business decisions.

Companies will locate any eWorld activity anywhere, wherever they can find the best bargains of skills and productivity. Developing countries will increasingly perform online services, monitoring security screens, running call centres, writing software, and sell them to the industrial countries that produce such services domestically.

The irrelevance of size

Small companies will offer services that, in the past, only giants had the scale and scope to provide. Individuals with substantive ideas, initiative and strong business plans will attract global venture capital and convert their ideas into viable businesses.

Improved connections

Most people will eventually have access to the eWorld. While the eWorld will continue to exist in its present form, it will also be converted into other services, such as the telephone and television.

Increased value of brand

The popularity of a product, or the latest financial data, will attract greater rewards. The costs of producing or promoting these items will not change, but the potential market will increase greatly.

Increased value in niches

The power of the eWorld to search, identify and classify people according to similar needs and tastes will create sustainable markets for many niche products. Niche players will increase, as consumers' demand for their customized goods and services expands.

Bonding of communities

The bonds among people performing the same job or speaking the same language in different parts of the world will strengthen. Common interests and experiences will bind these communities together in the eWorld.

More open markets

Many more companies and customers will have access to accurate price information. This will curtail excessive profits, enhance competition and help to curb inflation, resulting in prosperity. It will be easier to find buyers, but hard to make excessive margins.

Increased mobility

In the eWorld every form of communication will be available for mobile or remote use. While connections such as cable will offer greater capacity and speed, wireless will be used, not just to send a signal over a large region, but to carry it from a fixed point to users in a relatively small radius. Satellite transmission will allow people to use a single mobile telephone anywhere in the world, and the differentiation between fixed and mobile equipment will be reduced.

More global reach, more local provision

While small companies find it easier to reach markets around the world, large companies will more readily offer high-quality local services. By putting customers in one part of the world directly in touch with expertise in other parts, they will be able to monitor the quality of the local arrangement.

More informed businesses

The eWorld networks, rather than rigid management structures, will hold companies together. Many companies will become networks of independent specialists; more employees will therefore work in smaller units or at home. Loyalty, trust and open communications will reshape the nature of customer and supplier contracts: suppliers will draw directly on information held in databases by their customers, working as closely and seamlessly as an in-house supplier now does. Technologies such as email and computerized billing will reduce the costs of dealing with consumers and suppliers, no matter what the distance.

More Davids – more Goliaths

The cost of starting new businesses will decline, and companies will contract out services, consequently enabling more small companies to set up in support. The eWorld extends the strength of brands and the power of networks. Major organizations that develop a sustainable eWorld strategy will prosper.

The home and office

As more people work from home or from small, purpose-built offices, the line between work and home life will change. The office will become a typical part of the house.

The development of ideas

New ideas and information will travel faster to the remotest corners of the world. Third World countries will have access to knowledge that the industrial world has long enjoyed. Long-distance education programmes will help people to find better education and acquire new skills.

A new trust

Since it will be easier to check whether people and companies deliver what they have promised, many services will become more reliable and people will be more likely to trust each other to honour their word. However, those who fail to deliver will quickly lose that trust, which would become very difficult to regain.

The value of people

The key challenge for companies will be to hire and retain good people, extracting value from them, rather than allowing them to keep all the value they create for themselves. A company will constantly need to convince its best employees that working for them increases each other's individual value.

Loss of privacy

Governments and companies will easily monitor people's movements. Computers will recognize physical attributes like a voice or fingerprint. The Civil Liberties groups will be concerned, but others will accept the loss as a fair exchange for the reduction of crime, including fraud. In the eWorld, there will be hardly any true privacy and hardly any unsolved crime.

Redistribution of wages

Low-wage competition will reduce the earning power of many people in rich countries employed in routine computer tasks, but the reward for certain skills will increase. People with skills that are in demand will earn similar amounts wherever they live in the world. Consequently income differences within countries will grow, and income differences between countries will narrow.

Less need for immigration and emigration

Poorer countries with good communications technology will be able to retain their skilled workers, who will be less likely to emigrate to countries with higher costs of living if they can earn top wages in their own country and pay prices for everyday necessities at home. Therefore inexpensive communications may reduce some of the pressure to emigrate.

A market for everyone

The greater freedom to operate anywhere will cause havoc with taxation. Savers will be able to compare global investment rates and easily shift money abroad. High-income earners and profitable companies will be able to move away from hefty government-imposed taxes. Governments will compete to bring down tax rates and to attract businesses and savers.

Rebirth of our cities

As individuals spend less time in the office and more time working from home, our cities will transform from concentrations of office blocks to centres of entertainment and culture. In contrast, some poor countries will curtail the movement from the countryside to cities by using low-cost communications to provide rural communities with better medical services, jobs, education and entertainment.

The English language

The global role of English as a second language will intensify, as it becomes the common standard in the eWorld for business and commerce. Many more countries, especially in the developing world, will therefore adopt English as a second language.

Improved writing and reading skills

Email will induce young people to express themselves effectively in writing and to appreciate clear creative writing. Inept or confused writers will fail in the eWorld.

Rebalance of political power

People will communicate their views on government more directly. Governments will become more sensitive and more responsive to lobbying and public opinion polls.

The effect on jobs and incomes

As the eWorld expands, the world will become much more like a single giant national economy. For many products and services, global markets will eventually be more important than national ones. Any service that can be offered in the eWorld will be able to locate almost anywhere in the world. Time zones will matter more than distance. The consequence will be to create global competition in industries that have up to now thought of themselves as local or national. The conclusion will be some job losses, but also many job gains. New industries will spring up. Call centres, which barely existed 10 years ago, now employ millions. There will be wider income differentials, as companies compete to acquire the best talent, rather than make do with what is available locally. Between countries, incomes will become similar, as people worldwide will earn equal salaries for identical jobs, no matter where they are located.

> **Tips, tricks and trivia**
>
> **Time taken to its eWorld extreme**
>
> View and print year calendars through to 2004. Count down second by second to Y2K from ANYWHERE on the globe (and learn who's getting there first!) Find the time in any country and virtually any city. And create your own bank of clocks covering any cities you want.
>
> **http://www.timeanddate.com**

10

Strategies for selling online

- Creating trust in eBusiness
- Which products sell best online?
- Planning the perfect eWorld shop
- Consumer confidence
- Common mistakes and how to rectify them
- EWorld advertising

Before you take the plunge into eCommerce, or even after you've tested the waters slightly, you must consider developing a strategy for your business. A well thought out strategy will be your benchmark in monitoring your goals.

This chapter brings you strategies for business planning and product positioning that should take your online business to the next level.

Creating trust in eBusiness

Companies can use the eWorld to communicate with partners, to remotely connect to back-end data systems, and to perform other eBusiness functions. However, companies wishing to sell online are faced with security issues, which must be addressed in order to protect sensitive information and make their customers feel confident in giving their credit card details to completing a transaction.

The lack of user confidence in electronic business transactions is the greatest obstacle in the growth of eCommerce. The industry at large recognizes that efforts must be made to reduce that level of uncertainty if the eWorld is to reach its full potential as an indispensable medium for business. IBM are at the forefront in trying to make the eWorld more secure for online trading. They have recently announced that customers who are using their Home Page Creator program, as detailed in Chapter 6, and are using the Secure Credit Card Authentication facility will be entitled to display on their Web site the IBM 'eBusiness Mark'.

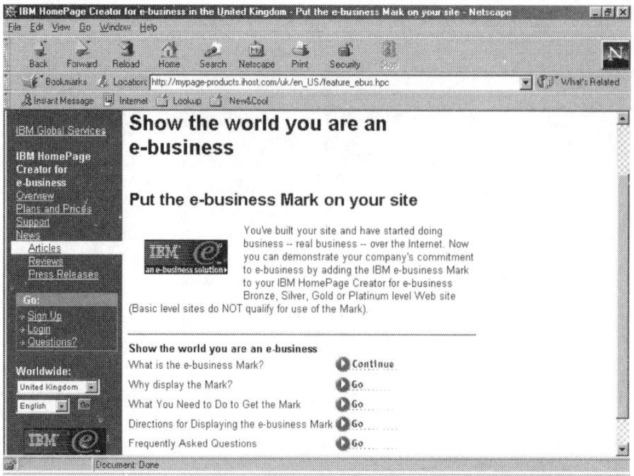

The IBM 'eBusiness Mark' is a 'Web button' which is a tangible way to show end users that your site is using IBM eBusiness products and services, and that these services may help make the site more reliable, scalable and secure.

A growing number of organizations are building public key infrastructures to solve eBusiness security issues. A public key infrastructure (PKI) will protect data through encryption and authenticate users through a certificate-based framework of digital signatures.

What is PKI?

A PKI is a system of certification authorities (CA), registration authorities, certificate management services, and directories. The CA establishes security policies and issues digital certificates to users. Registration authorities register users into a particular domain. A certificate management system is used to manage certificate life cycles. Directories contain the public encryption keys, and certificates that are used in verifying digital certificates, credentials and digital signatures. However, implementing a public key infrastructure is not enough. Once a digital certificate is issued to an individual or organization it must be protected in much the same way as you protect your credit cards.

Storing digital certificates on the LAN or on your computer makes it fairly easy for others to copy the certificate and then use it to impersonate you.

The smart card solution

Storing multiple digital credentials such as certificates, private keys, logon IDs and passwords on a smart card solves a number of the security and portability issues. Smart cards are an ideal secure storage device. They are simple to use and almost impossible to duplicate. A user merely inserts the smart card into a reader, enters a PIN to unlock the card, the credentials are presented to the application(s) and access is granted, just like using an ATM machine.

Smart cards make it easy to carry digital credentials and use them with other computers at home, in remote offices or on public access terminals. Smart cards enable consolidation of passwords for their PC, LAN, mainframe, mail system and multiple applications.

Businesses and consumers are mesmerized by the promise of the eWorld but are also facing the realities of security and authentication. Companies that utilize smart card and public key infrastructure (PKI) technology to address eCommerce security issues will create user confidence in electronic business transactions and will become the driving force behind the widespread adoption and growth of the electronic economy.

Outsourcing the task

You can build your online store yourself, but the advantages of outsourcing the task can't be ignored. You don't have to worry if your store receives more visitors than anticipated or if some of the equipment fails. An eCommerce service provider will focus on the back-end, processing orders, calculating taxes and getting credit card authorization. On top of that, they will make sure you are online 24 hours a day, 365 days a year.

ECommerce service providers will allow complete flexibility and creativity on the front-end, where it belongs. They'll support store sites built by anyone, using any tools or technology and hosted anywhere. Then they'll provide full-featured, industrial-strength order management and payment processing on the back-end, delivered as a service over the eWorld.

The three main benefits

- **Cost savings** Because you don't have to buy and maintain hardware and software and operate the system seven days a week, you will have more functionality and better reliability for 90 per cent less cost.
- **Gets you online faster** Because there is nothing to install or learn, they can turn a marketing site into a selling site in literally less than an hour.
- **Reduced risk** They won't have to store credit cards on their site, and because they rely on experts who serve hundreds of merchants, they won't have to worry about their technology choice becoming obsolete, their site not working properly, or their success exceeding the scale of their installation.

In the end, it comes down to focusing your attention on your business instead of worrying about all the technical problems.

Which products sell best online?

You've read about the success of eCommerce giants like Amazon.com and Dell Computer. You've seen America Online attract more than 10 million subscribers. And now, you'd like to measure the chances of your own business's online success and to develop a winning strategy for generating your own big-volume sales.

Let's first start by understanding your target market. In the eWorld, people tend to be relatively knowledgeable in their purchasing choices. You can expect a well-informed consumer who is aware of multiple sources from which to buy. Your first strategic move is to evaluate your competition in terms of finding ways to distinguish your own offerings from the rest.

> **Tips, tricks and trivia**
>
> **Who else can sell you both a washer and some stock?**
>
> First, online brokerages came along, threatening to make stockbrokers obsolete. Now we have companies like Home Depot, which sells its own stock over the Web at
>
> **http://www.homedepot.com**
>
> If other companies follow suit, maybe online brokerages will become obsolete! The Home Depot site is loaded with other great features, not the least of which is its extensive Project How-To section. As far as I know, this is the only place in the eWorld where you can purchase stock AND learn how to fix a leaky toilet. How can brokerages even pretend to compete?

Price and added-value

There are two main ways to distinguish your products from your competitors. The first is on the basis of price. In general, it would make sense for shoppers to pay less for an identical product. For this reason, the second way to distinguish your products is to provide 'value-added' features where consumers may be willing to pay slightly more for an equivalent product, if they feel that they are getting an additional benefit.

For example, superior customer support, easy exchange policies and express delivery might sway consumers in your favour. If you are offering value-added features, make sure to let visitors to your site know that clearly and quickly.

Fewer unknowns

Another strategy of online product positioning is eliminating unknowns. In general, consumer confidence levels have been steadily improving so far as purchasing directly in the eWorld is concerned. However, offering standard, brand-name products has made the consumer's choice to purchase online even easier. Generic or less well known products increase the number of 'unknowns' and may result in online 'window shopping' and comparing rather than actual purchasing.

The 'order by phone' alternative

It's true that direct sales online are skyrocketing. The latest reports claim that consumers are spending over $4 billion in eWorld shopping. However, successful online storeowners will tell you that approximately half their orders are actually processed by phone, after the consumer has browsed their Web site. So, in addition to providing an online credit card processing mechanism, part of your online strategy should include a plan to provide personal phone support. Keep in mind that the eWorld is 'open' 24 hours a day, so include the hours during which shoppers can expect to reach an order processor, next to the phone number on your site.

Handling and shipping issues

The 'back-end' issues of product handling and shipping should also play a role in your strategy. If shipping charges will significantly impact on the price of the product, then shoppers might prefer to do their purchasing at a retail outlet, rather than online.

Also, ease of shipping on your part is an additional factor. To handle volume orders, standard product size might be of great importance. For example, music CDs are well suited for online selling because they are all of similar size and weight, allowing the merchant to plan for standard shipping boxes and less time spent in handling and preparing to ship.

What will sell?

While it may be tempting to think that all products sell equally well offline as on the Internet, it's important to make an objective assessment as to whether your products are suitable for sale online. Rather than wasting resources on developing an online store to sell a product which is not well suited for sale in the eWorld, it is usually preferable to set out your strategy in advance and make a more productive choice from the beginning. Also, remember that just because your competitors have Web sites that offer products similar to yours, it does not mean that they are actually getting orders for their products. Some products may be better suited for marketing and promotion in the eWorld, rather than for direct sales.

Planning the perfect eWorld shop

A well-designed site, in terms of content as well as presentation, can give your online store the edge you need to succeed.

Clarity and ease of navigation

Many of the big retail Web sites, such as Amazon.com, Dell etc., make it clear to the shopper which categories of products are available, and provide easy site-navigation links. From anywhere in these sites, the shopper can easily proceed to browse more products without having to waste time searching. It would seem fairly obvious that a good navigation system is required for a successful eCommerce site, but as you may have noticed, many sites in the eWorld are desperately lacking in this respect.

Fast-loading pages

The vast majority of consumers connect to the eWorld from their homes with relatively slow modems. This is especially true in the case of international shoppers. For this reason, the perfect online store would be fast-loading, not bogged down by overly long content or graphics. One strategy, which has become very popular, is to show small product 'thumbnails' with an initial product description, and then giving the shopper the option of clicking on the thumbnail for a larger graphic.

Shopper privacy

When purchasing online, shoppers are often required to provide personal information, including a mailing address, phone number, email address and billing information. In general, requiring these disclosures can discourage shoppers from purchasing directly online. To lessen shoppers' privacy concerns, the better-designed sites provide guarantees that shoppers' personal information will not be sold to other companies for mailing lists and other questionnaire purposes.

Technical support

Often, online shoppers are wary of poor customer support, wondering if the merchant will respond to issues that may arise after the purchase has been made. The concern is whether the online merchant has the expertise or personnel required to resolve technical issues relating to the set-up or use of the product. The perfect store would post its technical support policies clearly to address shoppers' potential concerns.

Return and exchange policies

Another factor affecting consumer confidence is a concern that they will be dissatisfied with the product purchased without the benefit of examining the product physically before purchase. The perfect online store would advertise an unconditional exchange or refund policy to boost consumer confidence.

The right look and feel

Marketing is a crucial part of the sales process. Ultimately, the online store must captivate potential shoppers to make a purchase. To a great extent, sites accomplish this with well-planned graphic design. The perfect site would feature a pleasant colour scheme and tasteful design elements, which serve to highlight the products being offered without overshadowing or conflicting with them. Remember, graphics do not have to be overly large in file size or be flashy to be effective. A quick-loading site is a must.

Consumer confidence

You know which products you want to sell online. Like any other retailer, you have carried out research on your products, and established relationships that enable you to offer shoppers quality merchandise at a low price.

You have spent the time and money in building an attractive Web site, and it looks great. You've installed the latest shopping cart software on your site, so you can display your merchandise, take orders, and accept payments from Internet shoppers. You've even registered with a few search engines and invested in some non-Internet media advertising to help promote your Web site. You've got a great Web marketing strategy, and based on the number of hits to your site, it certainly appears to be working.

There's only one problem. For the most part, the people visiting your site are only 'window shopping.' Lots of people are looking, but they're just not placing their orders with YOU. What could possibly be wrong? You sell brand-name products that people already recognize and use. It's not like you're trying to get consumers to try an unfamiliar product, or one from a new or untried manufacturer. Your prices are in line with your competitors. As a matter of fact, in many cases your prices are even lower than your competitors. Still, you're not getting the number of online purchases you should be, and you just don't know why. Well, the problem is lack of consumer confidence!

Boosting consumer confidence

The main difference between walking into a shop to make a purchase and buying in the eWorld is the element of human involvement. Many people simply need to know that if they have a problem with their purchase after the sale, there will be a 'live person' available to tend to their customer service needs. Very few, if any, consumers are going to risk making a purchase if they think a problem with, or question about, their order will only be handled by email communication. So how does the eWorld merchant solve this problem? Here are some tips to help eWorld merchants boost consumer confidence in their online stores:

- In addition to listing your email address on your Web site, tell people where you are located. Include your company's address, telephone and fax numbers on your Web site.
- If your telephone is not answered by a 'live person' 24 hours a day, let people know which days and hours they can speak with a customer service representative. If you have your phone answered by an answering machine or voice mail, leave a message that tells the caller when they can expect their call to be returned.
- Invest in a free telephone number and list it on your site. This is a relatively inexpensive way to raise the level of consumer confidence. It sends out a strong message that your company cares about hearing from its customers. If someone has the need to discuss a discrepancy with their purchase, they'll likely be more patient, and inclined to listen to your point of view, if they are not paying for the

call. This strategy also gives online merchants an excellent opportunity to turn a 'negative' into a positive opportunity, by building a better relationship with their customers.

- If you offer a money-back or a satisfaction guarantee, display it clearly on your site. If you do not offer such guarantees, list your terms of sale and your return policy and procedures on your site. Buyers want to understand the terms of their purchase before they push the 'order now' button.
- Let people know how long it takes to deliver their order. Post which method of shipping you use, and how much you charge for shipping. Also, be sure to disclose any additional charges, including sales tax.

Despite all the planning that goes into a Web merchant's marketing and sales strategy, a clear customer service guarantee is easy to overlook.

Common mistakes and how to rectify them

Over-engineering

A common mistake is to attempt to develop a site that turns out to be too complex ever to be implemented. Often, well-intentioned projects never get off the ground due to unrealistic and complex plans. In many cases, the challenges created by new and unfamiliar technologies may be too great to overcome initially, and the new online store can be greatly delayed or abandoned altogether, as technical costs mount.

To avoid over-engineering, start simply by identifying the most basic goals of your online store and first implement those. When the basic system is in place, you can always add on all the bells and whistles.

Tips, tricks and trivia

SciCentral provides a 'gateway' to help you locate some of the best science and engineering resources in the eWorld. One point of access is the search feature, which allows you to select Boolean operators from drop-down lists. You can also browse subject areas to find specialized journals online, check out bulletin boards, find information on teaching science, and read about science news. SciCentral recently started a service to deliver science news to subscribers through email.

http://www.scicentral.com

Taking on more than you can cope with

ECommerce can involve a highly complex combination of equipment choices, Web site building and hosting issues, as well as security and billing technologies, etc. It is easy to attempt to resolve all these issues when setting up shop, but the more prudent strategy may be different. Instead of biting off more than anyone can cope with, choose an eCommerce service provider that has turnkey solutions.

For example, when starting, why not use a service like IBM HomePage Creator, which takes care of all the 'big decisions' and highly technical issues? Instead of trying to become an expert in all these areas, let IBM, or any other high-quality store-hosting service, worry about fending off Internet hackers, as well as hardware and software issues that only the top computer networking gurus can handle. In this way, you can concentrate on selling your product while delegating many of the technical chores to others.

Neglecting security issues

Internet hackers have become a household word lately, and reports of electronic theft and sabotage seem to be increasing at alarming rates. If you host your own eCommerce site, you need to make network security a top priority even before your eCommerce site goes live. Computer network experts are probably already aware of the pressing need to install the Windows NT service pack and of the dangers of leaving the pre-packaged CGI scripts in place. If you are an intermediate user, you should seriously consider retaining the services of a network security consultant as well as installing specialized security software. If you are a beginner, you should let an experienced hosting service take care of security issues.

Going it alone

ECommerce pioneers generally share an innovative and entrepreneurial spirit, which may well be the underlying secret of their success. However, when considering the vast complexity of eCommerce issues, it would be a mistake not to outsource some of the eCommerce set-up tasks, as needed.

In many cases, even when using a turnkey hosting service like HomePage Creator, many new eCommerce stores fail due to a lack of professional design and marketing know-how. Rather than undertaking a long and difficult process of planning, only to stumble on the final design and presentation of the store, consider retaining an eCommerce-oriented Web development agency. Don't 'go it alone', if you have the option of having professional, experienced backup.

Design mistakes

To run an online store, sophisticated technologies are installed on the host Web server or, as it is often termed, the 'back-end'. However, ultimately, the prospective online shopper only sees the 'front-end', i.e. what is displayed in the shopper's Web browser. For this reason, a well-designed interface is needed. Without a professional, marketing-oriented and easy-to-use page layout, even the most sophisticated back-end technologies will be of no use in encouraging sales.

Cluttered Web pages that make it difficult to navigate your site, or make it difficult for the shopper to know how to place an order, can cause an online store to fail. If you are serious about building a successful eCommerce site, make sure that your site works to your advantage, rather than be a cause of lost sales opportunities.

Neglecting the telephone number

It is a little-known fact that for many online stores the point of sale is not online at all. Rather, a typical scenario might be that the shopper browses through the site, researches and compares values, but then finally places the actual purchase order over the phone. Yet, many sites fail to make a phone number available for ordering.

To respond to shoppers' preferences, a phone number should be listed prominently on every page of the site. By nature, the eWorld is a global medium and a free telephone number would be highly recommended. It helps convey to the shopper you are a reliable source, and helps boost confidence that you will be there to provide customer service, if necessary.

EWorld advertising

EWorld advertising continues to be a burning topic of discussion, capturing the attention of traditional and direct marketers, and for good reason. The size of the EWorld market is enormous and growing at double-digit rates as both individual companies and online service providers rush to make their connections.

For the advertiser, costs of online advertising can be nominal while the returns can be significant. However, since the eWorld advertising market is so new, it can be very difficult to predict rate of response or the return on investment of the advertisement without first testing a variety of online vendor services and staying with them for prolonged periods of time.

There is an even more difficult question facing advertisers: How do I get my audience to see my product in the eWorld? This chapter will examine some simple and economical methods for advertisers to test this growing market, without spending an extensive amount of time or money.

> **Tips, tricks and trivia**
>
> **Information, ad, or both?**
>
> Earlier this year, AltaVista announced plans to auction off top placement in results for given queries. Many people who use the eWorld for research are concerned that this practice may affect the quality of citations they can find with the search engine. However, AltaVista says that it will only sell up to two placements per search and that these will be clearly marked as advertisements. You can read AltaVista's explanation of the program, called Relevant Paid Links, at
>
> **http://www.altavista.com/av/content/paid_placement.html**

Until recently, navigating the eWorld meant you had to learn UNIX, the operating language of the eWorld, along with its essential navigating commands. Now, software makes this challenge less difficult. Still, the vast majority of potential eWorld users that make up this growing market don't know how to get around in the eWorld. Many of the advertisers are drawn in by hype regarding response and by the reported size of the audience in the eWorld at any given time.

It's easy to get carried away into believing that just because you advertise in the eWorld, millions of people are going to see your ad, just because it's there. The truth of the matter is that it just isn't so. First, people have to know your advertisement exists and the locations where you can go and find it. Secondly, people have to have the ability to go and read it. It will still be some time before a large enough segment of the market possesses the software and becomes familiar and comfortable with its usage.

Advertisers are beginning to realize that not everyone's an expert. As you plan your eWorld advertising strategy, it's worth knowing the lowest common denominator of online proficiency among computer users today.

Ask yourself what kinds of software, hardware, and level of usage skills the largest and broadest segment of online users possesses. One of the main reasons an advertisement doesn't work is that the advertiser does not properly estimate the audience's size and ability with online usage.

For the advertiser to ignore this basic principle would be like choosing to place a billboard on Mount Everest because it's the tallest mountain in the world, and so anything you put on it must be visible to millions of people.

It is true that the eWorld is used by millions of people, but by the same token the vast majority don't know the first thing about navigating it or even have the right software to use.

How do companies use it cost-effectively?

Auto-response email

While there are various kinds of options and sources you can access that will give you information about how to go commercial in the eWorld, one advertising method that is easy to use and is used by thousands of companies is known simply as auto-response email. Instead of trying to direct your audience to your advertisement, auto-response email allows your advertisement to come to them instead. Moreover, users don't need to own any sophisticated software, graphical interfaces or high-speed modems. All they need to do is simply address an email message and their work is done.

Using auto-response email allows businesses to tap into the enormous population that is not connected through one source or another to the eWorld. A business can set up numerous addresses, each of which is pre-programmed by the advertiser to send a different file or document back to the requesting party. This is much the same as fax-on-demand. Naturally, you'll want to provide your prospects with your email address, along with your telephone number and physical address as well.

By using auto-response email, an individual simply addresses a piece of email and sends it to an address, which may look like info@xyz.com. Nothing more has to be said in the body of the email message because the receiving reply to that email is pre-programmed to reply to the email

> **Tips, tricks and trivia**
>
> **Don't be fooled by the name**
>
> It may be called Useless Knowledge, but it actually turns out to be one of the most useful and informative pages in the eWorld:
>
> **http://www.uselessknowledge.com**
>
> Each day, one sweep of the home page gives you a solid quote, a great fact, an out-of-the-ordinary but extremely useful word, a historical event that occurred on the current date, and the number of days until the years 2000 and 3000. If this isn't enough edification, you can click through archives for all the categories, take a series of trivia quizzes, or get the answers to various 'imponderables' (such as 'Why is the sky blue?' or 'Why do bees buzz?'). Every site should be so useless.

address of 'info', by sending back a specific document or file to the person who sent the request. No one on the receiving end will ever even see the email request or have to answer it manually.

This makes sense for two reasons:

- There is no danger of information getting lost in the overload of data already stored in the thousands of eWorld user groups.
- Auto-response email needs no special skills because the information is sent directly to the party who requested it, no matter where they are.

A potential respondent or buyer can access your information from virtually any bulletin board system, commercial online system, university, or in the eWorld through an independent access provider. No technical skills, eWorld navigation skills or UNIX skills are needed.

There are basically two ways to incorporate auto-response email into your operations. First, there are a number of Internet service providers that can offer you this service. Some have fixed rates while others have rates based on the number of requests made for your document or your file. This is a popular method because it prevents the auto-response provider from risking financial ruin if his system were to send out your document to the one million people who requested it.

In addition to supplying equipment and know-how, the Internet service provider is also paying for the telephone time to transmit your document to the requesting party each time.

Another alternative is to use the services of a company that has established a track record with auto-response classified advertising. Using this approach, your information will be packaged along with others in a similar category, so that everyone requesting information dealing with your product or service will also receive information for other products and services as well. In addition to a much lower price, this alternative also requires you to be far less proficient in knowing how to navigate the eWorld.

Additionally, a professional classified provider will normally help to create and type in your data so you don't have to upload your information to him.

I requested and received an auto-response email document recently on CompuServe. You can request a document be sent via auto-response email from any online service. In my case it took a total of eight seconds for the sender to download the entire file containing commercial information into our emailbox.

Once you begin using auto-response email, you'll appreciate how it can effortlessly speed up your operation of sending information to potential customers and receiving responses from the customers to the supplier.

Some do's and dont's for eWorld advertisers

The do's

- Do examine the skills and computer equipment belonging to your friends, business associates, neighbours, and people with whom you work.
- Do examine your own proficiency with the software and the online service. Do you really know how to use your software and can you find your way around the various areas of your favourite online service?
- Do examine your product. Are you selling a course on quantum physics to thousands of scientists who navigate the eWorld regularly, or a product that appeals to someone like yourself? Observe methods employed by other advertisers with similar products.
- Do quantify your audience. How many people do you need to reach, what percentage of the market does your favourite online service actually address? Tailor your message as closely to your audience's demographics as possible.

Define your objectives

Are you willing to give less or more time to tests, compared with your other media? Will the exposure combined with the image your product conveys play a role in your online strategy?

The don'ts

- Don't place an advertisement in the eWorld if the audience cannot conveniently access your advertisement at a particular location.
- Don't assume that most people have the navigational skills to access your advertisement.
- Don't overestimate the attention span of your typical online respondent. Most users will willingly download text if you don't overload them.
- Don't underestimate the message. Clarity, brevity, realism and a restrained sales pitch should be sent to your audience.
- Don't be unaware of your audience's idiosyncrasies regarding viewing commercial messages. Don't assume that all online advertising is unobtrusive to users.

Using methods such as auto-response e-mail can increase the chance that your audience will read your message by giving respondents the feeling of control to select only that product information that they feel has considerable value.

EWorld strategy is not static, it is an ongoing process. Putting a site in the eWorld is not the end of your journey, it is the beginning.

11

Making your Web site work for you

- Some do's and dont's
- Designing information
- How eWorld advertising is different
- Learning in the eWorld
- Three steps to putting your business on the net
- Six ways to make your Web site sell!
- How to write ad copy for the Web
- Auto-responders serve your customers around the clock

Make your Web site sell! Web site prices are coming down, with many services offering free Web space; it makes sense for every small business to have a Web site. Unfortunately, many people are finding that their Web site doesn't do much for sales. Here are a few important things to bear in mind in making your Web site more effective.

Your Web site should clearly communicate its purpose to readers in the very first frame. Tell people what you do or sell, what your page is about, and what benefit they'll get from reading it. Put that information right at the top of the first page.

Some do's and dont's

Make sure your Web site offers lots of FREE information

Remember that word 'free.' It's almost impossible to sell anything in the eWorld unless readers can get free and helpful information from you. By giving away some information, readers are much more likely to want to BUY more from you.

Keep your site simple

Lots of whiz-bang graphics can look attractive, but make your site slow to download. As you surf the eWorld you will come across so many sites that have:

- unprofessional look and feel;
- weak branding;
- poor graphical consistency;
- poor overall usability;
- poor navigation.

As I surf the eWorld I have come across many sites where I have struggled to make sense of them, and then tried to find some relevant information. These sites seem to have been created by some designer who must have been under the influence of hallucinogens. The eye can take about 3.2 seconds worth and then you click your mouse, never to return.

Technological confusion

Who invented splash pages? Who could possibly enjoy sitting through a download of some pointless animation or logo before you can get to a site's front page? A Teletubby would lose patience.

Whose bright idea was it to have extra windows popping up and floating around over what I want to read? Why should I load up my computer with plug-ins so I can be distracted by what usually adds little more than window dressing to a site? I know that Shockwave is like handing a wonderful box of electronic crayons to digital designers and programmers. But too often, the flash ends up being the content.

> **Tips, tricks and trivia**
>
> **A waste**
>
> The Internet's Largest Waste of Space is an empty Web page of some 40 million pixels square:
>
> **http://www.geocities.com/~sampieri/waste.htm**
>
> To help you sense the full magnitude of the waste, the site's creator tells us, 'If you had a load of 21-inch monitors with the resolution set to display 1280 pixels by 1024 pixels then to show the full space, you'd have to stack them 39,063 high and 31,250 wide.' Little does this person know that less creative people are wasting space on the Web without even trying.

Designing information

If you are contemplating a new site or think your current site needs improvement, find a developer with an appreciation for information design. Their passion for making information user-friendly should be at least as powerful as their wish to create something visually breathtaking.

When they talk about 'user experience', be sure they are referring to the ability of users to easily find what they are looking for, understand it, and act on it confi-

> **Tips, tricks and trivia**
>
> **Your Web site, in syndication**
>
> Where can a Webmaster go to fill holes in his or her site's content? To iSyndicate, the company whose modest goal is to 'syndicate the Internet':
>
> **http://www.isyndicate.com**
>
> Thanks to iSyndicate, you can perk up your site with news, weather, sports, stock quotes, horoscopes, entertainment, etc. from a stable of established Web sites. I predict it won't be long before you see an entire site made up of syndicated content.

dently. If your site can't do that, all the visually breathtaking features in the world won't make a scrap of difference.

A prominent member of your Web development team should be what's called an 'information architect'. The role of that person is to fully understand your business and all the information you want your customers to have access to, as well as what you want your customers to be able to do on your site; these are called 'user tasks'.

An information architect should be able to help you define your information requirements and tell you exactly how they fit into an overall concept for your site. And that person should be accountable for that concept at every step of the design process.

Defining the concept

By concept, I do not mean 'look and feel,' which unfortunately are what many Web developers focus on. To put look and feel first is to put the cart before the horse, and before you know it, you're getting the Shockwave treatment. You'll end up with a site that doesn't do what you want for your customers, which is to communicate clearly and be easy to use.

Choosing a Web developer

You must be firm when you choose an agency to create or overhaul your Web site. Insist on the following:

- Their proposal must show an adequate understanding of your business objectives and marketing strategy.
- The team members working on your site must exhibit the brain power and attention span to grasp all of the information that needs to go on your site.
- Their team should include an information architect with the ability to organize your site's content logically so that it's all easy to find.
- Someone on their team should have the writing skills to transfer your copy to the Web plainly, simply, concisely and clearly, so that it's easy to understand.

How eWorld advertising is different

The eWorld provides an exciting marketing tool for small businesses. Nowhere else can you grab hold of a major advertising media for FREE. It's not all a bed of roses, though. Many business owners come to me with a common question. After their Web site has been in place for a few months, they notice that it sells differently. It has to do with the ease of visiting online merchants. In the 'real' world, you have to get in your car and drive to a location to buy something. Once you're in the store, you've already committed time, effort and fuel. In the eWorld, it takes only minutes to browse through dozens of online stores, and you do it all without leaving your chair. For that reason, eWorld shoppers don't feel as committed to buy. You must bring them back several times to get the sale.

Learning in the eWorld

There's an old saying that education is wasted on the young. Many times, we go into business wishing we knew more about marketing, finance, taxes, or life in general. The eWorld is making learning easier. It is also demanding that all of us become life-long learners, continuing to add to our knowledge of skills and ideas. Facts, figures, tips and insights are everywhere in the eWorld. Many Web sites, ranging from IBM to your local consultant, are putting up pages with lots of helpful resources for small business owners. The ease and speed of placing a new article on a Web site leaves books, manuals and videos falling well behind. Colleges and universities are getting into the act. Your learning choices range from venerable institutions to the very innovative and non-traditional Summit University at **http://www.summitunivofla.edu**.

Communicating via email and in chat rooms, entrepreneurs can connect with experts, writers, coaches and professors. Yahoo does an excellent job of keeping up with eWorld learning sources.

Three steps to putting your business on the net

'How do I get my business on the eWorld?' It's a common question that more and more business owners are asking. The eWorld's massive power and very low cost is particularly attractive to small businesses and home-based entrepreneurs. Here's a simple three-step method that has worked for countless businesses entering into the eWorld community:

1. Build a Web site. With so many people shouting their messages on the eWorld, it's important to have a place where people can go to get to know you and your business.
2. Offer a free report filled with information that people want. Nothing draws attention better in the eWorld.
3. Advertise your free report aggressively in free ads, appropriate newsgroups, and in email newsletter classifieds. None of this has to be expensive. You can build your Web site yourself or you can have a small site built for a few hundred euros. Above all, remember that the eWorld is crowded and you must promote to get results.

Six ways to make your Web site sell!

I call it the 'Six Months Later' curve. Almost all of us get it about six months after we put up a Web site. You build some attractive Web pages, you promote them in the eWorld, lots of people come to visit, BUT you don't sell anything. Here are some simple ideas you can use now to get your Web site sales going.

- How many times have you visited a Web site that looks promising, but you can't quite comprehend what they're selling? Odd but true, many Web sites have a hard time telling you WHY they are there. Tell the reader in very clear terms what you are selling. Make sure your 'what I'm selling' message is the very first thing the readers see. Many sites get carried away with graphics. They believe that you'll love the look so much you will be happy to click around for 10 minutes to find out what's being sold. Most people don't have that kind of time or patience. Remember that all readers come to your site asking, 'What's in this for me?' Tell readers, from the start, what they will get out of your site. List the benefits of reading further and buying from you.

- **Tell readers who you are.** EWorld commerce is still new and many people don't quite trust it yet. This is typical for any new media still in its early stages. Before anyone will spend a penny with you, they have to have some idea of who they're doing business with. I'm often surprised at how many Web site designers go for a cold corporate look that provides little information of who is behind the site. That's maybe all right for Coca-Cola or Pepsi, companies that are household names. For the rest of us the reader wants to know who we are. Give the reader your name, your email address (in a link they can click on to write to you), your phone number, and in most cases a physical business address. I believe that no one in their right mind is going to send money to someone they don't know and can't get in touch with easily. I also feel it's a good idea to include some pictures. It might be a picture of you working with others, your workshop, or your showroom. Pictures communicate a lot of information and go a long way towards putting eWorld shoppers at ease.

> **Tips, tricks and trivia**
>
> **How to be witty**
>
> Ever wonder how your friends come up with those little facts and witticisms they include in their email signatures? Perhaps they subscribe to Coolsig, home to some 2,729 signature files at my last visit:
>
> **http://www.coolsig.com**
>
> Sign up, and every Wednesday you'll receive a list of ready-to-use signatures, culled from the thousands submitted weekly to the site. If you have a Web site, you can also download something called the Coolsig Randomizer, which if you're not afraid to cut and paste a little HTML code, will display a different signature on your home page every time someone 'hits' it. Even if you couldn't care less about signatures, you can have some fun just reading through this site.

- **Make sure it's easy for readers to find your order page,** find your purchasing information, and locate a number to call to order. If your Web site's main goal is to sell something, put ORDER INFORMATION in an easily seen link on every page. I like to make it as clear as possible: Click here for prices and how to order.
- **Give readers several different ways to buy:** an online order form, with a phone number, or by writing a letter. I'm always surprised at the number of people who still prefer the old-fashioned method. Most consumers will give you a credit card number.

- **Include comments from satisfied customers.** Before people do anything, they look to see who else is doing it. It's human nature. Be sure to pepper your Web site with testimonials. They can be short or can go into more detail about the benefits the buyer got from your business. Your testimonials will be more believable if they include the author's full name, business name, and address.
- **Promote your site**. Because eWorld commerce is new, it takes a lot more visitors through your site before you get a sale. Increase the number of visitors and you increase sales. Advertise in email newsletters, on newsgroups that accept ads, trade links with other sites like yours, get into a co-op banner arrangement, and build your own house mailing list by offering a free report or newsletter. Finally, remember that the eWorld is an information-based media. People go online to find good FREE information. Put some articles on your site that tell readers more about your speciality. These articles don't need to be long. A few paragraphs often do the job for hurried readers. You can increase sales today by keeping these simple points in mind when designing or updating your Web site.

How to write ad copy for the Web

Reading an article or ad in the eWorld is very different from reading the same copy in a magazine, newspaper or book. While a newspaper lets you quickly scan your eyes over lots of stories, pictures and ads, a computer screen limits your vision to just a few inches. Informed Web writers are beginning to discover better ways to write copy for the eWorld. Information needs to be grouped into brief, self-contained packages. Give the reader a few three-sentence paragraphs

Tips, tricks and trivia

A Poet's Potential Friend

Having trouble completing your rhymes? The Semantic Rhyming Dictionary may help you. Point your browser to

http://www.link.cs.cmu.edu/dougb/rhyme-doc.html

and type in a word, and you could get scores of rhymes, plus links to related words, and even a Web search of *pictures* of the word in question; maybe there's such a thing as being too comprehensive, after all.

that can stand alone as an individual piece of helpful information. Web designers also like to keep pages short. Readers shouldn't have to scroll down more than two screens' worth of material before clicking to another page. With all this clicking, it's important to limit the number of graphics so the page will load quickly. Some designers have taken the 'keep things short' attitude too far. Many expensive Web sites now suffer from not enough copy. They make it hard for readers to understand what the business is selling.

Auto-responders serve your customers around the clock

Auto-responders are very clever devices. You send email to them and they send a pre-composed message back to you. Smart businesses are using these simple tools to distribute all kinds of things: sales letters, price lists, free articles, product updates, and tips. Studies show that almost everyone in the eWorld is using email. Twenty per cent of those people rarely or never check out a Web site. Auto responders give you a way of sending large amounts of information to people who only use email. Some Web sites now provide a summary of their information via auto responder. If a visitor doesn't have time to read through the entire Web site, they can access an auto responder for information of what's there. Auto responders are inexpensive. The best Web site packages come with plenty of auto-responders included. Services such as **http://www.infoback.com** provide them at low cost. Some companies offer free auto-responders. Many larger Web site packages come with unlimited auto-responders. Keep in mind that you don't have to buy stamps to send email. It costs the same to send a short note as it does to send a 12-page sales letter.

> **Tips, tricks and trivia**
>
> **Yoyo mode**
>
> When your harried IT manager stomps around the office complaining that 'the server is in yoyo mode', what is he talking about? He means that the computer is going down, then coming back up, then going down again, then coming back up again, many times in rapid succession. It also means you should be nice to him, because he's not having a very good day.

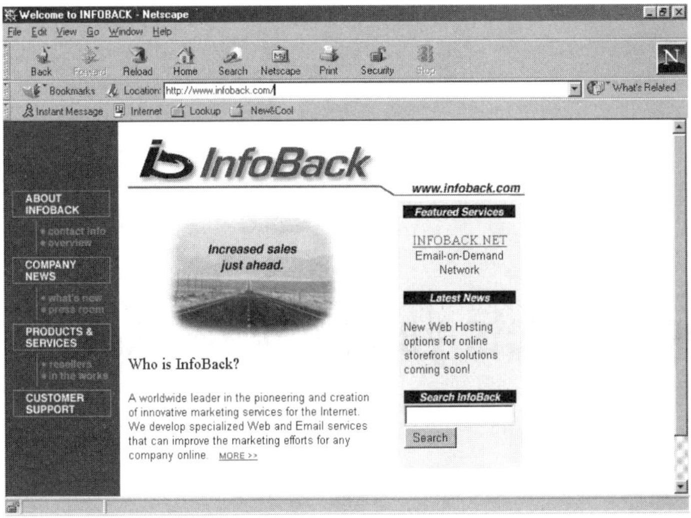
Welcome to INFOBACK - Netscape
File Edit View Go Window Help
Back Forward Reload Home Search Netscape Print Security Stop
Bookmarks Location: http://www.infoback.com/
What's Related
Instant Message Internet Lookup New&Cool
InfoBack
www.infoback.com
ABOUT INFOBACK
contact info
overview
COMPANY NEWS
what's new
press room
PRODUCTS & SERVICES
resellers
in the works
CUSTOMER SUPPORT
Increased sales just ahead.
Who is InfoBack?
A worldwide leader in the pioneering and creation of innovative marketing services for the Internet. We develop specialized Web and Email services that can improve the marketing efforts for any company online. MORE >>
Featured Services
INFOBACK.NET
Email-on-Demand Network
Latest News
New Web Hosting options for online storefront solutions coming soon!
Search InfoBack
Search

12

Search engine facts you need to know

- Information and knowledge is power in the eWorld
- General information
- Why are relatively few pages indexed?
- Spamdexing
- Points to consider
- Six major search engines

Information and knowledge is power in the eWorld

There are some interesting facts about search engines and the eWorld that you should be aware of in order to use this information to promote your site through the search engines more effectively. There are many more ways you can market your eWorld site, but the most effective both in results and in costs is getting included in the search engines and getting a good rank in searches for your products or services. That's because getting listed in a search engine is free, and if you are placed well, the traffic from an engine will increase your number of hits and potential sales considerably. Search engines are the most popular tools that users use to find new information in the eWorld.

> **Tips, tricks and trivia**
>
> **Get found**
>
> Many Web services offer to register your site with as many as 100 search engines; Did-it.com has a different approach: Instead of listing you with 100 search engines, it makes absolutely sure you get listed with the top 10. The site also lets you know how your site ranks in searches based on certain keywords and provides tips for improving that ranking.
>
> **http://www.did-it.com**

General information

Forrester Research estimates that there are 500 to 600 million pages on the Internet and that number is growing fast. However, the largest search engine, AltaVista, only has about 150 million pages indexed (about 27 per cent of the eWorld), with Excite and Lycos at only about 50 million indexed (about 10 per cent of the eWorld). In the past year none of the search engines increased in size significantly, despite the fact that the eWorld continued to grow. To a Webmaster, these are shocking statistics.

Why are relatively few pages indexed?

- The eWorld is growing faster than the engines can keep up with.
- Many Webmasters do not know how to design and submit their pages correctly.

Getting and staying indexed well in a search engine takes a little more work than most people assume. You need a four-step approach.

1. Make sure all your eWorld pages can be reached from your home page within three clicks. Most engines will only crawl three levels deep when indexing your site. Also, make sure all your pages have TITLE tags and META description and keyword tags, as most engines now use these. It is also highly advisable to have META category, language, and robot revisit tags, and ALT tags on all your images. Don't just slap these into your pages. Put some thought into them. For example, the text in the TITLE tag for a particular page should start with a word that summarizes the entire page (a keyword). Say you have a page that has information on vacations in Marbella, Spain. Your TITLE tag should read something like 'Marbella vacations, tours, and travels in Spain. Packages include diving ...'. The word 'Marbella' starts the sentence, and the rest of the sentence is made up of keywords that are related to the content of the page. This goes a long way toward getting you better rankings; same thing with the META tag text. If you use frames on your site, make sure you use good NOFRAMES tags since not all major engines support frames. If you don't, those engines simply will not index your pages. If you use image maps, make sure you have a text links navigation bar somewhere on the same page, as not all major engines support image maps either. Quick note: the TITLE tag text should be at most 200 characters long, with the first 80 characters being the most important, as these are the ones most engines focus on in ranking and results display. Do not simply repeat keywords in the title tag. Make some grammatical sense out of the sentences but ensure that the keywords feature early and are not diluted by too many 'junk' words.

Tips, tricks and trivia

Because the only link that matters is the one to *your* site

Having trouble getting the search engines to notice you? All I Know About Specific Search Engines, at

http://www.geocities.com/~laisha/

is one Web designer's volumes of experience on how to get your site 'ranked' on the big-name portals. By all means, read the detailed instructions, but I also encourage you to heed the Webmaster's plea for rationality: 'While it is important to be listed, it is equally important not to mislead. Keep in mind that searches are actually more for searchers than submitters, and if you misrepresent your pages in order to rank high, you ultimately degrade a large part of the Internet.' I couldn't agree more.

2. Submit only your home page and perhaps one other major page and then let the engines crawl your site. I will explain this in depth below. (The only exception is Infoseek. Infoseek does not crawl so you must submit every page on your site to it manually.)
3. Monitor your submission and resubmit your home page every couple of weeks. The engine may have taken your submission but dropped it later (this happens a lot with Excite), gone to your site and found it unavailable at the time, or just not indexed your site due to a technical error on its part. Resubmitting and checking on your submission every two weeks will ensure that you will eventually get in and stay in the index.
4. You need to get as many people linking to your site as possible. Visit related sites and ask for a link to your site. There is a trend by the engines increasingly to use link popularity and traffic as an indicator of relevance. What this means is that the more people link to your page relative to your competitors' pages, the more highly you will rank on the engines. Not only will getting many incoming links get you a better rank on the engines, but it will also get you a lot of traffic (following links is the second most popular way people find new sites). Furthermore, on Excite, HotBot and Lycos, link popularity also determines whether the engine will crawl deep into your site and index more pages or not. Do not ignore this fourth step, no matter how hard it sounds!

Tips, tricks and trivia

Direct hits by popularity

Direct Hit has developed a 'Popularity Engine', which helps sort search results in order of relevance. Its criteria include how often people visit sites selected from a search results list and the amount of time spent at these sites. Web sites visited frequently and explored for a longer time are ranked higher than other sites. HotBot and Lycos are among the popular search sites that use Direct Hit technology. You can also try out Direct Hit directly at

http://www.directhit.com

For the major engines, do not leave the submission process to automated programs and services. The major search engines are too important and the automated services sometimes do it incorrectly. You are only submitting the home page and one other major page to Excite, Lycos, AltaVista, Infoseek, Northern Light and HotBot; that is not much work to do manually every two weeks!

Spamdexing

Because the search engines are so overwhelmed, they are coming up with more ways to make their job easier and weed out pages they feel are not worth indexing. One of the new developments is that most engines now insist or highly recommend that you only submit your home page to them and let the engine crawl through your site and index the pages it finds. If you decide to go against this recommendation and submit a whole list of pages through the online submission forms, you will risk being tagged a 'spamdexer' (index spammer). There is also an indication that engines like AltaVista give a higher ranking to crawled pages than submitted pages. So for your own interests, you want your pages crawled so that they have a higher score. Other engines like Excite will take the same amount of time to add your pages to their index whether you submit them manually or let it crawl to them from your home page. So not only will you be wasting your time submitting each and every page you have to Excite, but you will risk spamming that engine.

Points to consider

Submit only your home page and one other major page and let the engines crawl your site. The only exception is Infoseek. Infoseek does not crawl so you must submit every page on your site to it manually. You can make a list of URLs to your pages and email that to Infoseek if you have more than 50 pages you wish to submit (see their submission page for more details).

There are a few other things to watch for to avoid having your pages excluded from the engines. The following make an engine tag a particular page as spam and therefore not index it. Make sure that none of your pages has any of these.

- **Keyword stuffing** This is the repeated use of a word to increase its frequency on a page. Search engines have the ability to analyze a page and determine whether the frequency is above a 'normal' level in proportion to the rest of the words in the document.

- **Invisible text** Some Webmasters stuff keywords at the bottom of a page and make their text colour the same as that of the page background. This is also detectable by the engines.
- **Tiny text** Same as invisible text but with tiny, illegible text.
- **Page redirects** Some engines, especially Infoseek, do not like pages that take the user to another page without his or her intervention, e.g. using META refresh tags, CGI scripts, Java, JavaScript, or server side techniques. If you use redirection, it should have a delay of about seven seconds.
- **META tags stuffing** Do not repeat your keywords in the META tags more than one to three times, and do not use keywords that are unrelated to the content of your site.

Do not submit the same page more than once on the same day to the same search engine.

Do not submit virtually identical pages, i.e. do not simply duplicate a Web page, give the copies different file names, and submit them all. That will be interpreted as an attempt to flood the engine.

Below are several useful facts and tips for each major search engine that you can use to improve your search engine marketing.

Six major search engines

AltaVista http://www.altavista.com

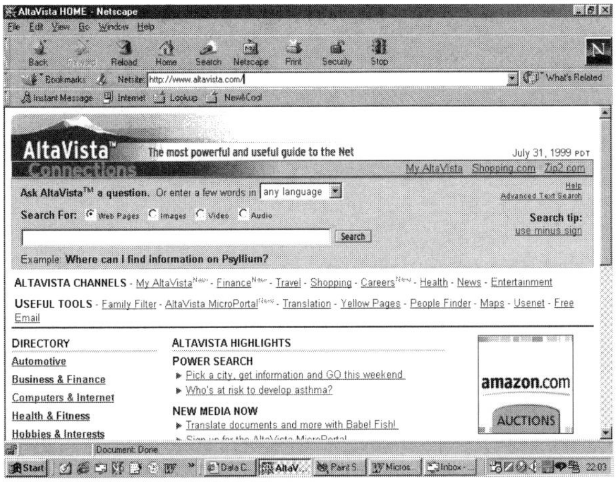

Altavista facts

Pages in index in millions: 150

Time it takes to index a submitted page: 1–2 days

Time it takes to index crawled pages (may take longer than indicated): 1 day to 1 month

How to check if your page is on the index: In the search box, type: '+url: yourcompany.com/yourpage.htm'.

How to check how many pages link to your site: In the search box, type: 'link: yourcompany.com'. You can narrow your search to a particular directory or page like: 'link: yourcompany.com/ourpage.htm'.

To eliminate from the results all the pages within your own domain that link to each other, use the -url command: 'link: yourcompany.com -url: yourcompany.com'

Supports frame pages: Yes

Supports image maps: Yes

■ HotBot http://www.hotbot.com

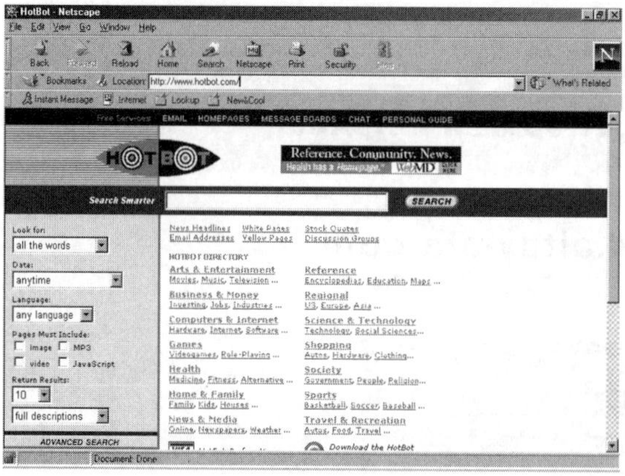

HotBot facts

Pages in index in millions: 110

Time it takes to index a submitted page: 2 days to 2 weeks

Time it takes to index crawled pages (may take longer than indicated): About 2 weeks

How to check if your page is on the index: Select the advanced search options and enter your page's URL.

How to check how many pages link to your site: In the search box, type: 'linkdomain: yourcompany.com'.

To eliminate from the results all the pages within your own domain that link to each other, use the -domain command like: 'linkdomain: yourcompany.com -domain: yourcompany.com'. These methods get you all the pages linking to your domain.

To find the links to only a particular page, enter your URL into the search box, then choose the 'links to this URL' options.

Supports frame pages: No

Supports image maps: No

Infoseek http://www.infoseek.com

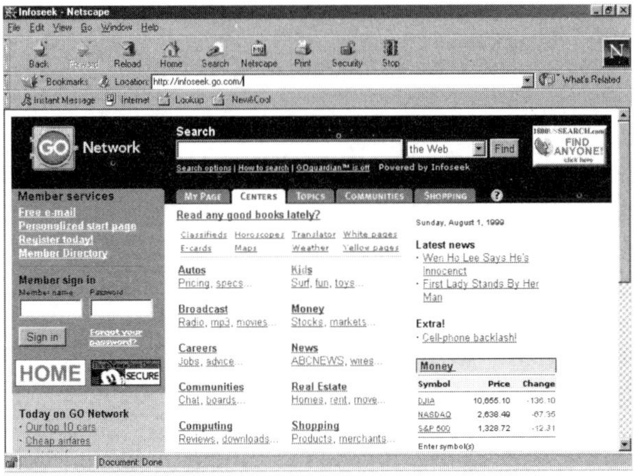

Infoseek facts

Pages in index in millions: 75

Time it takes to index a submitted page: 1 day for pages submitted online, 7 days for email submissions.

Time it takes to index crawled pages (may take longer than indicated): Rarely spiders, if it does then 1–2 months.

How to check if your page is on the index: In the search box, type: 'URL: http://www.yourcompany.com/page.htm'.

How to check how many pages link to your site: In the search box, type: 'link: yourcompany.com'. You can narrow your search to a particular directory or page like: 'link: yourcompany.com/ourpage.htm'.

To eliminate from the results all the pages within your own domain that link to each other, use the -url command like: 'link: yourcompany.com -url: yourcompany.com'.

Supports frame pages: No

Supports image maps: Yes

Excite http://www.excite.com

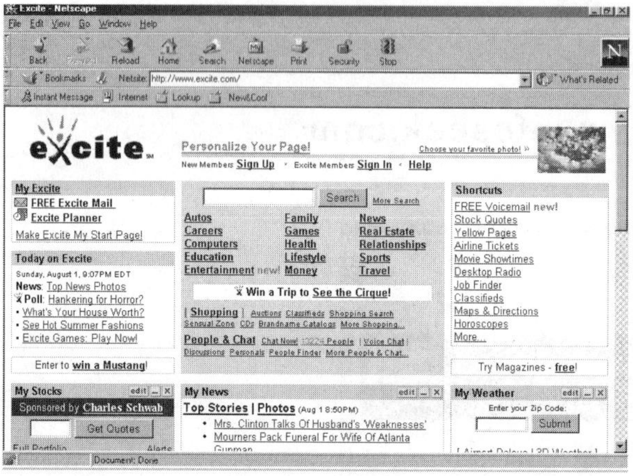

Tips, tricks and trivia

Excite guides families through the eworld

Excite beefed up the Family section of its portal recently. Excite Family offers links to tools like a Baby Namer and genealogy search engines. You can also download safe-surfing software at no cost through links to the site (on going to press, ZeekSafe was the featured kid-friendly program). The site also encourages families to get involved with links to special eWorld activity pages for kids and chats for teens. The obligatory search engine allows you to search Excite's resources or the entire Web.

http://www.excite.com/family/

Excite facts

Pages in index in millions: 55

Time it takes to index a submitted page: About 2 weeks

Time it takes to index crawled pages (may take longer than indicated): Up to 6 weeks.

How to check if your page is on the index: In the search box, type in the full URL of the page.

How to check how many pages link to your site: N/A

Supports frame pages: No

Supports image maps: No

Lycos http://www.lycos.com

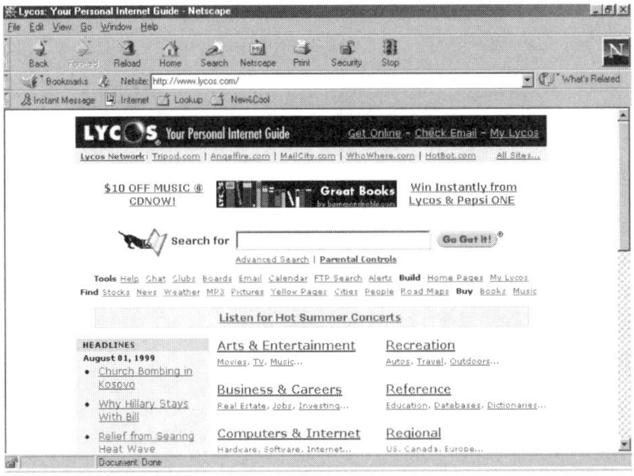

Lycos facts

Pages in index in millions: 50

Time it takes to index a submitted page: 2–4 weeks

Time it takes to index crawled pages (may take longer than indicated): 2–4 weeks

How to check if your page is on the index: N/A

How to check how many pages link to your site: N/A

Supports frame pages: No (limited)

Supports image maps: No

> **Tips, tricks and trivia**
>
> **Images and pictures**
>
> The Lycos Image Gallery is probably the largest source of free art in the eWorld. The gallery contains 80,000 FREE images. Note: There are restrictions on using the photos, so read the disclaimers carefully.
>
> **http://www.lycos.com/picturethis/**

Yahoo http://www.yahoo.com

Yahoo! facts

Yahoo! is the most popular directory on the eWorld. Many people have problems getting their site listed. A rough estimate is that only one out of every 10 submissions gets listed, if that. Moreover, it takes an estimated 4–15 weeks to be listed for those who actually get listed! Those who get listed have to resubmit their site an estimated four times over several weeks or months before getting listed (resubmitting often is spamming, by the

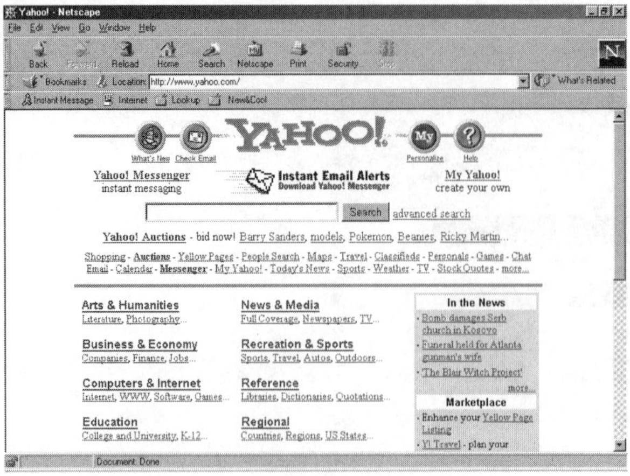

way). One thing is for sure – you must get into Yahoo! Yahoo! actually brings some sites over 50 per cent of their business. Yahoo! now has an express submission service whereby you pay $199 for a response to your submission within seven days. It doesn't guarantee that you will be listed with them, but at least you get to know within seven days whether you are in or if not, why. Here is a set of links that you need to visit to learn how to get into Yahoo! successfully.

http://help.yahoo.com/help/search/url/

http://howto.yahoo.com/chapters/10/1.html

You may feel overwhelmed with all this information. You may feel as if you don't really want to bother and follow all of the above. That would be a big mistake! Consider what it's worth in this way: The top search engines each charge €52,000 and upwards for banner ads tied to a keyword. They make it expensive because they know it's effective and valuable. Now, if you were positioned in the top 10 or 30 results, free of charge, using Web pages that you submit to the top five search engines, that would be comparable to paying for €260,000 worth of advertising per keyword! But all you have to do is take a few simple steps that most Webmasters fail to take advantage of and you get this for no cost bar a few minutes of your time.

The statistics referred to in this section were correct as at June 1999.

13

The euro and its impact on eCommerce

I want the whole of Europe to have one currency.

NAPOLEON BONAPARTE
1769–1821

- Advantages
- Resources on the euro
- What does the euro mean for your business?
- The euro changeover

The euro, Europe's single currency, is with us (http://europa.eu.int/euro), after more than a decade of planning and preparations. On 1 January 1999 the euro created the largest single economy in the world with a larger share of global trade and a greater number of consumers than the US and Japan combined.

> **Tips, tricks and trivia**
>
> Whether you call it Bungee, Bungy, Le Benji, or Suicide Practice, Bungee Jumping is a growing sport. The Bungee Zone is at
>
> **http://www.bungeezone.com**
>
> Among the site's many features is the Worldwide Bungee Club List.

Eleven countries have now achieved this goal. EU currencies like the German mark, French franc and Italian lira are now blending to become the euro. It includes all European Union countries except the UK, Sweden, Denmark and Greece. Norway and Switzerland are not members of the European Union, and neither are Eastern European countries.

The timetable of the euro is:

- **1 January 1999**: the euro became an official currency.
- **1999–2002**: existing national currencies and the euro operate side by side at fixed rates. The euro is not imposed as currency, but inter-bank transfers can be made in euros.
- **By January 2002**, new euro notes and coins will circulate.
- **By July 2002**, at the latest, local currencies are completely phased out and no longer allowed. Only euro transactions (cash or transfer) are possible.

Advantages

There are many economic benefits. The euro will:

- **lower prices** by making them transparent across Europe;
- **create a genuine single market** by ending barriers to trade caused by transaction costs and fluctuating currencies;
- **enhance competition** by forcing companies to concentrate on price, quality and production instead of hiding behind weak currencies;

- **benefit small and medium-sized businesses and consumers** by making it easier for the former to enter 'foreign' markets, and allowing the latter, increasingly via the eWorld, to shop in the lowest priced markets;
- **bring inflation and interest rate stability** via the new European Central Bank; and
- **lower the costs of doing business** through lower prices, lower interest rates, no transaction costs or loss through exchanging currencies, and the absence of exchange rate fluctuations.

The single currency will significantly increase competition, lower costs, and bring about greater confidence. This pressure will introduce much-needed structural reforms in Europe. Almost every aspect of Europe's business and political environment will be affected.

More importantly, marketing and pricing strategies need rethinking. The euro allows easy price-comparison across Europe, especially in the eWorld, which will quickly reveal the differences between higher and lower priced markets.

For those selling in the eWorld, the euro will make it easier to do business, and give enormous assistance to companies selling to European customers. This makes the decision process easier. Since Europeans will now be able to shop and compare prices at a click of a mouse, the advantages of the eWorld become obvious.

As Europeans will now be able to shop internationally at the click of a mouse, they will become aware of other choices and prices for the same product that were not previously available. Competition will increase for the consumer's euro, and this will put a downward pressure on prices.

Inter-European eCommerce

The benefits of inter-European eCommerce are enormous. Many analysts claim that the euro will have more impact on the integration and unification of the single market than any other force. From a European business's perspective, eCommerce is more likely to be accepted when it involves trading with our neighbouring countries than when it means selling to the US or Asia.

The advance of smart cards in Europe should make it possible to use in purchasing things online, by using a card reader, which is relatively inexpensive, from Gemplus **http://www.gemplus.com** which you then connect to an online PC.

Already in Belgium, the Proton cash card is a great success; one can add cash to it and spend such eCash almost anywhere in Belgium. Hopefully,

Tips, tricks and trivia

Two wolves

Don't be put off by the totally inappropriate name: Ginger's Exotic WolfCam is an entirely wholesome, if often uneventful, Web site. Here you can look in on the lives of Ginger's two wolves, Angus and Brianna. The image of their 'campground' environment (they sleep in a tent) updates every 15 to 30 seconds. My advice is to visit in the morning; the wolves are pretty scarce after noon. And don't forget to click the ads on the site, which help keep the wolves fed.

http://www.nidlink.com/~ugholl/pages/wc 1.html

the card will be able to be used later this year for online purchases. And the use of smart cards will become more available in Europe, after such a success in Belgium.

The implications of using cash less and less, either in the physical or online world, are staggering. Even the European Union has come out and said that they support a move to a cashless society. Your Web site will be competing with same-subject European Web sites for the attention of Europeans. Obviously, you will need to use euros as a currency on the site, as well your own currency.

If you want to offer your prices on your Web site in both dollars and euros, use the HTML code € or € to obtain the 'euro' sign (€), though be aware that it is not yet available on all computer and browser fonts.

You will need to promote your Web site in European languages. To get the attention of online Europeans, you have to attract them to your Web site in their own language. Once they arrive and their interest has been stimulated, many will be able to follow it in English. But the initial change from the previous online subject to your Web site has to happen in their

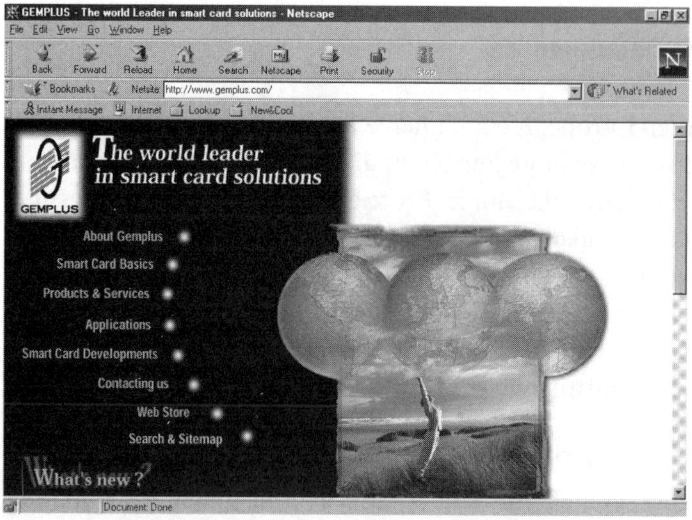

language, since there's a 99 per cent chance they are accessing the Internet in their own language.

Many European companies are internationally orientated and already deal with the issues of pan-European trade. These companies have a definite advantage.

Resources on the euro

- **EMU Net http://www.euro-emu.co.uk**. Perhaps the best single site for information about the euro. Current news, official documents, links to euro-currency events, and online forums.
- **Official EU site for the Euro http://europa.eu.int/euro/**
- *Financial Times* collection of articles about the euro. **http://www.ft.com/emu/**
- **TrueType Core Fonts for the Web** include the euro symbol. These can be downloaded from the Microsoft site for Arial, Times Roman, Verdana, Courier New, etc. **http://www.microsoft.com/typography/fontpack**
- **The Euro Currency Symbol** from Microsoft gives you links to downloads that update various operating systems for the Euro. **http://www.microsoft.com/typography/faq/faq12.htm**
- If you use Windows 95, you will need a patch to your operating system to be able to display the euro symbol (€), which you can find at **www.microsoft.com/windows/euro.asp**.

No matter how you look at it, the euro is going to have immense implications on world business, and especially on online business. Your strategy for including the euro on your Web site is a very important issue.

What does the euro mean for your business?

The most common concerns that eWorld merchants have is whether they should offer prices in euros on their sites. I do not understand their concerns when you consider the euro will initially be potentially accessible by

374 million Europeans. If you add to this equation 287 million Americans, you have a potential market of some 661 million people. And this already huge number is likely to continue to grow as other countries sign up for the euro, for example the United Kingdom, the remainder of the Scandinavian countries, and even possibly Russia.

There are, however, some problems to be overcome before eWorld merchants can start pricing their goods in euros.

There are the limitations built into much of the eCommerce software currently in use. Most merchants considering offering euro prices will want to do so in addition to their current currency of choice.

There are few eCommerce software packages available that will handle multiple currencies, particularly at the lower end of the market. Not only that, merchants who plan to make a complete switch by offering euro pricing only will have problems to resolve, as it is likely that their eCommerce software, and most of their customers' Web browsers, will be unable to display the euro currency symbol.

There are also restrictions associated with credit card merchant accounts. Many holders of merchant accounts will find that they are only able to process one currency through them, normally the currency of the country in which their business is based.

Even holders of merchant accounts issued by European banks who want to switch to the euro may well face problems as they find their card processing software and hardware unable to cope with the new currency.

Then there is the issue of exchange rate fluctuations. One of the goals of the new European Central Bank will no doubt be to try to hold the euro steady against the US dollar; the exchange rate will nevertheless fluctuate. There are, of course, methods that a business can use to limit its exposure to the impact of currency fluctuations. But many small businesses may well determine that they are in the business of selling goods and services, and not in the business of underwriting international finance.

European retailers whose merchant account limits them to trading in their own national currency, and whose customers are mainly in Europe, should investigate switching to the euro as soon as possible.

In addition to the challenges detailed above, there are still economists who are convinced that the euro will fail.

A stable, strong pan-European currency will without doubt provide a major advance to global electronic commerce.

I suggest that you keep a close eye on developments with the new currency; merchants should begin a dialogue now with the providers of their eCommerce software and their credit card merchant providers.

Easier to do business

If the benefits promised by the EMU governments come true, EMU will make it easier to do business.

It should provide greater economic stability, ease entry into other member state markets and subsequently result in the creation of an even more competitive trading environment.

Some of these projected benefits of EMU are:

- Cross-border trading will not involve the need and cost of changing currencies.
- No risk of exchange rate fluctuation.
- Prospect of lower interest rates.
- Markets will grow together or be created.
- New sales channels reaching wider markets will be opened.
- Goods and services which were previously not worth exporting to certain countries because of exchange rate implications on profit margins may now find new markets.
- Price transparency will allow consumers an easy comparison of the prices of goods and services from one country to the next.

These factors will greatly accelerate the growth of electronic commerce, eBusiness and the Internet. For full details of how IBM can help, see **http://www-5.ibm.com/euro/**.

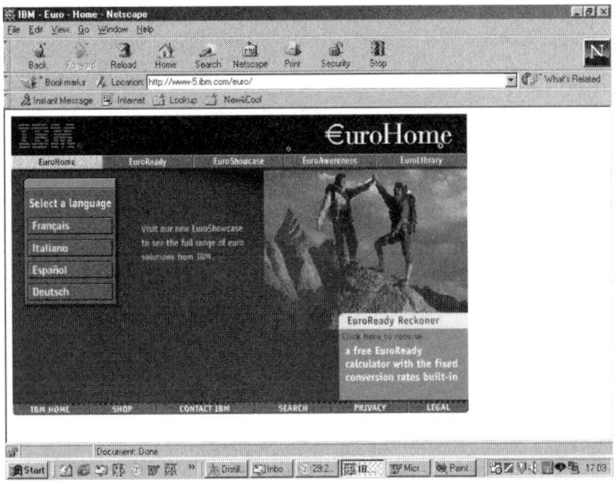

Your competitors are already positioning themselves before you do. To take any advantage you have to plan ahead.

The euro changeover

Organizations will need to examine the way they intend to handle financial amounts in relation to both the national currency and the euro.

These cover:

- **payments to suppliers and from customers;**
- **customer information, for example euro conversion of price lists;**
- **pricing strategies – strategic price points which affect consumers will have to be thought out; for example, a product priced at 9.99 in national currency may not translate well into euros;**
- **human resources, salaries, social security, income tax deductions, pensions, life and health insurances;**
- **financing, funds, cash management, short-and long-term financing; statutory reporting; accounting ledgers, shares, corporate taxes.**

This high degree of change will affect large numbers of people within every organization and their trading partners and customers. Companies will need to construct awareness, training and information programmes and help facilities to ensure that their overall EMU programmes are successful.

Other implications

Price transparency will mean that country price differentials will be harder to sustain. The already controversial car pricing difference across European borders will be increasingly heightened when the euro allows direct comparisons to be made. As the euro becomes more widely used during the transformation period, prices of heavily traded products will be set in euros. While these EMU-driven issues are appearing, other developments, such as electronic commerce and the eWorld, will open up new strategy options for many organizations.

Prepare now

Many companies are not preparing for the euro, which is absolute foolishness. Companies are at risk if they do nothing or delay preparation until the last minute, as they will find they have no time to think the process through. The cost involved as a result of not acting now may be substantially higher. In fact, companies could be put at a substantial competitive disadvantage as they struggle merely to comply.

If there is undue delay, there may not be time to make all the necessary changes. This will affect all areas of commerce. Systems and staff need to be trained to handle at least two currencies. Companies will, by 2002, have to deal with both currencies simultaneously as well as invoicing in more than one currency.

Start now before your competition does.

Tips, tricks and trivia

Need to lose a few pounds?

More and more people are trying to lose weight by the Paleolithic Diet, a diet that emulates the eating habits of our oldest *Homo sapiens* ancestors. The logic isn't that cavemen were rarely fat but that their diet was mankind's first and most natural, and one from which we've only recently (in the grand scheme of things) strayed. If you really enjoy fruits, vegetables and lean meats, and can do without dairy products and breads, take a look at:

http://www.paleodiet.com

14

Ten simple tips on setting up an eWorld shop

- The three basics

Can you make money in the eWorld? Thousands of people are making money and saving money in this new marketing medium every day. But if you want to set up shop in the eWorld, it's important for you to be just as professional, businesslike and cautious as you would be in any other new venture.

I suggest taking time to get to know the eWorld and develop a sustainable strategy. Here a few tips that you should consider before you get started.

1. **Get to know the eWorld.** Do plenty of exploring. If you're already in the eWorld, you're way ahead of the pack. You need to know what you're getting into. You can hire someone to set up a Web site for you. There is nothing wrong with that. But remember this is your business, and you should have a good feel for how it's being promoted. You know your business better than anyone else does. Because of that, you're going to find the appropriate ways of getting it to work for you, ways that no consultant could ever think of. Here's my advice: go do it. Join in some electronic discussion groups. Surf the eWorld. Start communicating by email. Don't wait. Do it now.

> **Tips, tricks and trivia**
>
> Lynx is a *text-based* Web browser. When you browse with Lynx, you can see all the text and tables in a Web site but not the pictures, animations, Java elements, mouseovers, and so on. With Lynx, you miss all the sizzle of the Web, but you get there much faster.
>
> **http://lynx.browser.org/**

2. **Be a resource.** E-world users expect information. So make sure your message is more than just hype. Add value. Be an information provider. Participate in online discussion groups, and be helpful. If you have a Web site, provide useful background information about your industry, your specialities, and your areas of expertise.
3. **Don't send out unsolicited email marketing messages.** This won't help your business and will just get recipients angry. There are much better ways to market your product or service. Electronic mail is different from postal mail. For one thing, sending out a conventional direct-mail package costs you, the sender. But often your electronic mail message will cost the recipient money! If you become a regular user of email, you'll see how annoying it would be if your mailbox got filled up every day with email advertising. There's nothing to be gained by this.
4. **Use online discussion groups for 'soft-selling'.** Newsgroups and email discussion groups can be fertile fields for marketing. But watch out.

Most groups don't tolerate commercial postings. Instead of barging in to hype your product, be a real participant. Prowl and listen. Answer questions and offer help. Include a signature block at the end of your postings to let people know how to get in touch with you. You'll be surprised how often this will bring in leads from potential clients or customers.

5. **Check your email regularly.** People on the eWorld expect fast responses. I recommend checking your email messages twice a day. Respond as quickly as possible. This shows that you're serious about your eWorld presence and that you care.
6. **Plan your site first.** Because the Web allows graphical presentations, it's easy to get caught up in designing something you like, but that does nothing to sell your product. Make sure your site communicates and offers value to the user. Make sure it's readable and that it's easy to get around. Your Web site doesn't have to be boring. You can be clever, and you can be visual.
7. **Keep your Web site changing, so people will come back.** Repeat visitors are more likely to become clients or buyers, and they're more likely to recommend your site to others. To draw users back to your site, you need to keep it changing. Update your material. Take advantage of new technology as it appears. Add new features, new resources and new information.
8. **Use correct spelling punctuation and grammar.** I'm surprised how much poorly written copy I see in the eWorld. Project a professional image by correct writing. Even if it's a basic email message, double-check it for typos or vague language.
9. **Include clear instructions in your message.** What do you want the user to do after he or she has followed your presentation? Purchase a product? Request a proposal and price quotation? Join a mailing list? Ask for more information? Let them know what you want them to do, and ask them to do it in clear, direct terms. Make it easy for them to respond. Set up a response mechanism, a direct email link, a form to fill out, and a button to click. The more direct and immediate, the better. A phone number, a fax number, or a postal mail address is a MUST.
10. **Promote your eWorld presence through offline channels.** Let your regular customers and the public know about your eWorld presence. Put your email address and URL on your business cards, stationery,

ads, brochures and packaging, anything you can think of. Send out press releases. Get the word out. Selling over the eWorld can bring results. Get to know the medium. Work up a sound strategy. Seek out appropriate online marketing methods that will get your selling message across while respecting other eWorld users.

The three basics

The age of global marketing through the eWorld has let businesses progress very quickly and it has given them unprecedented visibility.

Getting someone to know you exist in the first place is difficult enough. Keeping his or her attention is an even greater feat. Think about that: you go through the task of making your presence and services available globally, but if the people you are trying to reach don't know what to do once they visit you, what's the point? When you create an eWorld site, there are three basic points you should consider:

1. Why are you making the site? Do you have something to offer? Do you have something that people really need?
2. What are you trying to say? The message of your service MUST be clear.
3. Who are you trying to reach? You must cater to your target audience.

Once you can successfully answer those main issues, you must then package your concept in such a fashion that even someone who stumbles across you by accident will know what to do when he hits your site. Granted, he might not need anything you provide, but he might know someone who does and your chances of him saying to that person, 'Remember when you told me you were looking for (whatever)? I found a great site that does just that!', increase dramatically. You can't buy that kind of advertising.

It all boils down to this: If anyone has a reason to keep clicking when they hit your site, and

Tips, tricks and trivia

It is only rock 'n' roll

UBL, the Ultimate Band List, helps connect people to info on their favourite rock 'n' roll bands. Just type the name of the band and click the Find button. You can also select Album or Resources to locate that information through the search engine. UBL is a great way to find links, but the site is also happy to sell you related merchandise.

http://ubl.com

they know WHY they are still clicking, and know what to do after each click, they are going to stay. They will always stay longer if they find what they want and it is easy to understand. The chances of them bookmarking you improve greatly as well. Then if they are happy with you, they are going to refer you to all their friends with similar interests. Now they all become visitors to your site and possible users of your services.

Part III

Users with special needs

15

Internet users who have special needs

The eWorld has created an opportunity for many to think and act without handicap and will give many that so inspiring motivation – Hope.

CHRISTOPHER LYNAS 1999
WHILE RESEARCHING *THE eWORLD HANDBOOK*

- Users' needs
- Why a computer?
- Adaptive and alternative technologies
- Help with speed and accuracy
- Person-to-person communication
- No easy options
- What does this mean for employers?

The eWorld, this revolution in all our lives, will be the greatest boost for the disabled community and those with special needs, by simply creating equal opportunities; it will create an environment where few special accommodations need to be made. It will produce an opportunity for many to think and act without handicap. It will create an environment where everyone is able to work, play and most importantly communicate. In the eWorld any disability is invisible and irrelevant.

Disabled people fall into two categories: those who have become recently disabled and are struggling to cope, and those who have come to terms with their disability and are fighting back to take control of their lives. The eWorld helps both of these categories overcome these issues and to advance at their own pace. The eWorld will give them more freedom and the opportunity to lead full, independent lives.

While researching this section I was humbled by the information and knowledge that I gained from this research. It made me realize that the eWorld will change many people's lives in many different ways. The eWorld is a great equalizer, putting people with disabilities on an equal footing with people without disabilities. There are hardware and software products appropriate for people with special needs, and this technology is currently being implemented in education, rehabilitation, and workplaces around the world. It can provide many solutions to many of the problems facing people with disabilities today.

Over the past 10 years, IBM has been one of the largest corporate contributors of cash, equipment and people to non-profit organizations and educational institutions around the world. IBM's efforts to help people use information technology and to improve the quality of their lives are commendable. Before I researched this section I had no knowledge of IBM's commitment in this field. To all those involved at IBM and to everyone else in the world that is contributing in this area, well done.

Tips, tricks and trivia

The Guide to Disability Resources on the Internet is sponsored by the Disability Resources Monthly newsletter. Here you can find articles from the newsletter, plus links to a vast amount of information available on the Internet. The site is searchable and can be accessed through an index. A great way to get started is to browse the DRM WebWatcher section, which highlights 'interesting topics' and new or updated sites on the Web. You can also find specific information on disability resources, as well as information for parents of, and advocates for, people with disabilities.

http://www.geocities.com/drm/

IBM's commitment goes beyond simple chequebook philanthropy. They are working hand-in-hand with public and non-profit organizations designing technology solutions that address these specific problems.

They have created databases full of human services agencies. IBM experts from all over the world have helped in the development of assistive technology, and they have founded a broad range of information and services online for the disabled community. They have overcome many challenges in trying to provide people with various disabilities full access to the information in the eWorld. See **http://www.austin.ibm.com/sns/**.

> **NOTE**
>
> **A note to Web site designers:**
> **Do remember that the deaf can't enjoy sound and the blind haven't much use for pictures. Graphical and audio information should be presented in text form: pictures can be described, spoken information can be captioned. Most of the disability sites I have seen are text only.**

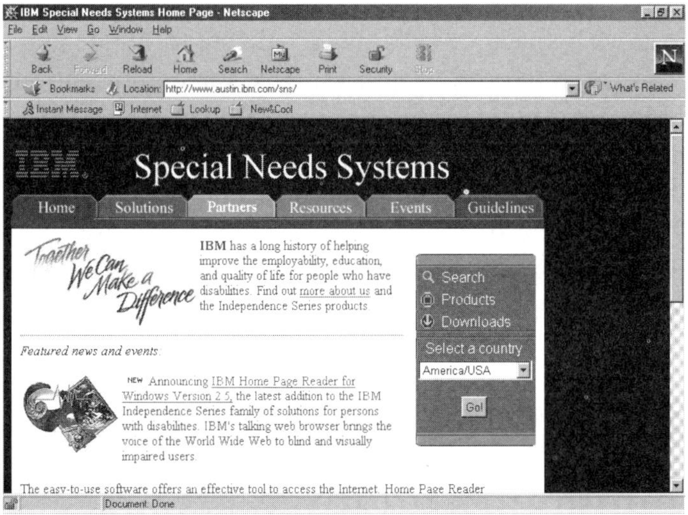

Users' needs

The blind cannot use a mouse because it is a hand–eye coordinated device, so every application must be operable with just the keyboard. The blind and others with dyslexia and low vision also rely on assistive technology known as a screen reader that reads the screen's information, controls, buttons and text to the user. Today's screen readers transform the visual interface into an audio interface.

Those users with low vision and colour blindness have difficulty recognizing information that is presented by differences in colour, contrast, depth, size, location or font differences alone.

The deaf and hard of hearing have many of the same needs as those users who do not have a sound card or who work in a noisy environment and need information presented visually in addition to the audio means. For example, closed captions, blinking error messages, and transcripts of the speaking audio are necessary for the deaf and hard of hearing.

Users with hand, arm and other mobility impairments may not be able to use multiple simultaneous keystrokes such as Ctrl+Alt+Del and therefore rely on special keyboard enhancements in the operating system. Some users must rely on voice input and navigation where possible. Others rely on changing settings to allow them time to enter the information at their own pace, one keystroke at a time.

It would be impossible in this section to cover every aspect of the computer and those with special needs but I will try to make some important points, cover the basic concepts and give some information. However, there will be items not covered, but you will find at the end of this section a comprehensive list of very useful URLs which will point you in the right direction for more detailed information. The sheer number of disability sites speaks volumes of the various requirements of the disabled, and to the many organizations that supply disability-related services.

Why a computer?

Disability can limit an individual's range of communication and independence in all manners of day-to-day life. An ordinary personal computer can make a major contribution to the quality of these lives as an instrument that can be used as an alternative to pen and paper. It can be a means of writing for people who have physical disabilities, a means to organize and store personal information, a means of speech, a means of reading and, through the eWorld, a means of communication.

Adaptive and alternative technologies

Adaptive and alternative technology is terminology used to describe hardware and software that can overcome an apparent disability to give full access to a computer, and to what it can do. The computer is just an ordinary computer, but the means of using it are different. Each individual, disabled or otherwise, should, and can, choose the method of computer use that suits them best. A varied and interesting industry has created hundreds of 'adaptive' solutions. Many of these solutions are cheap and are remarkably effective.

Alternatives to the standard keyboard

For some people, the computer keyboard can be a difficult device to use. The keys are usually arranged in straight rows, but fingers are different lengths. In order to use one of these conventional keyboards you have to distort your fingers and use sensitive touch. Many operations require two keys to be pressed simultaneously, and if there are difficulties with the hands, wrists or upper arms this can present significant difficulties. However, there are many adaptations and modifications that can be made, for example:

- Keyboards can be adapted so that they react less quickly, for people who take longer on each keystroke. Software is available that will 'hold down' the shift and other control keys for people who cannot hit two keys together. A rigid key guard, with holes above each key, will allow a user to rest their hands above the keys while they locate a finger or stick above the key they want.
- Greater accuracy and less effort make up for any apparent slowing down of keystrokes for those who use a stick in the mouth, or on the forehead, and there are small and specially shaped keyboards that can be placed in the most comfortable position. Small and large keyboards provide a whole range of alternative ergonomic designs and hand positions for maximum comfort with minimum effort.

Alternatives to the standard mouse

With the increasing use of Windows and other graphical user interface (GUI) techniques, people think they need to use a mouse. But a mouse can be uncomfortable, or even impossible for some people. To use it effectively, you have to have access to a flat surface, grip the device, move it around to locate areas on the screen and hold it still while you hit a switch. There are alternatives which can be used:

- **Keyboard alternatives** exist for most mouse pointing actions and they can be very efficient – but few people know about them. A tracker ball is a device which is stationary, unlike a mouse, and is operated by fingertip movement of a ball on the top. It can be placed wherever is comfortable. A range of joysticks offer similar advantages and there are devices specially designed for disabled people, including pointing devices operated by head movement.

Keyboard emulation

For some people, the best possible keyboard can be an exhausting or even an impossible proposition. Keyboard emulation makes it possible to do everything with the minimum of effort and movement. Selections can be made from a 'keyboard' on the computer screen or sometimes a separate unit, using one or more switches operated with whatever body movement is most comfortable; a puff of breath; or any of the mouse alternatives mentioned above.

Many of these systems are sophisticated products that can be tailored and tuned to suit each user.

Help with speed and accuracy

Many people, disabled or not, would like to improve the speed and accuracy with which they type. This is a special requirement for people with hand or arm difficulties or problems with the written language. Computers with word processing software can always provide some advantages. Text can be reviewed and corrected before printing. Pieces of text can be stored and reused. Spelling can be checked and corrected, and word-processed text looks more professional than handwritten alternatives.

But there are additional techniques that apply directly to the needs of disabled people. As with all 'adaptive' approaches, the solutions come in a variety of forms at a variety of prices! A keyboard user can save up to 50 per cent of keystrokes with techniques like word prediction, phrase prediction, word endings, and paragraph store.

- **Word prediction** As you begin a word, the computer suggests a range of words that are likely to include the one you want. Each word has a number code beside it and with one keystroke the computer will replace your letters with a complete word of your choice.
- **Phrase prediction** The computer suggests a range of phrases when you type a key word or series of letters. For example if 'ASAP' was typed then the computer might suggest 'as soon as possible'. By selecting the appropriate numeric code this phrase will replace your previous 'ASAP', saving you time and effort.
- **Word endings** In a similar way the computer can add endings like 'ing' or 'ed' with one keystroke and apply the right spelling rules in the process.
- **Paragraph store** This is rather like phrase prediction, typing whole paragraphs prompted by the entry of a two- or three-letter abbreviation.

It is often useful to combine these ideas with other alternative approaches like a replacement keyboard or a switch input device.

Person-to-person communication

A computer can enable people who would normally find it difficult to express themselves through writing. Additionally there are adaptations and modifications which can be made to enable people with impaired speech to communicate effectively.

Speech synthesis

Speech synthesis added to any computer can act as a very effective communication aid. Text written in advance can be read to an audience or the above ideas can also be used to produce conversational speech quickly and easily.

> **Tips, tricks and trivia**
>
> **The love calculator**
>
> The self-styled Dr Love, whose motto is 'NOMEN EST OMEN', believes that lovers' names are an accurate predictor of the success of their relationship. Which pairs of names have the best chances of bliss? Only the Doctor knows for sure, but he's been kind enough to share his knowledge in The Love Calculator, at
>
> **http://www.lovecalculator.com**
>
> Type in two names, click a button, and presto – you get the probability (in percentage terms) that this pair can tear up the prenuptial agreement for good. Or use the Mass Calculation feature to match one name against several possible mates' names.

> **Tips, tricks and trivia**
>
> You have probably heard the term MP3 bandied about of late, and you probably know it has something to do with digital audio. Well, here's the rest of the story: MP3 (which stands, loosely, for 'MPEG audio layer 3') is an extension of the MPEG compression scheme that compresses sound from a CD by a factor of 12, without sacrificing the quality of the sound. MP3 is the biggest step yet toward making downloading entire songs or albums from the Web to your computer practical.

The eWorld is opened up if a computer is attached to a telephone line through a modem and an Internet browser. The computer user can then exchange news, views and information with a vast interconnected community worldwide. Any disability is invisible and irrelevant in the eWorld.

Voice recognition

Voice or speech recognition is a technology that allows computers to be used by voice alone. A range of products is available with different capabilities at different prices. The more sophisticated of these will understand dictation at speeds of approximately 40 words per minute and will learn about your speech and vocabulary the more you use them.

Prices have decreased markedly over the past few years and voice input is a more accessible option. It is also being used more frequently by able-bodied people simply for its comfort and speed – and the more this happens the better it is for disabled people, as their best choices become more routine and better known. New versions and new products are becoming available all the time. Make sure you get good, independent advice when you explore these possibilities.

For those with impaired vision

When impaired vision makes reading and writing difficult it may seem that computer use is impossible. This is not true!

Making the right choice of background colour, type colour and style can help by increasing the contrast of the text. Large screens are available and can be ideal for many visually impaired people while special software can enlarge the image on the computer screen.

Two major technologies provide other solutions. The computer screen can be read to the user through a speech synthesizer or be presented in Braille. There are a wide range of alternative products.

Braille is relatively expensive – €5,000 and above.

Screen reading systems can be bought for anything from €285 to €2,850 depending on their complexity. They are extremely effective, enabling thousands of visually impaired people to work in their chosen professions.

There have been many exciting developments in this area. It is now quite feasible for visually impaired people to have access to DOS, Windows 95/98 and Windows NT, as well as to CD-ROMs and the eWorld. A simple addition to the computer allows a blind person to have total access to Teletext and electronic newspapers. More information is being made available in a computer-readable form, and OCR/scanning allows a computer to read paper documents, store them for use in the computer and read them out in synthesized speech or Braille.

Smaller and smaller

We have laptop computers and now the new generation of notebooks and palm-tops, some with built-in speech output. Using these very small but powerful computers, all the facilities mentioned above could be used, making the user more independent and mobile. However, these are not right for everybody; they can be expensive and heavy to carry around. The screen is generally smaller and therefore may not be so clear for some users. The keyboards are not ergonomically designed.

No easy options

The technology available today to enlarge and enhance the lives of disabled people is extensive, varied, exciting stuff – but there are no easy options here. Good independent advice is essential to ensure that the correct choices are made. Some solutions take flexibility, patience, training and commitment, so be prepared for the possibility of a steep learning curve!

Computers are an important communication tool. In an increasing number of jobs, adaptive and alternative technologies can make a computer accessible to people with disabilities. However, these adaptations and modifications can only be made when the alternatives are known about and understood. There are many adaptations that can be made freely to a standard computer system.

What does this mean for employers?

They should:

- make simple adaptations available, such as alternative keyboards and mice, where necessary;
- organize proper assessments of needs and options for employees with disabilities;
- implement an IT strategy that accommodates the most frequently needed adaptations and alternatives.

16

Dyslexia and computer use

- Planning
- Using a keyboard
- Spell checking
- Voice recognition
- Scanning with Optical Character Recognition (OCR)

Dyslexia is a general term for disorders that involve difficulty in learning to read or interpret words, letters and other symbols, but that do not affect IQ. Dyslexics may find it difficult to realize their full potential if they have to depend on reading and writing for communication.

Computers can enable dyslexics to address some of these difficulties with the use of powerful word processors, predictive spelling, and grammar and spell checkers. Speech input can enable text input with dictation and speech output enables the computer to read back text to the user. This is technology that can help dyslexics to communicate effectively and accurately.

No two people are alike. The best solution for each person is likely to be a selection from the ideas described. Ideally one would like people with these types of difficulties to have an opportunity to see and try them all – but in the real world this may not be possible. Thankfully some of them are free, or relatively inexpensive.

The examples below are based on IBM-compatible PCs running Windows.

Tips, tricks and trivia

Give each letter of the alphabet a number, a=1, b=2, etc. If you add up the letters of the alphabet in the word 'Attitude' this is the result:

A	=	1
T	=	20
T	=	20
I	=	9
T	=	20
U	=	21
D	=	4
E	=	5

Attitude is 100%

Planning

It really does help most people if they decide what they want to say before they start writing. This could mean talking through what is to be written first, making brief written notes, or even drawing a diagram. Some word processing packages have a facility that displays an outline before starting to write. An example is the 'outline' facility in Microsoft Word.

Using a keyboard

For some people the task of handwriting can be hard work, demanding concentration and mental energy. Consequently, the decision about what to write is often less important. The use of a keyboard can make a positive difference, allowing the user to concentrate on the content without worrying about the clarity of the handwriting. The printed word always looks more professional than the handwritten word.

Coloured and bigger key tops

Large, coloured, alphabetic and numeric characters placed on the key tops can help the user to locate the keys more quickly and with less effort. They can be fixed easily onto the keys of any keyboard.

Coloured, larger, and easier-to-read text on the screen

If you have a colour monitor then you can usually select your own colour combinations for the background and the text. Many people find this simple adjustment can make a big difference.

Letter size can be varied by changing the font size or by magnifying the screen by using a 'zoom' control and this can sometimes be helpful because less information is displayed on the screen and it can appear to be less 'cluttered'.

Changing the font style can also help. Some fonts are less clear than others, particularly on the screen. The choice of font should be made by the individual concerned; it is a matter of personal preference.

Increasing the spacing between the lines of text, known as 'leading' in some software, can improve legibility. Remember you can always return the document to its original line spacing before printing.

Your system and software manuals or online help systems will show you how to implement most of these ideas.

Spell checking

Most word processing systems have built-in spell checkers. These are not designed for the specific difficulties of dyslexics, and they may not suggest the correct word if the spelling is obscure. For example, if the word tomorrow is spelt with some of the letters transposed, i.e. toworrom, then the spell checker might not have any suggestions for a correct spelling.

However, research has shown that spelling is generally improved for most people with the use of a standard spell checker simply because commonly misspelt words appear repeatedly until the user is familiar with the correct spelling.

Note that spell checkers improve a little with each new version of word processing software.

Special and automatic spell checking

Some word processing systems have the ability to spot and automatically correct spelling errors as you write. In Microsoft Word, for example, this facility is called AutoCorrect. One can very easily make a list of incorrect spellings and difficult words to type. These words will be automatically corrected as the user continues to type.

Special additional spell checking programs

These programs address more significant spelling difficulties. They suggest a wider range of alternative words for incorrectly spelt words. They will not necessarily suggest words that begin with the same letter, for example: nite may be written for knight, and most spell checkers would suggest words beginning with NIT---. Some of these programs also include synthesized speech output to reinforce reading skills and phonetics.

Expanding abbreviations

Some word processors have functions that can be used to speed up your typing – by adding abbreviations to an AutoText or AutoCorrect list, the computer will insert the complete word when the abbreviation is typed; for example, storing 'ys' as 'yours sincerely' can save time.

In Microsoft Word, for example, there are several methods built into the program such as the AutoCorrect facility (mentioned previously). AutoText works in a similar way but you deliberately call for the AutoText item you want, and create 'macros' that are small routines that run when you select a designated key or button. These are particularly useful if you are repeating a set of actions such as cut and paste in a file; the macro records the actions and repeats them when the designated key or button is selected.

Speech output or text review

With a sound card, or alternative speech output device, in your computer you can get the computer to read back, in synthesized speech, all or part of what has been written. This might well reveal errors that would otherwise be missed – even by a spell checker. For example: the writer types 'They was lots men there' when he wants 'There were lots of men there'. The spell checker won't help with this, but the problems may be obvious when listened to, giving a second chance to get it right – perhaps by listening to this phrase again, or each word in turn. Alternatives that give speech output include Text Assist, which gives a range of very clear voices, both male and female, that will read whole documents, or any piece of highlighted text. If you have a SoundBlaster card you may already have this software.

Prediction

There are a number of separate programs that run alongside word processing packages and will predict, or 'guess', what you are about to type, completing the word or phrase for you. These systems can add words or phrases as you type, or you can add the words and phrases you want predicted (or both). For example: you type the letter 't' and the system offers the alternatives:

1. thank
2. the
3. theory
4. thank you
5. thank you for your letter

Typing the number makes the computer type your choice! Examples of these types of predictive software are:

Applied Human Factors' SoothSayer Word Prediction.

http://www.ahf-net.com/

'Aurora 2.0' for Windows 3.1 and Windows 95.

A word prediction package for Windows, with face-to-face communication options. Works with Microsoft Works, WordPerfect, Microsoft Word, Ami Pro, WordPad.

http://www.djtech.com/Aurora/info/awin.htm

'Co:Writer' for the Macintosh.

An intelligent word prediction program that operates in conjunction with word processors and other applications that require text entry. Can be used for correspondence, reports, schoolwork, business and personal writing.

http://www.donjohnston.com/

Help with words that sound similar but are spelt differently

Another program that runs alongside a word processor is one that will highlight any word that may be confused with another because of its similar sound and will offer possible alternatives, with explanations. Some alternatives and explanations are part of the program when you get it; others can be added to meet individual needs. These can be any words that are confused, such as similarly spelt words.

For example, if the user types 'bought', the system puts on the screen:

1. **bought – with money**
2. **brought – did bring**

These were put into the checker in this form by or for this user. The user is given the two suggestions and they have to select 1 or 2 to type the correct word automatically. Other familiar examples may be 'weather/whether', and 'their/there/they're'.

Tips, tricks and trivia

The crossword solver

Having trouble finishing that crossword, jumble, or cryptic crossword? The final answers you need are no further than The Jumble and Crossword Solver, at:

http://ull.chemistry.uakron.edu/cbower/jumble.html

Type your scrambled or partial word into the blank and click a button; in a few seconds (actually, a slower Internet connection might take more than a few seconds), you have at least one, and usually several, alternative solution words. Each solution word is linked to its definition in Webster's Online Dictionary, so you can be sure you're choosing the word with the correct meaning.

Voice recognition

Modern voice recognition systems, running on personal computers, are remarkable in their ability to understand spoken words and type them. Until recently the words had to be spoken separately, with a small gap between them, and this will still be the best technique for many people, but there are now systems that take 'natural' or continuous speech. If properly used, the system will become more accurate and faster with use.

There is no voice recognition system that gives 100 per cent accuracy. But they will get better and better. If recognition errors are not properly corrected the system will not improve. So the user must either be able to recognize errors and spell the right word properly, or must achieve the same result with help. Learning to use the system effectively requires a real commitment.

Scanning with Optical Character Recognition (OCR)

Equipment attached to a computer can reliably 'read' typed or printed documents and make them available to you in your word processor. This could be used to put a piece of printed information into a document without retyping, or with the help of text-to-speech software it could be read back to you. This technology can be expensive.

17

Hearing or visual impairment

- Using a computer with a hearing impairment
- Visual impairment – an overview
- Simple first considerations
- Making text easier to see
- Working without vision
- Portable systems
- Other helpful technology

Using a computer with a hearing impairment

As computers have been introduced into both the working and home environment they have opened up far more possibilities for people who are hard of hearing or deaf, as a hearing impairment alone will not restrict an individual from making effective use of a computer. Text telephone systems like the Minicom can now be linked to a standard PC, enabling more communication opportunities than ever before.

Computers have been fitted with internal speakers for many years. Sound has often been used to alert the user to errors or to signify task completion or that an input is required. These extra settings allow a hearing user to have a better understanding of their computer environment, but for those who cannot hear the sounds, alternatives are often required.

Software is available which can change system sounds into visual signals on the screen. The two components available for Windows 95 are called SoundSentry and ShowSounds. SoundSentry generates visual signals whenever the computer makes a sound and ShowSounds displays captions for those items that either speak or make a specific sound. These systems can be effective for a novice user, but may cause distraction, so it can easily be deactivated when not required.

Visual impairment – an overview

The following information is a basic overview and is intended to introduce the approaches used to address the needs of people with impairments of vision who use or wish to use a computer. They are not intended to be detailed or comprehensive. These approaches can be used singly or in combination to enable a visually impaired person to use a computer effectively.

Simple first considerations

Access to the keyboard

Typically the letters on a computer keyboard are small and difficult to see. Large print key-top stickers in several colour combinations are available. Acquiring reasonable touch-typing skills is most desirable except where a physical impairment prevents this. Touch-typing tutors are available in large print, on tape and as a speaking computer program.

Screen placement

The placement of the screen can be important. Glare and window light can make unusable a computer that would otherwise be manageable.

Colour

Many people with impaired vision can see some colour combinations better than others. Many software packages enable the user to change the text and background colour and most operating systems have preferences, which include changing the colours used for highlighting, labelling, backgrounds etc.

Screen size

Large screens

Larger than normal screens (VDU displays, monitors) produce a larger than normal image. Dealers should be able to tell you about the standard screens available for your computer.

Specialist manufacturers make screens that are very large – up to 30" diagonal. Some users get the image size they need without having to learn any new or additional computer techniques.

Tips, tricks and trivia

Themeland

You may be tempted to say that desktop themes are a penny a dozen. Well, at FreeThemes they don't even cost a penny per million. Here it's just free theme after free theme, including all the parts that go into a theme: screen savers, wallpapers, icons, cursors, and even fonts. Check out the weekly theme or just search for the topic that interests you, because it is almost surely here. And, of course, pay nothing.

http://www.freethemes.com

Laptop screens

The screens on portable computers vary in quality. 'TFT' or Active Matrix technology offers the best visibility and contrast and is available in sizes up to 14.1" on some models of laptop.

Making text easier to see

Choice of font, style and size

A font such as Helvetica or Arial may be easier to read, especially on screen, than a serif font (with feet at the base of the uprights) like Times or a fixed space font like Courier.

In Windows 95/98/NT a number of colour schemes include larger text up to three times the normal size.

The mouse pointer

In most cases it is quite easy to change the colour of the mouse pointer (arrow) and enlarge it by up to three times. A wider range of sizes and colours and high visibility effects can be achieved with specialist software.

Enlarging the text

Zooming in

A number of programs such as word processors allow the user to increase the size of the text in the window where the document appears quite considerably. This does not affect the size in which the text is printed out. Most buttons on the toolbar (the row of small pictures at the top of the screen that can perform an operation when clicked on with a mouse pointer) can also be enlarged by choosing the right option within the program.

Magnification software

A number of products are available that produce an enlarged image of the computer's screen. The sizes of enlargement possible, the image quality and the method of control vary. Enlarging characters in this way always means that only a portion of the whole screen is visible at any one time. Use of such software is relatively simple and is available for DOS and Windows 95/98/NT as well as other operating systems. There are also a number of word processing packages specifically designed for use with large characters.

Working without vision

Screen-reading using speech output

It is often thought that a graphical user interface such as Windows, with its pictures and icons, is not accessible to those without vision. In fact these operating systems are still, in reality, text-based and often pictures are purely cosmetic or accompanied by a text label.

A blind computer user can know what is on the screen by having the necessary information spoken by a synthetic voice. This could include having each character or word echoed back as you type. On computers that can produce sounds and music the speech output can be produced in a similar way, through the main speakers. In other instances a separate piece of equipment may be required to make the computer talk.

The software programs that control the speech (called screen-readers) vary in their reliability and sophistication. The more sophisticated software packages allow the user effective and reliable 'eyes-free' use of the vast majority of DOS and Windows 95/98/NT programs (as well as some running under other operating systems).

Tips, tricks and trivia

Home Page Reader 2.0 from IBM Special Needs Systems is a speech-enabled browser and email package for blind and visually impaired users. Home Page Reader has an unlimited vocabulary and reads Web pages out loud, verbalizing text on Web sites with a male voice, and highlighted links with a female voice. Home Page Reader comes on a CD that includes the Netscape Navigator browser, IBM's ViaVoice OutLoud text-to-speech engine, and complete documentation. Several products are available through IBM to enhance the quality of life of people with disabilities. Contact Special Needs Systems at:

www.ibm.com/sns

Screen-reading using Braille output

As well as offering speech output, screen-reading software can also produce Braille readout of the text on the screen. What would otherwise be spoken is displayed on an electromechanical strip of typically 20–40 cells situated close to the keyboard. Braille output can be used alone or combined with speech output.

■ Screen-reading access to the Internet

A program called a Web browser is used to view individual pages or Web sites on the Internet. These pages contain mostly textual information, images, video, or audio clips. It is important to choose the right software to get the best access to the Internet.

There are some specialist Web browsers that enlarge text and speak the contents of a Web page. Also, some combinations of screen-readers and Web browsers have the ability to make the reading of pages with complex structures and layouts even easier than the specialist Web browsing programs.

Portable systems

■ Portable computers and note-takers

Visually impaired people may wish to have a portable solution to their computer needs. There are many portable devices that offer note-taking, word processing, diary and address book facilities.

Some are specialist machines that have been designed to give speech and/or Braille output and have either Braille or Qwerty keyboards. Others are essentially laptop computers running screen-reading software with speech output or a Braille display added.

Other helpful technology

■ OCR scanning

A scanner looks like a small photocopier on which you can place a page of text or an opened book. The text on the page is converted from a picture into text which can be edited, magnified, spoken back, etc. in a word processor.

There are many specialist scanners that can read the printed page and automatically speak back the contents. Mainstream scanners, however, are now typically sold with the necessary optical character recognition software, at a fraction of the cost, and can easily be used by someone who already has a computer with speech output, Braille or enlarged image output.

No scanner can read handwritten text.

Closed circuit television – CCTV

Closed circuit television systems are devices that enlarge print or handwritten text as required by the user. They may or may not be attached to the computer.

Most common are standalone models. They comprise a single unit, with a screen above a moveable table on which is placed the item to be read.

Portable versions are available with small hand-held cameras that connect to a television or computer. Those connecting to a computer give the user the option to view the CCTV image, or the computer image, or both in a split-screen view.

Combined approaches

These solutions need not be thought of in isolation. For many visually impaired users the best solution might be a combination of the strategies mentioned.

18

Voice recognition

How well do these systems work?

There are many people who use voice recognition systems successfully and productively. Having said that, it is important to realize that they are not magic wands. To get the most out of voice recognition it is important to:

- choose the right system;
- choose an appropriate supplier;
- have realistic expectations;
- take the time and make the effort to learn new skills and a new system;
- get adequate training and support.

Can they understand you?

We all speak differently, so voice recognition systems store 'voice models' for each user. These systems have a vocabulary of words that frequently occur in speech and they match your spoken words to words in the vocabulary. At first this is not 100 per cent accurate and you will need to correct mistakes. However, as you make corrections the systems learn and become more accurate.

To begin this process of adaptation, some systems require you to do an initial word match, where you have to read to the computer before starting to use the software.

Vocabulary size

Each of the voice recognition systems has a built-in vocabulary that is referenced during speech input. Although words are sometimes not recognized, the inserted word is always correctly spelt. You can add words to the standard vocabulary simply by saying the word and then spelling it in.

The systems vary in the number of words they keep in memory. A typical vocabulary is 30,000 words. Those working in highly technical occupations may choose to have a larger vocabulary or to purchase a specialized vocabulary (e.g. medical, legal and so on).

Discrete and continuous speech

There are a number of continuous speech recognition products that allow you to dictate using natural speech; you can pause as and when you like. However, these systems work best when speech is at a predictable rate and some additional effort is made to speak each syllable spoken.

Continuous speech systems look at groups of words and use statistical models of your speech to improve accuracy. These systems are capable of higher levels of accuracy than the older discrete speech products. People who have speech impairments are likely to have more success using discrete speech products.

Dictating, 'command and control' and hands-free use

All of the voice recognition systems mentioned allow you to dictate words into a word processor and some have additional features that allow you to control other software applications by voice. For example, you could say 'computer, go to Excel' to start your spreadsheet and 'file, send mail' to send an electronic mail. This is known as 'command and control' and is particularly useful to people who have difficulty in using a mouse and keyboard. For a system to be deemed 'hands-free' we would expect to be able to start programs, modify settings, make corrections and have a method of moving the mouse pointer, all by voice.

If you are happy with some keyboard use and only want to make use of voice recognition for writing text, you may find that one of the dictation-only systems will meet your needs.

Macros

The majority of voice recognition systems have facilities for you to add your own macros. Macros allow you to insert standard pieces of text quickly and can allow you to link together a number of operations. For example 'sign-me-off' could insert 'yours sincerely', six blank lines, your name and title. Macros are a powerful way of speeding up your dictation and can make your system easier to use.

Microphones and soundcards

Recognition accuracy can be improved by making sure that you use a good microphone and soundcard. Most of the systems detailed here are supplied with a headset microphone. These keep the microphone a fixed distance from your mouth while allowing you to move around. There are other choices in microphones; for example, clip-on microphones and radio microphones as well as microphones fixed on a stand. Some of these would be more suitable if you have difficulty taking a headset microphone on and off.

The soundcard in your computer passes the microphone signal on to the speech recognition software. Soundcards vary in quality and it is worth checking that your soundcard is compatible and of reasonable quality.

IBM ViaVoice 98

NOTE

ViaVoice requires Windows 95 or Windows NT.

ViaVoice 98 is the current continuous speech recognition product from IBM. The older products were ViaVoice and ViaVoice Gold. ViaVoice 98 has its own simple word processor called SpeakPad which can be used for dictation.

ViaVoice 98 Executive

This is the most hands-free ViaVoice product. It is possible to correct by voice and to identify words to be changed simply by saying 'select' followed by the word or phrase. Unlike the old version of ViaVoice, there is no separate 'dictation mode'; you can dictate, make corrections, and apply formatting without needing to issue additional commands to 'swap modes'.

A similar level of hands-free use is available in Word 97. It is possible to dictate directly into other applications using ViaVoice Direct. However, this can be more awkward to do hands-free and it can be easier to dictate into SpeakPad and then cut and paste.

Correcting in ViaVoice 98

ViaVoice 98 allows you to start, close and control applications by voice. It is able to identify all the menu items associated with an application, so rather than having to say 'file' then 'print' you can just say 'print'. ViaVoice 98 has a 'vocabulary expander' which will add new words from existing files.

It keeps a recording of your speech which you can play back and also has a synthetic text-to-speech facility, ViaVoice OutLoud, that will play back the recognized speech.

ViaVoice 98 Home Edition

This is aimed at the home market and is a good system for dictation. You can dictate into Word 97 and SpeakPad. Errors can be corrected by voice, but there is no overall command and control.

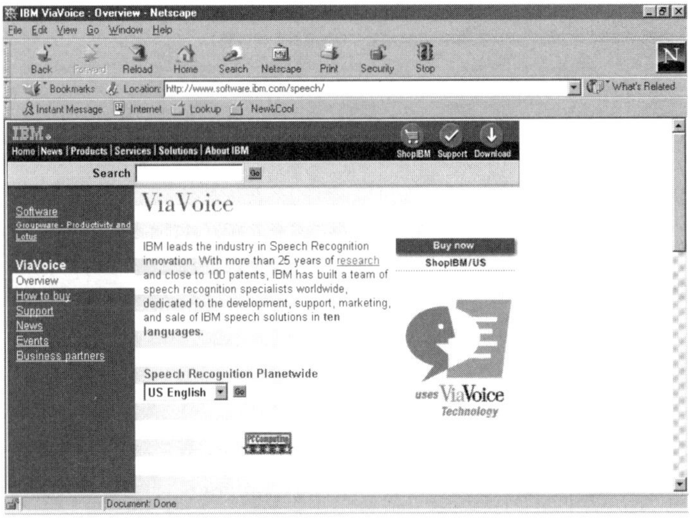

19

Communication aids

- What is a communication aid?
- Why computers?
- Choosing a communication aid

What is a communication aid?

A communication aid is a device that helps an individual to communicate more effectively. This could be as simple as a letter board or as sophisticated as computer equipment.

Computer as a communication aid. How do I choose?

A dedicated communication aid is a device that has been tailor-made for the job, and does nothing else. A computer-based communication aid is a standard computer (notebook etc.) running a piece of specialist software. It has similar characteristics to the dedicated communication aid, with the added functionality of being a computer as well. In order to use either type of communication aid it is not essential for the user to be able to read text. Many aids are graphics based and still provide full functionality in order to communicate with others.

Why computers?

Personal computers have become more common for communication over the past decade, and many software packages are easily available. The benefits of a computerized communication aid are extensive. However, the computer's flexibility is probably the most important. The user has the ability to customize and manipulate a range of options, making it more accessible. A major consideration of the computer-based system is its weight, size and cost, which in the past have made computer-based communication aids restrictive to some. As technology improves there are cheaper, lighter, improved products available.

There are some computer systems that have been specifically designed to withstand the rigours of daily use whilst mounted on an electric wheelchair. Although expensive, they can offer a high level of functionality, for example the equipment used by Professor Stephen Hawking.

Choosing a communication aid

Selection of the correct communication aid is very important. Where possible, we recommend talking to a communication aids specialist about the most suitable devices for your needs. There are a number of Communication Aids Centres around Europe, who would be able to help you. Below are a few questions you may wish to consider before you contact a centre.

NOTE

Centres sometimes require a referral from a medical body.

Answers to these questions will be useful when talking to an assessor:

- How is the equipment going to be used (typing, touch, switch, pointer etc.)?
- Where is it going to be used?
- What is it going to be used for?
- Does it need to be graphic or text based?
- Does the user have any previous experience that may be of relevance?

Links to other sources of information

International sites ■
Europe ■

Many centres have created databases of links to relevant sites with material of interest to people with disabilities. You will find below a list of those sites, plus some other useful international contacts.

If you have a site which you feel may benefit others by being listed here, please get in touch with me and I shall use it in future editions of this Handbook and I will post it on the European Internet Users Handbook Web site **http://www.eurohandbook.com**.

Yuri Rubinsky Insight Foundation. One of the most well known resource sites for people with disabilities on the Internet. **http://www.yuri.org/webable/**

WAACIS – The Wigram Augmentative and Alternative Communication for Internet Surfers: Project providing access to the Internet for people with physical or speech disabilities. **http://www.tcns.co.uk/waacis/for-disabled-surfers/welcome.html**

BECTA – British Education Communications and Technology Agency. Information on the education area of special needs. Formerly the National Council for Education Technology (NCET). **http://www.becta.org.uk**

Scope – The main UK charity for people with cerebral palsy (CP). This site contains information for people with CP or their families, and care workers. It also contains information about the services available through Scope. **http://www.scope.org.uk/**

Microsoft's disability and technology pages. **http://www.microsoft.com/enable**

Mardis: supplies the ORAC communication system. Site is part of the Lancaster University site. **http://www.lancs.ac.uk/users/mardis/**

Disability Net. Information service, forum, shopping and resource database for the UK. **http://www.disabilitynet.co.uk/**

SDRU – Sensory Disabilities Research Unit. A study on how new technology can assist disabled and elderly people. **http://phoenix.herts.ac.uk/PsyDocs/sdru/index.html**

AbilityNet – **http://www.abilitynet.co.uk**

Ability Web Directory and Internet Resources Site – Including an extensive link site. **http://www.ability.org/**

Action for ME Support. **http://www.afme.org.uk/welcome.html**

Assistive Technology On-Line. **http://www.asel.udel.edu/at-online/assistive.html**

Bobby – Web site accessibility analyzer by Cast. **http://www.cast.org/bobby/**

Charity UK. **http://www.foremost.u-net.com/charityuk.html**

Computing Out Loud – An independent site to help people using speech recognition software. **http://www.out-loud.com/**

Connections Disability, Information, News and Community Centre. **http://cil.gcal.ac.uk/connectd/home.html**

CRDC – Choices and Rights Disability Coalition. **http://www.dtop.demon.co.uk/crdc/educate.html**

CTI Human Services – Southampton University. **http://www.soton.ac.uk/~chst/**

Dancing Dots – Music and Braille. **http://www.netaxs.communication/~ddots/**

Disabled Net. **http://www.disabilitynet.co.uk**

Disability Now – The award-winning newspaper for everyone with an interest in disability. **http://www.disabilitynow.org.uk**

Disability on the Agenda – The government's Disability Discrimination Act and DfEE information site. **http://www.disability.gov.uk/**

DOS Web Browsers – DOS is not dead! **http://ibc.wustl.edu/~hugh/dos-www.html**

Esmerel's Collection of Disability Resources on the Internet. **http://www.esmerel.communication/library/disabled**

Guide Dogs for the Blind Association. **http://www.gbda.org.uk/graphics/index.html**

HAFAD – Hammersmith and Fulham Action for Disability. **http://dialspace.dial.pipex.com/town/street/xga79**

Heart 'n Soul Music Theatre – A leading disability arts group. **http://www.heartnsoul.co.uk/index.html**

Inter-link – Disabled goods, advice, news and links. **http://www.itdirect.com/disabled/charity.html**

MedWeb – Disability Resource Pages. **http://www.gen.emory.edu/medweb/medweb.disabled.html**

Multiple Sclerosis Society. **http://glaxocentre.mersyside.org/mss.html**

National Autistic Society – UK resource guide. **http://www.jaymuggs.demon.co.uk/resource.htm**

Osmond Group – Ergonomically designed office products. **http://www.ergonomics.co.uk/frconten.htm**

Royal National Institute for the Blind (RNIB). **http://www.rnib.org**

Scope – The national charity for people with cerebral palsy. **http://www.scope.org.uk/**

Scottish Sensory Centre – for everyone who is involved in the education of children and young people with sensory impairment. **http://www.ssc.mhie.ac.uk/**

Special Needs Research and Development Centre. **http://www.canterbury.ac.uk/xplanatory/xplan.htm**

Stroke Association. **http://glaxocentre.merseyside.org/stroke.html**

Sun Technology and Research – Enabling Technologies. **http://www.sun.com/tech/access**

UK Charities – Useful information on UK charities. **http://pitch.phon.ucl.ac.uk/home/dave/toc_h/charities/**

Widgit Software for literacy and special needs. **http://widgit.com/**

International sites

Ability Network – Canada's Cross Disability Magazine. **http://www.ability.ns.ca/**

Ability Online Support Network – An American electronic mail system that connects young people with disabilities or chronic illness to disabled and non-disabled peers and mentors. **http://www.ablelink.org/**

ADA Disability Information – One of America's foremost resource sites for disabled people. **http://www.public.iastate.edu/~sbilling/ada.html**

Blazie Engineering – Manufacturers of Braille 'N Speak. **http://blazie.com/**

Disabled Peoples International. **http://www.escape.ca/~dpi/links.html**

EASI – Equal Access to Software and Information. **http://www.rit.edu:80/~easi/**

Gladnet – Global Applied Disability Research and Information Network for Employment and Training. **http://www.gladnet.org/**

IBM Special Needs Systems. **http://www.austin.ibm.com/sns**

LC Technologies – Creators of the Eye-Gaze system. **http://www.lctinc.com/**

Makaton – Communication at your fingertips. **http://www.makaton.mta.ca/**

Microsoft Accessibility Page. **http://www.microsoft.com/enable/**

Reading with Phonics is Fun. Teaching reading by intensive phonics instruction. **http://www.ocs.com/phonics/computm.html**

Recording for the Blind and Dyslexic. America's education library for people with print disabilities. **http://www.rfbd.org/**

Solutions @ Disability.com – Linking people with disabilities and chronic health conditions to resources, products and services that promote active, healthy independent living. **http://www.eka.com**

The Disability Connection – Apple Macintosh's disability information site. **http://www2.apple.com/disability/welcome.html**

The Good, The Bad and The Ugly – Dedicated to Web page access. **http://www.usableweb.com/items/pcwbaddesign.html**

Thunderbeam – The parents' guide to children's software. Adaptive computer equipment for children with special needs. **http://www.thurnderbeam.com/w/f/adaptive.html**

Trace Centre. **http://trace.wisc.edu.**

Web Site Accessibility Guidelines. **http://trace.wisc.edu/text/guidelns/htmlgide/htmlgide.html**

World Association for Persons with Disabilities (WAPD). **http://www.wapd.org/**

WAPD Links page. **http://www.wapd.org/links/index.html**

W3C Accessibility Developments. **http://www.w3.org/wai/references/**

Europe

Austria

Bauen fr Behinderte **http://info.tuwien.ac.at:4324/histu/inst/as/0048300400.html**

Inst. f. Hochbau f. Architekten, TU Wien

Rehabilitation Technology Group at Vienna University
http://sun4.iaee.tuwien.ac.at/e359.3/abtb/abtb.html

Elektro- und Biomedizinische Technik, TU Graz
http://hyperg.tu-graz.ac.at:80/40094F1B/CForschung+TU-4450

■ France

Francophone Resources **http://www.ensmp.fr/scherer/handi/**
for Handicapped People in France.

Handicap Mission **http://handy.univ-lyon1.fr/eng/home.html**
University Claude Bernard, Lyon, France.

■ Finland

Disability resources on the Internet.
http://info.eunet.fi/gnn/wic/disab.02.html

Mood disorders.
http://www.avocado.pc.helsinki.fi/janne/mood/mood.html

Support depression. **http://www.avocado.pc.helsinki.fi**

■ Germany

Institute fuer Arbeitswiss. & Techn. Management, University of Stuttgart.
http://www.fhg.de

Blindness Info on the Web from Germany.
http://www.heim2.tu-clausthal.de/ortega/cgi-bin/starthtml?blind-e

■ Greece

TELDAT: A database on driving aids for people with special needs.
http://hermes.civil.auth.gr/teldat.html

TELSCAN: Telematic standards and coordination of ATT systems in relation to elderly and disabled travellers.
http://hermes.civil.auth.gr/telscan/telsc.html

European Assistive Technology Programs and Projects.
http://www.ics.forth.gr/proj/rti/

Hungary

Speech and Rehabilitation Technology Group at KFKI/MSzKI, Budapest, Hungary. **http://www.kfki.hu/mszkihp/info/RehTech/e_rehact.htm**

Ireland

Muscular Dystrophy from Ireland. **http://www.iol.ie/coreilly/mdi.html**

International Wheelchair Aviators Fly Me. **http://www.dsg.cs.tcd.ie/dsg_people/sloubtin/IWA.html**

Italy

Disability Information Point. **http://www.area.fi.cnr.it/hcap/first.htm**

Special Issue on Special-Purpose Architectures for Real-Time Imaging. **http://CM2.UniPR.IT/rti/**

Disabilita. **http://www.mi.cnr.it/IGST/Disabilita.html**

Informatici per la Didattica e l'Integrazione. **http://www.are.fi.cnr.it/hcap/auxi/catalogo.htm**

The Netherlands

The Handicap Institute. **http://www.metropolis.nl/handicapinfo/**

TNO Human Factors – An Institute occupied with research on driving – useful information on drivers with special needs. **http://www.tno.nl/instit/tm/**

Chronic Fatigue Syndrome. **http://huizen.dds.nl:80/cfs-news/**

Norway

SINTEF REHAB – Institutt for rehabilitering og ergonomi. **http://www.oslo.sintef.no/avd/32/**

Morten Tollefsen's Homepage Oslo, Norway. **http://hydra.unik.no/%7Emortent/forside.html**

Sweden

VTI. **http://www.vti.se**

University of Lund. **http://www.lth.se**

Switzerland

World Health Organization. **http://www.who.ch/Welcome.html**

Inst.Spec.Educ.Home Page. **http://pedcurmac13.unifr.ch/**

United Kingdom

SDRU – SATURN project.
http://phoenix.herts.ac.uk/Psydocs/SDRU/saturn/saturn.html

CTI Centre for Human Service.
http://ilc.ecs.soton.ac.uk/chst/hompaghs.html

DeafBlind Online. **http://198.234.201.48/dbonline.html**

MET Group Index Page. **http://hcrl.open.ac.uk/met/METHome.html**

Newcastle-upon-Tyne University,United Kingdom, Disability Research.
http://www.ncl.ac.uk/n4522992/reach.htm

The Will to Work: What People Struggle to Achieve.
http://www.demon.co.uk/solbaram/articles/willwork.html

SSENTSG. **http://call-centre.cogsci.ed.ac.uk/SSENTSG**

TURTLE Project. **http://www.tag.co.uk/turtle/**

What is Orthopaedics. **http://www.os.qub.ac.uk/whatis**

Disabilities Access (UK).
http://www.pavilion.co.uk/CommonRoom/DisabilitiesAccess/

Hearing Research. **http://ep56c.ep.susx.ac.uk:80/sussex_hearing.html**

Educational Technology Information and Resources.
http://www.csv.warwick.ac.uk/WWW/hefc/index.html

Dundee University MicroCentre.
http://alpha.mic.dundee.ac.uk/research4.html

Disabilities Access News Brought to you by *Now* magazine.
http://www.pavilion.co.uk/CommonRoom/DisabilitiesAccess/D-Access/DN_News.html

Blind Mobility Research Unit Home Page.
http://www.psyc.nott.ac.uk/bmru/home.html

Part IV

A pan-European guide to the Internet

21

Awareness of European Union resources

The only act of revolution left in a collective world, is thinking for yourself.

BOB GELDOF, IS THAT IT?

- EWorld and Europe
- EWorld vs. government control of information
- The freedom of information
- The future of Europe in the eWorld
- European Union resources

The eWorld is growing at a breathtaking speed in Europe. What kind of implications does this astonishing change in our lives have for Europe? What shall be Europe's role in the eWorld? Is the eWorld a threat or a promise for Europe?

History tells us that the rulers of Europe have always shown a considerable interest in controlling the flow of information. In medieval times, the Catholic Church endeavoured to control what the average European should hear and believe. Until recently, many European states have wanted to regulate the flow of information in their countries through the control of national TV and radio stations. We have recently witnessed a shattering of this government monopoly on information and nothing can illustrate this development more clearly than the spread of the eWorld. Today the amount of the information available in the eWorld is growing at a breathtaking speed and any attempts by any authority to control this flow are destined to fail. The spread of the eWorld raises questions: Are we dealing with an unknown that threatens to undermine the sovereignty of the European nation state as well as our cultural traditions? Or should we look at the eWorld as the opportunity to revive the European economy and our civil society?

EWorld and Europe

The heavily regulated European information infrastructure would have made it very difficult for the eWorld to be developed in Europe. When the eWorld finally came to Europe the Americans had already completed most aspects of its design. As a result the Europeans merely joined an existing system with little possibility to influence the way the network worked. Today Europeans can only boast that an Englishman in CERN, Switzerland developed the World Wide Web in 1991. But it is also evident that Tim Berners-Lee had an international eWorld community in mind when he designed

Tips, tricks and trivia

'404 Not Found'

Among the Internet and Web cognoscenti, a 404 is a link that takes you not to another Web page but to an error message – specifically, a '404 Not Found' error message, which means that the URL you requested cannot be found. '404 Not Found' is one of scores of original Internet status codes written and instituted by the founder of the World Wide Web, Tim Berners-Lee, in 1992.

the WWW standard and it was not Europe but America that first embraced this new standard. Still today the majority of all content on the eWorld is produced in English in America.

EWorld vs. government control of information

The eWorld has now become a marketplace of information and information is just one commodity among the many others that are being traded. The European states have traditionally safeguarded information as a way to guarantee internal as well as external security. Consequently, when the European Free Trade Association was created in 1959, an article was added to the Convention that gave the participating states an opportunity to keep control of certain key areas. Among these areas were the independent right to trade in arms and defence materials, the ability to take measures in times of war or in emergencies, undertakings aimed at maintaining international peace and security, and the safeguarding of information. The European nations have been able to preserve their sovereignty in military issues, but the possibility to control the flow of information has now been permanently lost. It has been the spread of the eWorld that has made people debate that the days of government control are now behind us and that they will never return.

The freedom of information

Today the eWorld is infiltrating European society at a breathtaking speed and critical and sceptical voices are becoming increasingly rare. Large businesses are lobbying politicians and the pressure to open national information to foreign competition is becoming ever greater. One major step in this area was taken in February 1997. The Group on Basic Telecommunications, organized under the direction of the World Trade Organization, completed negotiations on the world's first multilateral deal liberalizing international trade in basic telecommunication services. This deal was signed by 69 nations, including all 15 member states of the European Union. The participating 69 nations account for more than 90 per cent of the global market in telecommunications. This arrangement does not promise a complete overhaul of regulations but the fact that universality was endorsed by so many members of the WTO can be perceived as an important step towards a liberalized worldwide information market.

Tips, tricks and trivia

Evaluating Web information

Those of us who use the Web to do research know that some sites are more reliable and useful than others. The Ithaca College Library provides a good introduction to evaluating the information you find on the Web. Presented as a tutorial, 'The ICYouSee Guide to Critical Thinking About What You See on the Web' attempts to inspire surfers to think more critically about the information accessible through the eWorld.

http://www.ithaca.edu/library/Training/hott.html

The future of Europe in the eWorld

The European Union has a population, as of 1 January 1999, of 374,565,000 people. It also has 17 million small and medium-sized businesses (SMEs) which are the foundation of Europe's economic strength and a major instrument for job creation and innovation. They are the backbone for the development of new technologies and processes. It is therefore vitally important for the competitiveness of Europe that Europeans reap the benefits of the rapidly expanding eWorld.

Europe is now becoming a part of the eWorld society and at present nothing seems to threaten this development. The eWorld is still seen as a threat by some. It is not the economic promises of the eWorld that carry influence when important political decisions are made. Now the national governments as well as the European Union are coming to the conclusion that they must actually encourage the use of the eWorld if they wish to stay effective. But as Europe gradually embraces this new way of communicating, it also has to give way to its intrinsic values.

Tips, tricks and trivia

Champs Elysées

You can travel to the Champs Elysées and know your way around well enough to buy a loaf of bread! Before you make the journey to the world's most beautiful avenue visit it at:

http://www.champselysees.org

Here you can find the address of anything on this famous street, from automobile dealers to libraries and restaurants. The site is operated by Le Comité Des Champs Elysées.

The eWorld is a world where no organization or government has the right to dominate any other based on its superior position, be it based on economic, political or historical authority. Europeans have a long tradition of dominating others by power, but in the eWorld this approach definitely does not work. In the eWorld you can only influence others by giving your positive contribution. The same is true for all of the eWorld. There is no position in the eWorld reserved for Europeans which Americans, Africans or Asians could not occupy. The leading position that Europe still enjoys in the world can only be sustained if Europeans become active participants in the eWorld, willing to share with others what we have. As for government, there is no way back to the time when it was there to lay restrictive and conditional rules. In the eWorld the power is there to encourage people and companies to contribute and be creative.

European Union resources

During its brief history, the European Union has grown greatly in terms of the area it covers; it now numbers 15 member states. The founding Treaties have been revised three times: in 1987 (the Single Act), in 1992 (the Treaty on European Union) and in 1997 (the draft Treaty of Amsterdam).

The ultimate goal of the European Union is to create a closer union among the peoples of Europe, in which decisions are taken as closely as possible to the people. The objective is to promote economic and social advancement, which is balanced and sustainable, assert the European identity on the international scene and introduce a European citizenship for the nationals of the Member States.

The European Union is making an increasingly larger amount of information available on its various Web sites, and this trend will most certainly continue. In this section, while it would be impossible to give complete coverage of every European Union Web site, you will find a general overview of the major sites and a comprehensive list of URLs covering the majority of European resources.

The Europe Homepage **http://www.europa.eu.int/** offers multilingual information on the European Union's goals and policies. EUROPA represents the EU's institutions, and is run by the European Commission. Here are also links to official documents from the Union, publications, online services, statistics, news, and other Web servers of the area.

The Common Market's free database service, I*M-EUROPE (Information Market Europe), is set up to support the actions of DGXIII of

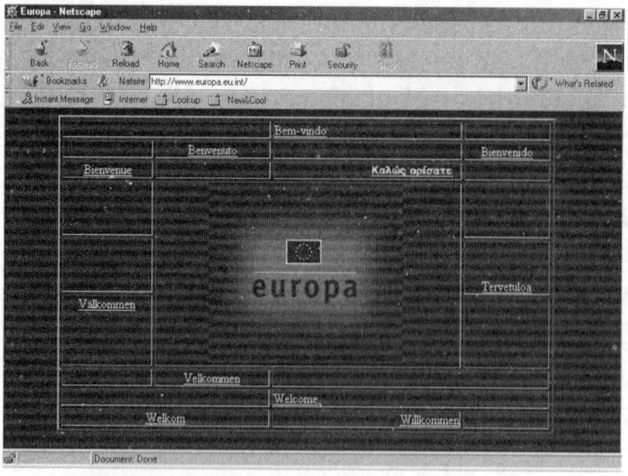

the European Commission in stimulating the European electronic information services market and multimedia content industries. It offers information on topics such as the Telematics Applications Programme, the INFO2000 programme, Task Force Multimedia Educational Software, and links to more EU organizations and programmes at **http://www.echo.lu/**.

The European Commission's CORDIS (Community Research and Development Information Service) is a database of all European Community information related to Research and Technological Development programmes. At **http://www.cordis.lu/** you're offered multilingual searches in databases on topics such as News, Programmes and for finding opportunities in your research areas. Projects for Who is doing What, Results for exploring Innovation, Partners for your Business Research, Publications for Key R&D, Published Items, Contacts to People who Can Help, Acronyms relevant to Community R&D, Understanding EU R&D decision making, and more. There are also links to R&D in the European Union.

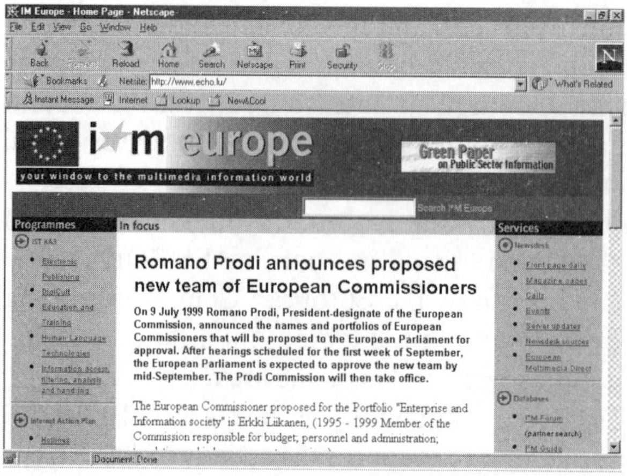

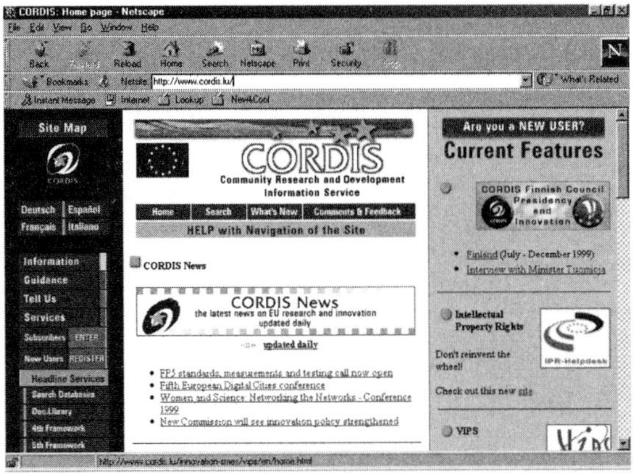

The EC's DANTE **http://www.dante.net/** provides advanced international computer network services for the European research community.

The WISE Information Board on R&D Activities in the European Union is at **http://www.igd.fhg.de/wise/**.

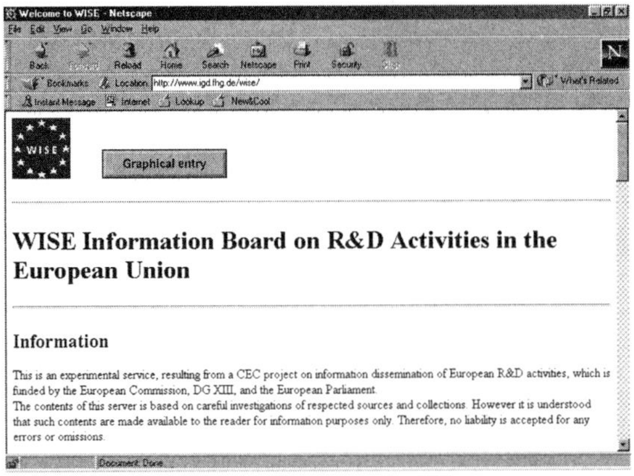

The Guide to European Legal Databases **http://www.llrx.com/features/europe.htm** provides links to European resources in the eWorld.

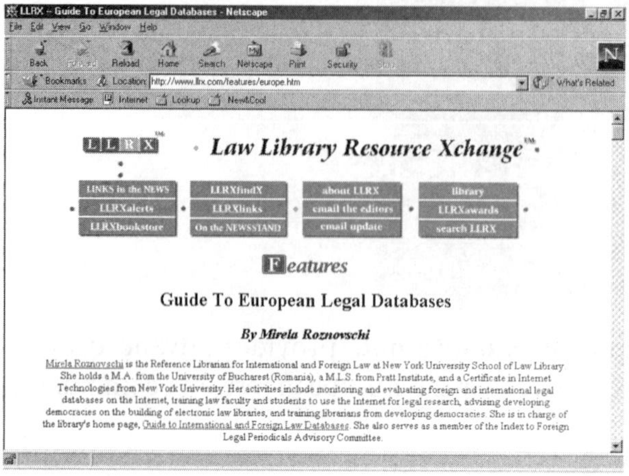

TED (Tenders Electronic Daily) **http://ted.eur-op.eu.int/index2.htm** is a database containing all European calls for tender published in the Official Journal Supplement S of the European Communities. It is the official information source for public procurement opportunities from the European Union, the European Economic Area and beyond. PLEASE NOTE: This interface takes a great deal of memory and uses Java.

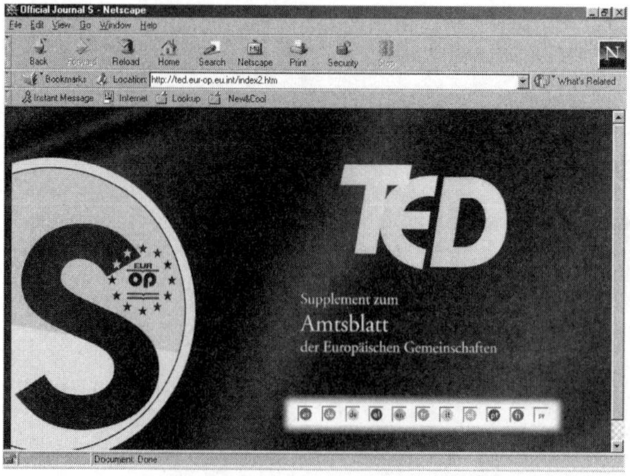

euroguide **http://www.euroguide.org/** will help you find your way through the maze of European information in the eWorld. Just click on a subject category to find lists of relevant sites and pages.

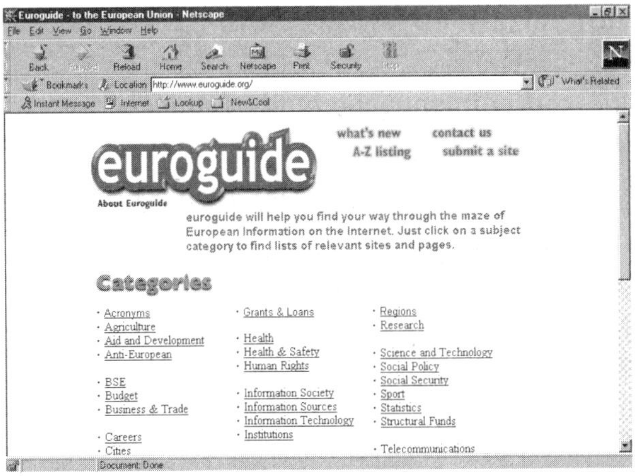

The European Business Directory **http://www.europages.com/** offers economic analyses and indicators on the main European markets, and practical information for doing business in Europe. Information is available in English, French, German, Italian and Spanish.

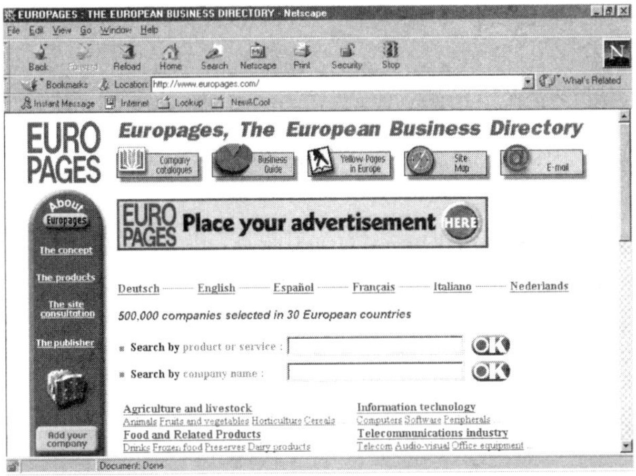

■ Web sites of the European Union

EUROPA **http://europa.eu.int** – European Commission/DG X

'IM EUROPE **http://www.echo.lu** – European Commission/DG XIII

ISPO **http://www.ispo.cec.be** – Information Society Project Office

CORDIS **http://www.cordis.lu** – Community Research and Development Information Service

EU offices/agencies/organizations

ECHO **http://www.echo.lu/echo/en/menuecho.html** – European Commission Host Organisation (Luxembourg)

EUI **http://www.iue.it** – European University Institute (Florence)

EUR-OP **http://europa.eu.int/comm/opoce/indexen.htm** – Office for Official Publications of the European Communities (Luxembourg)

EUROSTAT **http://europa.eu.int/eurostat.html** – Statistical Office of the European Communities (Luxembourg)

Other infosystems

AEGEE **http://www.uni-konstanz.de/studis/aegee** – Association des Etats Généraux des Etudiants de l'Europe

Britain in the European Union **http://www.fco.gov.uk/** – Foreign & Commonwealth Office (London, UK)

EUROPAGES **http://www.europages.com/home-de.html** – European directory of enterprises

European Information Association **http://www.eia.org.uk/index.html**

European Journalism Centre **http://www.ejc.nl** (Maastricht, The Netherlands)

Eurotext **http://eurotext.ulst.ac.uk: 8080/** – Extensive collection of online texts by the electronic Libraries Programme (eLIB)

ELSA **http://www.germany.elsa.org/** – European Law Students Association

The EU Employers Network **http://www.euen.co.uk**

EU Guide **http://www.sub.su.se/sam/euguide/eueng1.htm** – (Stockholm, S:)

European Patent Office **http://www.epo.co.at/epo/** (Vienna, Austria)

Eurotext **http://eurotext.ulst.ac.uk:8080/** – Access to key European Union full-text documents

Network: 'Women in Decision-Making' **http://www.reference.be/wo-mancracy/**

Student organizations **http://www.rwth-chen.de/zentral/aaaguide_studorgani.htm**

R&D infosystems

EHTO **http://www.ehto.be** – European Health Telematics Observatory European Union Research Programmes

ACTS Directory **http://www.lii.unitn.it/EU/Welcome.html**

ESPRIT **http://www.newcastle.research.ec.org/** – Networks of Excellence Information Service

RACE **http://www.race.analysys.co.uk/race.htm** – Server run by the INTERACT project to support the programme

WISE **http://www.igd.fhg.de/wise/wise.html** – Research and Development Activities in the EU

KoWi **http://www.kowi.de/welcome.htm** – EU liaison office of German scientific research organisation (Bonn, Germany)

European research institutions

C.A.P. **http://www.cap.uni-muenchen.de/** – Zentrum f. angewandte Politikforschung (Munich, Germany)

Centre for European Economic Politics **http://www.uni-trier.de/infos/ew/home.htm** (Trier, Germany)

Centre for European Union Studies **http://www.hull.ac.uk/Hull/CSS_Web/ceushomepage.html** – (Hull, UK)

CEPS **http://www.ceps.be** – Centre for European Policy Studies (Brussels, Belguim)

ECPR **http://www.essex.ac.uk/ECPR/** – European Consortium for Political Research (Essex, UK)

ECSA **http://www.ecsanet.org/index.html** – European Community Study Association

EPRU **http://les.man.ac.uk/government/research/epru/index.html** – European Policy Research Unit (Manchester, UK)

EuroInternet **http://fgr.wu-wien.ac.at/nentwich/euroint.htm** – University of Economics and Business Administration (Vienna, Austria)

European Centre for Social Welfare Policy and Research **http://www.euro.centre.org/causa/ec/** (Vienna, Austria)

ESF **http://www.esf.org/** European Science Foundation (Strasbourg, France)

ERCOMER **http://www.ercomer.org/** – European Research Centre on Migration and Ethnic Relations (Utrecht, The Netherlands)

Instead/CEPS **http://ceps-nt1.ceps.lu/** – Centre for Population, Poverty and Public Policy Studies (Luxembourg)

Joint Research Centre **http://www.jrc.org/**

MZES **http://www.mzes.uni-mannheim.de** – Mannheim Centre for European Social Research (Germany)

ZEI **http://www.zei.de/** – Centre for European Integration Studies (Bonn, Germany)

ZEUS **http://zeus.mzes.uni-mannheim.de** – Zentrum für Europäische Umfrageanalysen und Studien (Mannheim, Germany)

ZEW **http://www.zew.de** – Centre for European Economic Research (Mannheim, Germany)

Newsgroups

alt.politics.europe.misc news:alt.politics.europe.misc

alt.politics.ec news:alt.politics.ec

cl.europa.deutschland news:cl.europa.deutschland

cl.europa.diskussion news:cl.europa.diskussion

cl.europa.eu news:cl.europa.eu

eunet.politics news:eunet.politics

soc.culture.europe news:soc.culture.europe

talk.politics.european-union news:talk.politics.european-union

General overviews by countries

The European Directory **http://www3.ukshops.co.uk/cgi-bin/dycgi02.exe/site/index.stm**

European Maps **http://www.tradezone.com/mapslnks.htm**

Governments in the eWorld **http://www.gksoft.com/govt/**

Statistical Offices and Points of Information **/users/ddz/edz/net/state.html**

World Fact Book **http://www.odci.gov/cia/publications/factbook/index.html** – Basic information about European countries

International organizations

AI **http://www.amnesty.org** – Amnesty International

Council of Europe **http://www.coe.fr/index.asp** (Strasbourg)

EFTA (European Free Trade Association)
http://www.efta.int/structure/main/index.html

FAO **http://www.fao.org** – Food and Agricultural Organization of the UN

Greenpeace **http://www.greenpeace.org**

NATO **http://www.nato.int/**

OECD **http://www.oecd.org/**

OSCE **http://www.fsk.ethz.ch/osce/** (Swiss presidency)

UN **http://www.undcp.or.at/unlinks.html** – United Nations

UNESCO **http://firewall.unesco.org/**

Worldbank **http://www.worldbank.org**

West European Union **http://www.weu.int/eng/welcome.html**

WHO **http://www.who.org** – World Health Organization

WIPO **http://www.wipo.org** – World Intellectual Property Organization

WTO **http://www.wto.org** – World Trade Organization

22

Best practices

Trifles make perfection, but perfection is no trifle.

MICHAELANGELO (1475–1564)

In the course of my working week I spend a considerable amount of time with many large and small organizations helping their senior management establish some perspective of the business implications of the eWorld. More often than not I find that there is very little understanding as to what the eWorld is really all about. This may appear incredible considering you cannot pick up a newspaper or switch on a television without finding some article concerning the eWorld. Many of these senior managers feel confident in their successful businesses of today; many seem to be mystified by or apprehensive of the implications of the eWorld. Many sit back and argue that the eWorld will not affect them. It can never be an effective business system. It has all kinds of problems.

> **Tips, tricks and trivia**
>
> **Need a speaker?**
>
> If your company or organization needs speakers for special events, check out The London Speaker Bureau. This site will provide speakers' biographies indexed by topic and location. You can also find links to other agencies that can help you contact a professional speaker.
>
> **http://www.londonspeakerbureau.co.uk**

To those that are unaware and misinformed, I say, wake up! Every day, new hardware, software, standards and initiatives are being established in the eWorld. What is also apparent is the amount of venture capital that is now gushing into anything eWorld-related. This is ensuring that the eWorld is being propelled forward in ways that we can only begin to imagine. Financial institutions, software companies, governments, businesses – everyone is clambering to put in place the technology, standards, procedures and systems to enable the evolution of the eWorld.

The eWorld promises to wreak havoc throughout our economy. Anyone who chooses to remain complacent will have a very rude awakening in the next five years as these effects are felt.

The whole conception of the eWorld is really quite uncomplicated. It is the second phase of the civilized world's dependence on computer technology. The first phase, which is still ongoing, saw companies computerize their own businesses, learning how to take advantage of technology within their own working environment. This involved the introduction of office functions such as word processing and email. But more significantly, the first generation of computerization has involved the creation of systems for stock, purchasing, invoicing and payroll functions. Basically, we've spent the past 20 to 30 years converting many of our systems into an electronic system.

The second phase is the fundamental evolution of what we have done in the first phase; it takes these systems to our customers, business associates, trading partners, and others via the eWorld. In the eWorld, we are now starting to learn how to link our own computer systems and our businesses to those with whom we do business and everyone else in the terrestrial world that is linked to the eWorld. The potential and cost saving are enormous.

Unfortunately the eWorld is littered with Web sites that are pointless and ineffective. Many suffer from a wretched design that is destined to send visitors away as soon as they arrive. Many lack any consistent standard. Some form of standard must be put in place to promote a better quality and content in the eWorld and also to encourage potential customers to conduct business in the eWorld.

Having some form of 'best practice' criteria in this new and changing environment is a concept that must be encouraged.

There is also a need to understand which practices – online and offline underpin eBusiness success. KITE, which is a G8-funded European Initiative for small and medium-sized businesses, has gathered information on more than 130 SME eCommerce initiatives to show that this sector of the market can generate clever and money-spinning ideas. Some of these initiatives are more successful than others, and KITE is currently engaged in research to determine which factors influence this success. Having an excellent concept that suits the eWorld is an obvious factor, but, depending on the business objectives of the initiative, also important are: the ability to build up a trading community; to provide a Web site that is fast and easy to use; to have excellent integration between Web site and back-end systems; and to be able to promote the company's brand where its customers are – both in the eWorld and in the real world.

The full set of KITE SME eCommerce examples can be found in the KITE inventory at **http://kite.tsa.de**.

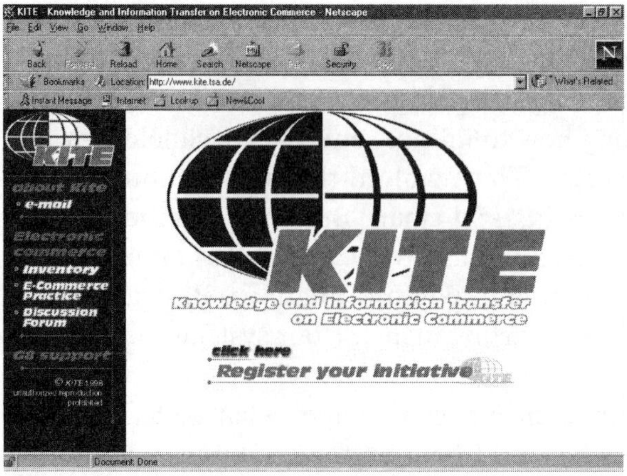

The European sites below all demonstrate practices that are up there with the best in the small and medium-sized enterprise market – and some have practices that would rank alongside those of very much larger companies with huge eCommerce budgets.

Buyonet sells software electronically. It has no physical inventory but sets up agreements with software publishers, which allow Buyonet to create copies of their software and distribute them over the Internet to consumers. Sales reports are sent monthly to each publisher and accounts settled electronically. Buyonet has also built into its commerce system a checking mechanism that publishers can use to check sales of their products. Buyonet has emerged from a small Swedish software distributor that struggled with the physical aspects of delivering software. It recognized the potential of the eWorld as a delivery mechanism, and worked out a concept that supported payment, delivery and sales reporting. **http://www.buyonet.com**

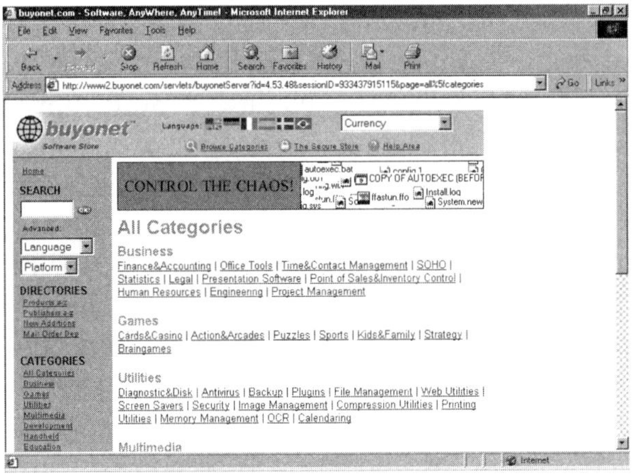

Tradezone is a third-party, business-to-business secure trading service. Its main focus is on purchasing business sundries (maintenance, repair, operations purchasing) where businesses can see immediate benefits in reduction of purchasing costs. The first franchise for the service is ONYX Internet Ltd. The initial suppliers are mainly based in the North East of England. However, the business case for Tradezone is based on a roll-out of franchises within the UK, Europe, North and South America and the Far East. Tradezone has a universal, multi-vendor distributed catalogue service that allows buyers to source from catalogues of competing suppliers wherever they are in the world. **www.tradezone.onyx.net**

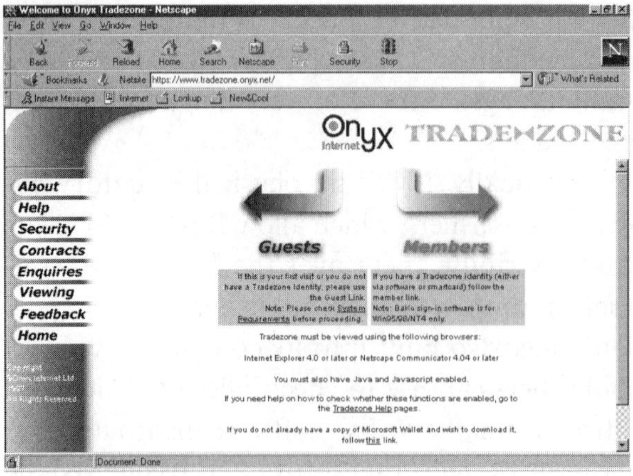

Based in Northern Ireland, **SailCoach Associates** brings together professional coaches across the world to provide services to individual sailors, sailing clubs, class associations and national federations. In order to compete at Olympic level, individuals and teams require increasingly sophisticated training programmes that draw on the skills of many expert coaches from different countries. National team coaches are becoming programme managers, identifying new talent, buying in professional coaching and giving top sailors budgets to pay for individual coaching programmes, all of which can be coordinated through SailCoach. SailCoach sees itself as a catalyst for better provision of coaching and coaching programmes across the world. Because the sailing coaching market is a global one, the Internet is the ideal channel to promote this service. SailCoach has developed a Web site that puts trainers and competitors in touch with one another, wherever they are in the world. It organizes the courses required and runs clinics for Olympic standard competitors. In the two and a half years the organization has been in existence, competitors from over 46 countries have contacted the site. SailCoach now reaches 80 per cent of its customers via the Internet. And competitors from as far away as New Zealand and Mexico have attended its clinics. SailCoach's multinational approach means that competitors of the same standard in smaller countries can share the same professional training available to those in larger, richer nations, making their training far more effective than would otherwise be achieved at their own national level. The SailCoach site contains a Web site shop for associated products. The site receives 300 hits a day and is linked to other specialist sailing sites to help build awareness and increase the effectiveness of its marketing. **http://www.sailcoach.com**

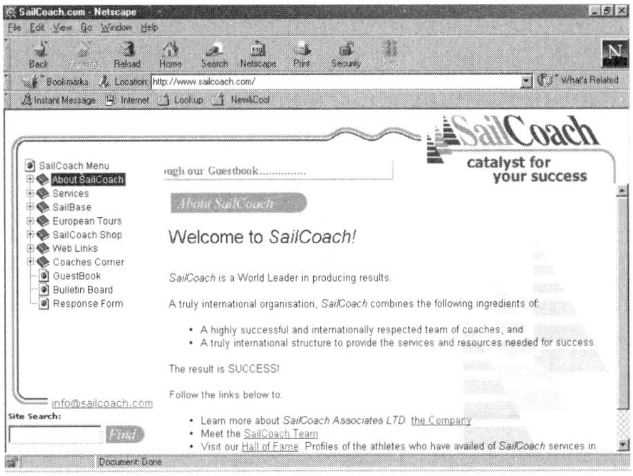

The Roland Collection, a collection of 650 films on the subject of art, art appreciation, architecture and contemporary literature, is marketed to the educational and museum sectors across the world. Anthony Roland started the collection 35 years ago and a new title is added each week, selected from the global output of 230 filmmakers. Traditionally, the Collection has been marketed through a printed catalogue, which is distributed periodically to around 150,000 customers in 75 countries. However, this catalogue is expensive to produce and, starting in 1996, the company has provided a preview service via its Web site, through which it has received orders for its titles from 82 countries as diverse as Russia and Papua New Guinea. **http://www.roland-collection.co.uk**

The Web Worker Group is a virtual network of specialists. For each project individual partners are grouped together in a virtual team. There is no office, all partners work from home. The team communicates electroni-

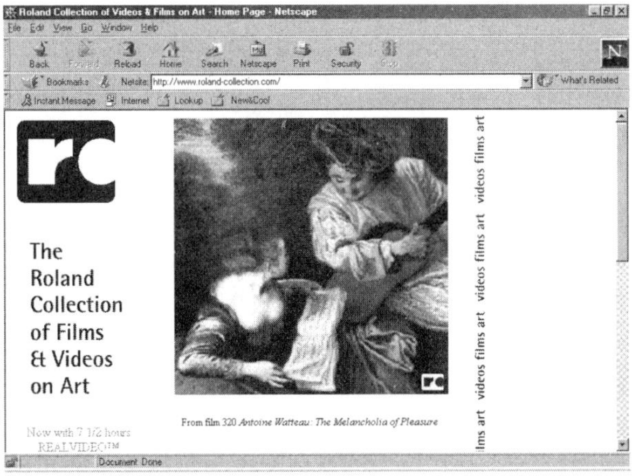

cally, by email, online-conferencing or fax or telephone. As the coordinating entity, TWG divides complex projects into single tasks. Each specific task is then undertaken by an individual team member with the corresponding expertise. The results are then put together, assuring an optimal overall project result. The main competence of TWG is to accompany restructuring in companies through information exchange on the possibilities of electronic business, to lower barriers and to prove through successful project work that the theories about the future of work are implementable in reality. **http://www.t-w-g.com**

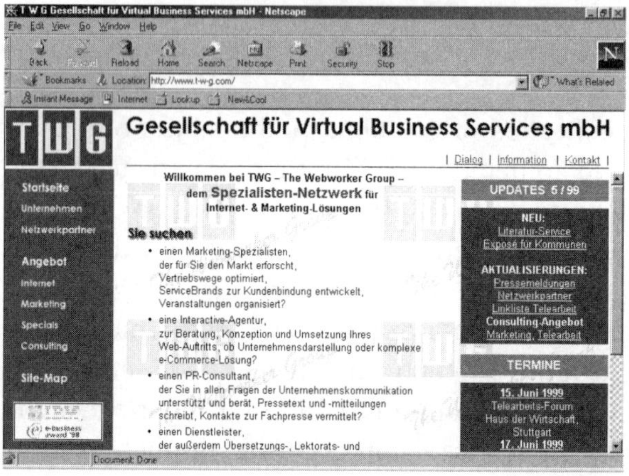

Ki Net is a virtual consultancy that carries out online market research for customers all over the world. It obtains high-quality information from anywhere in the world, analyzes it, and presents it to customers. Its unique selling point is that it can provide timely, tailored information to organizations when they need it, saving customers from information overload. At present, the company obtains around 30 per cent of its information directly from the Internet, and this proportion is growing all the time. However, it also has links to other online information sources. Ki Net finds customers through networks of personal contacts, and then builds up a relationship with potential leads via email. It has discovered that conventional sales and marketing techniques, such as cold calling, do not work for a virtual company. Ki Net does not make face-to-face visits to clients. It has three types of business partner: very large, global consultancies, which may subcontract to Ki Net for its expertise; small consultancies, which are not necessarily virtual; and organizations that are fully virtual, like Ki Net itself. **http://www.ki-net.co.uk**

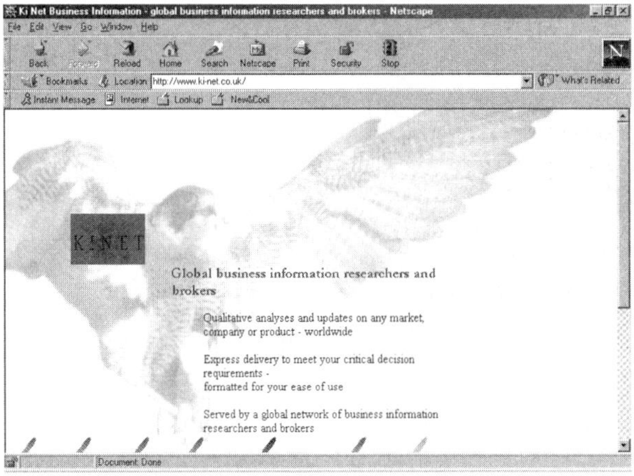

Smartmessage offers an advanced communication service: a personal smartbox which directly receives phone, fax, email and even SMS messages and forwards them upon request to the email address of the user. Faxes and phone messages can be accessed over the WWW. New messages are announced via a telephone (SMS) or pager. **http://www.msg-ag.de**

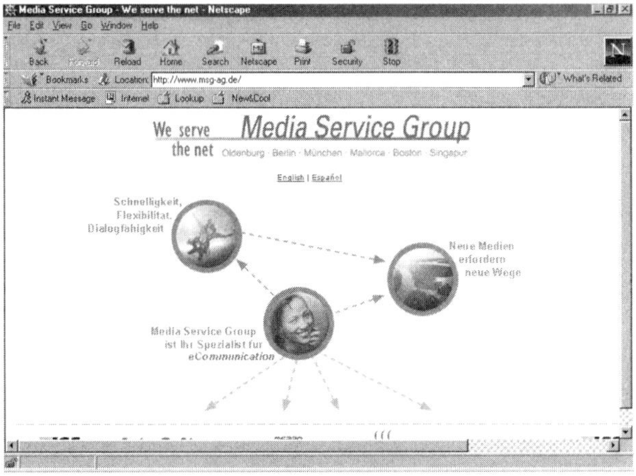

PrahaNet is a Czech site encouraging eCommerce activity, as well as providing an information point for visitors to the Czech Republic. PrahaNet hosts PrahaTour, a small travel agency, which takes bookings for hotel accommodation, sightseeing tours and transport in Prague over the Internet. PrahaNet also provides links to Web sites it has designed for other Czech SMEs, such as Classic, a distributor of classical music over the Internet, and VAMB, a Czech printing house. **http://www.prahanet.cz**

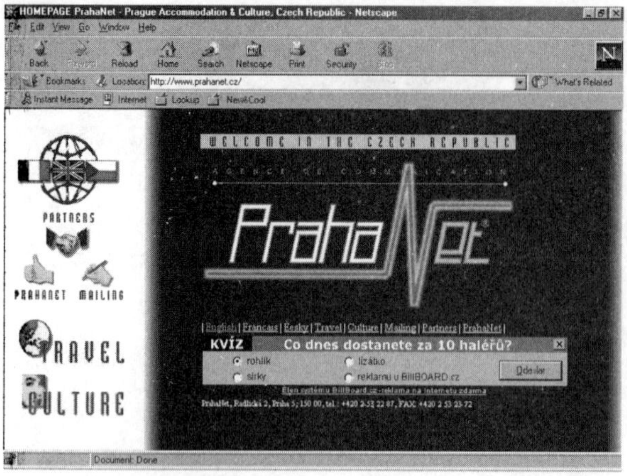

Cedlerts Fisk is a long-standing supplier of luxury seafood to Sweden's top restaurants and the Royal Court. When it started to explore ways of extending its business to the consumer market in 1997, the eWorld was the obvious choice of channel, rather than opening expensive retail stores. **http://www.cedlerts.se**

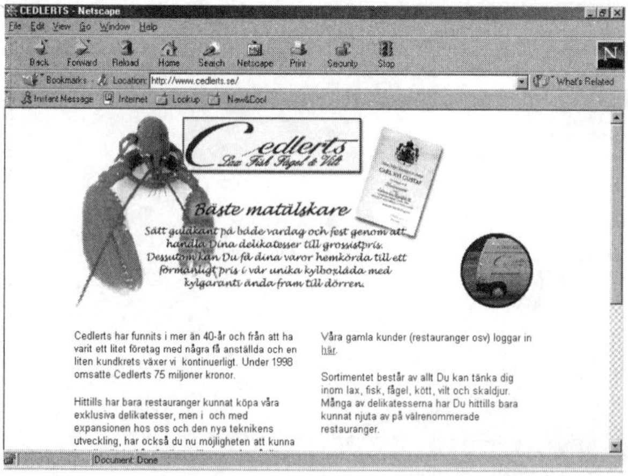

Quixell (QXL) is Europe's largest online auction site, offering computing, consumer electronic, jewellery and travel products direct from manufacturers and distributors. New categories of consumer products and services will be introduced in the coming months. Quixell was the first interactive auction site in Europe. Without registering, or giving any personal information, Web surfers can check all product specifications and images and see full details of others' bids and auction times. To participate, customers open an account on Quixell's secure server and then use a password to place firm bids. New lots come up several times a day and are open from between one hour and one week. If someone enters a higher bid that knocks the customer out of the auction, that customer receives an email alert, giving them the chance to increase their bid before the auction closes. Bidders can also ask the company's robot auctioneer to bid up to a set limit. Products are shipped to customers via UPS and are backed by guarantees and manufacturers' warranties. They carry an unconditional seven-day money-back guarantee. **http://www.QXL.com**

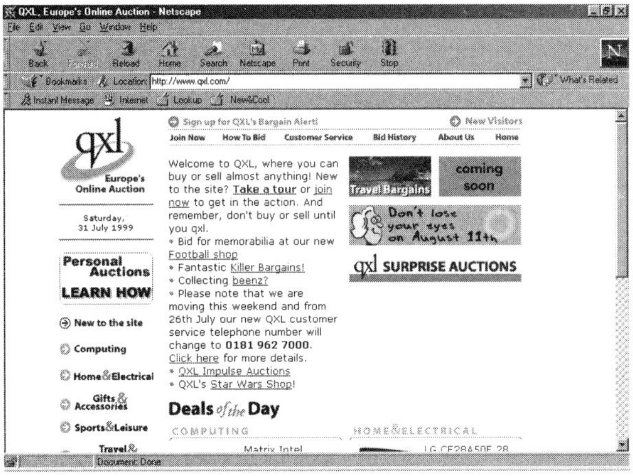

Band-X is a Web-based exchange for the trading of wholesale telecoms capacity – bandwidth, minutes and international telecommunications facilities space. Interested parties – buyers and sellers – put offers and bids anonymously on the Band-X site, with trading taking place offline (by telephone or email) by Band-X. Settlement also takes place offline. Deregulation round the world in telecommunications markets has enabled the rise of commodity trading in telecommunications minutes. Band-X was set up to exploit the new potential of this market by encouraging telecommunications companies to offer their tradeable assets, e.g. bandwidth, and to provide an accessible, central forum in which such trading can take place. Customers will be the winners as prices fall and investment rises through reduced risk. Small telecommunications companies will also be able to compete more effectively with larger players. **http://www.band-x.com**

Online eye test – the screen test for tired eyes. Working on the screen tires the eyes. To test the power of a user's vision, the company Lichtblick has developed an online eye test. The user can do it directly at the monitor of his workplace. The major advantage is that the eyes of the client, his glasses/lenses and the workplace/screen conditions, i.e. the relevant factors for working on a screen, are tested together. The test uses professional methods and guidelines. On the basis of the test it is possible to obtain a certificate of screen suitability. In addition the user can ask questions by email or set up an appointment for personal consultation. The test is available in several languages. **http://www.rhoen.net/Lichtblick/**

A Finnish company **Elcommerce.net** is building relationships between electronics manufacturers and their prospective and existing customers. The objective is to establish a business community on the Internet for the electronics industry. Current services include product information, daily

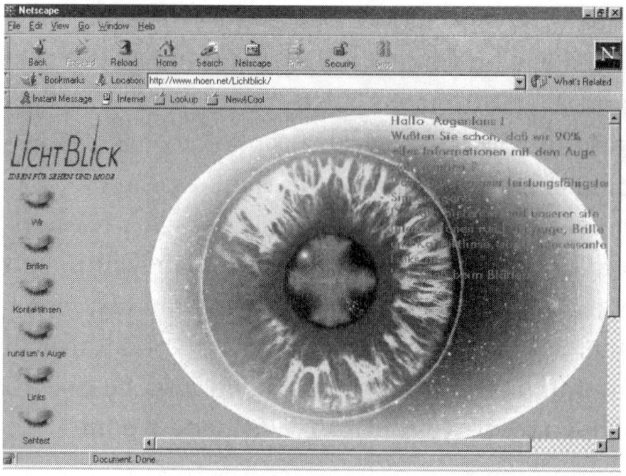

industry news, member company news, an industry news archive, member companies news archive, a news release centre, discussion groups, communication links and full technical support. **http:// www.elcommerce.net**

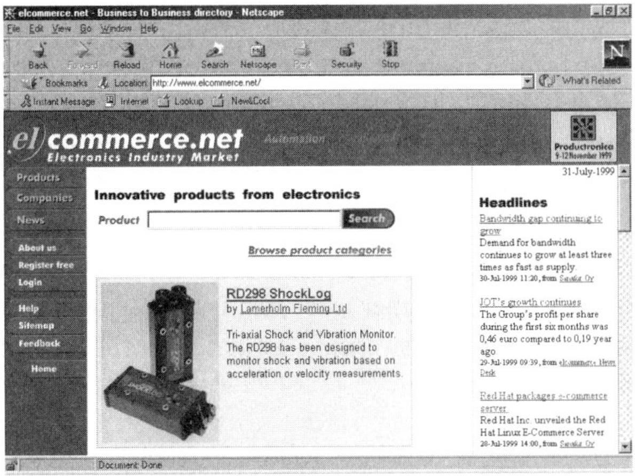

Based in Sweden, the vision of **Architecture Worldwide Network** is to provide a single focus point for everything related to architecture and people/companies interested in architecture. The business model is based on the assumption that revenues generated from selling advertising space to interested companies should generate enough turnover to maintain the site.

Today, the site features advertisements from architects throughout the world, as well as images and background information on the top architecture and building construction services. Architecture World is not strictly a community, as the entry of content is done by the management organization for Architecture World and not by subscribers themselves. **http://www.architectureWorld.net**

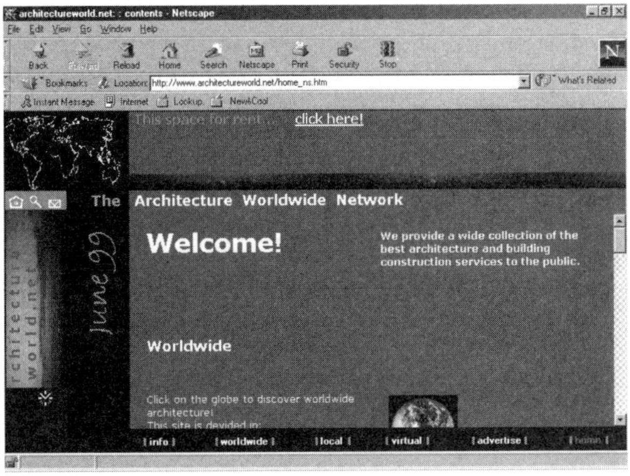

Mansfield Motors is an independent UK Land Rover specialist. It set up its Web site to extend its high-quality services to a wider customer base, including internationally, offering competitive pricing, fast turnaround time on orders, and the benefits of being part of a virtual Land Rover 'club'.

The garage's existing parts database, with over 4,000 high-quality (OEM) Land Rover parts and accessories, is available online and can be downloaded. The site has a 'club' feel to it: in addition to selling parts and accessories, the site provides a wealth of information about Land Rovers, a discussion board, advice column, links to other Land Rover club sites and classified ads. Each specialist mechanic has a photograph on the site, together with a personal email address – as does the manager's dog, which receives as many emails as the mechanics! The site is responsive to customer feedback, encouraging questions and comments, and has a policy of answering all queries on the day of receipt. **http:// www.mansfield-motors.com**

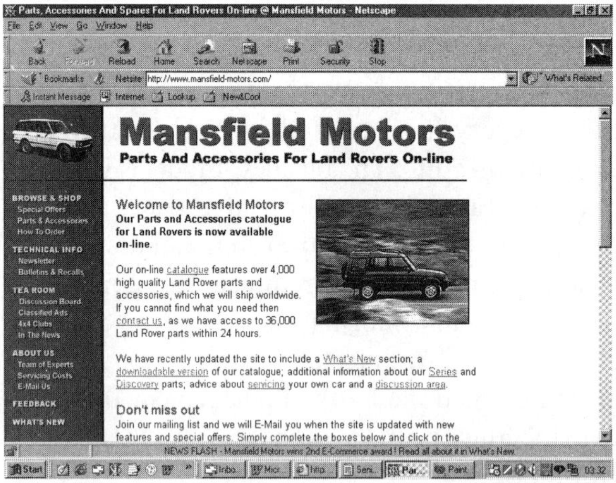

Sunglasses International is an eCommerce venture between Ottica Meloni, a family-run opticians business in Rome, and a UK Internet company, Openlink Services. The site was originally built by Ottica Meloni, but taken over for administrative and promotional purposes by Openlink Services when the volume of online business became too great for Ottica Meloni to handle on its own. Sunglasses International sells Italian designer sunglasses mainly to the North American market, which accounts for 75 per cent of sales. The company also has a mirror site in the premier US online fashion mall. Because of this, the company works with US credit card companies and banks in support of online payment. These are considerably more advanced than European banks, a critical factor in helping Sunglasses International exploit its online market niche. **Http://www.sunglasses-int.com**

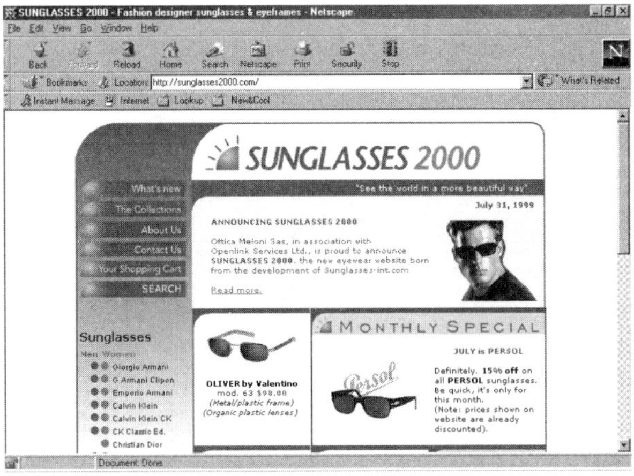

Food Ferry Online is an online grocery store. Currently customers can choose to access an online grocery catalogue or, to save telephone costs, they can browse a version of the catalogue on CD-ROM and prepare their order offline. Payment is made by credit card or cheque when the goods are delivered. Food Ferry does not have any physical retail outlets and its online/telephone food ordering and delivery service is currently only available within central London. Food Ferry expects its eWorld growth to at least match its overall growth, currently over 30 per cent a year. http://www.foodferry.co.uk

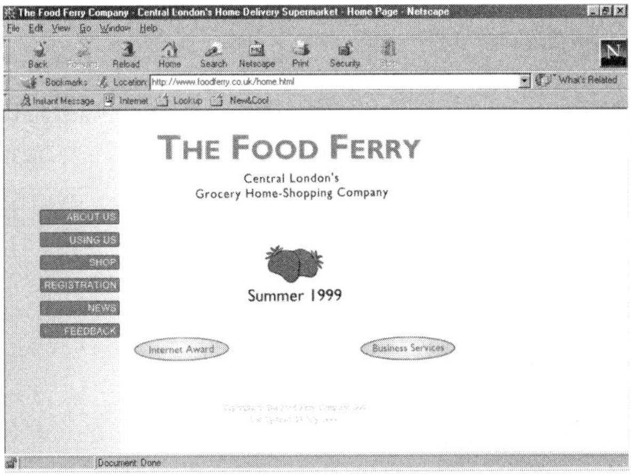

Fromages.com: if you like French cheese this is the site for you. http://www.fromages.com

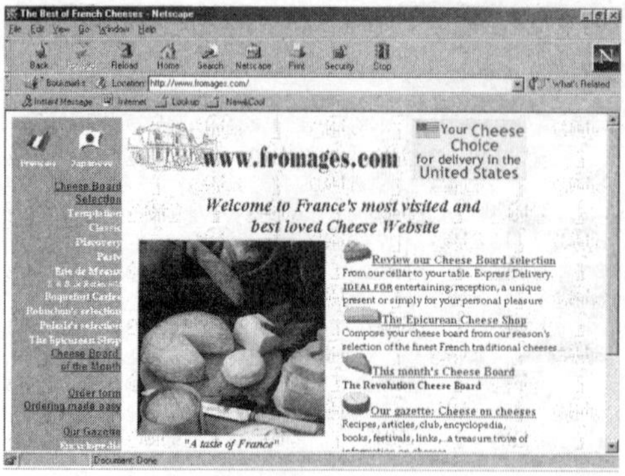

Fruitofcourse.com: A Belgian company specializing in high-end fruit and gourmet baskets. They feel fruit is more original, colourful and healthier than flowers as a gift. **http://www.fruitofcourse.com**

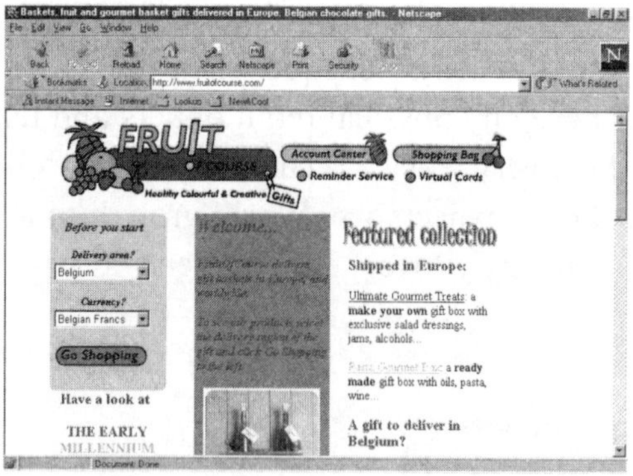

Biba Fantasia Bijoux Mall is the first Italian virtual shop specializing in the sale of handcrafted jewels made with natural semi-precious stones. **http://www.bigiotteria.com**

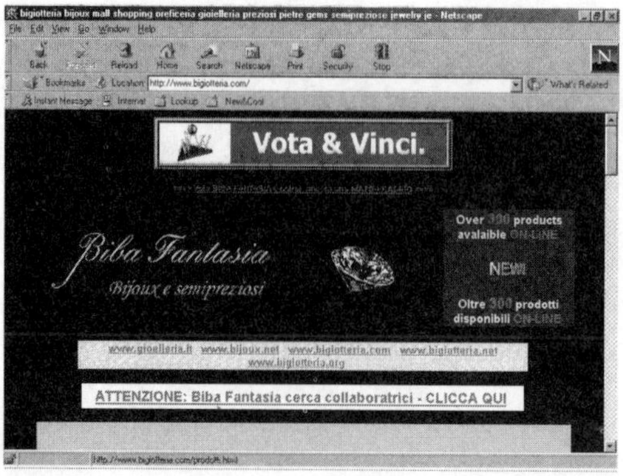

Choix.com is the first virtual hypermarket in France and Europe. They are an eCommerce company that allows consumers to shop in the eWorld. They also propose to permit distributors to sell their products via their site through advertising pages. **http://www.choix.com**

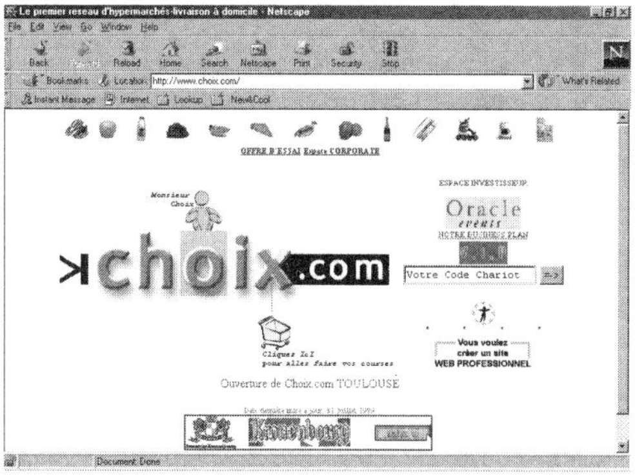

FatFace.co.uk is a retailer of lifestyle branded clothing. It has 25 stores in the UK and France and also sells via mail order. In keeping with its multichannel approach to retailing, it has set up a Web site to market the company's range of lifestyle products. Fat Face is using innovative technology – Hewlett-Packard's OpenPix ImageIgniter – to help sell its clothing range over the Internet. OpenPix enables customers to view items in great detail, enlarging clothing images to view buttons and stitching, for example. FatFace believes this helps customers feel comfortable about buying online because they can see what they are getting for their money. The site runs a 'fat calories' campaign to encourage sales and loyalty. Online visitors registered with the Fat Club earn fat calories for every £10 spent, redeemable against future online purchases and bargain offers. Customers are given unique, password-protected identities so that they can be greeted personally when they access the site and can view their purchases. **http://www.fatface.co.uk**

Mercato.it is a Cybermarket Mall and is one of the biggest and most active cyber malls in Italy, in terms of both number of shops (100) and products which are offered (25,000). **http://www.mercato.it**

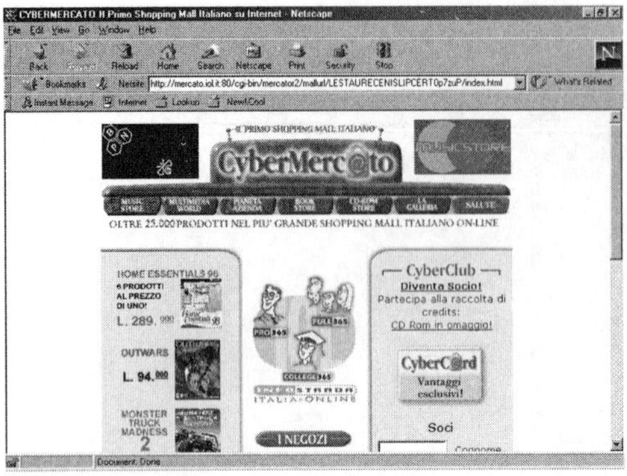

The **Owner-Driver Radio Taxi Service** is a London-based cooperative organization serving 2,000 self-employed London black taxicab drivers. It is currently piloting the first Internet-based real-time cab booking service in Europe with two large City-based organizations, before fully rolling out the service.

The online service allows corporate customers to access the Dial-a-Cab Web site, look at the availability of black cabs and make a booking online. The booking is automatically passed to the cab driver who acknowledges it via radio connection. Bookings can be made well in advance of a journey. Clients can also determine whether any cabs are currently in their vicinity. Payment will continue to be made through existing account channels, rather than over the Internet. Clients will, however, be able to review their account online, enabling them to analyze past and future bookings and associated charges. **http://www.dialacab.co.uk**

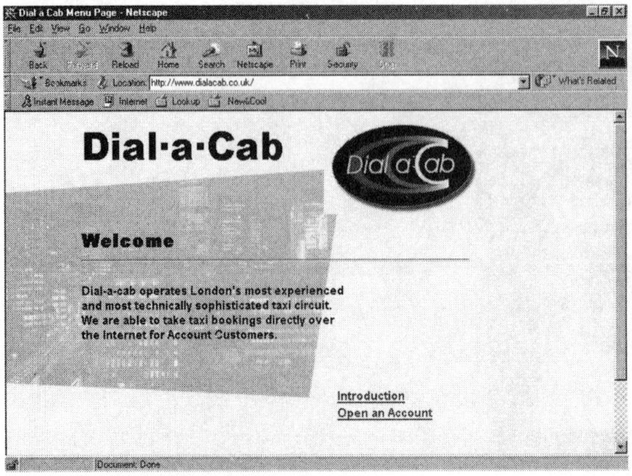

Silicon.com is an IT and television news service. **http://www.silicon.com**

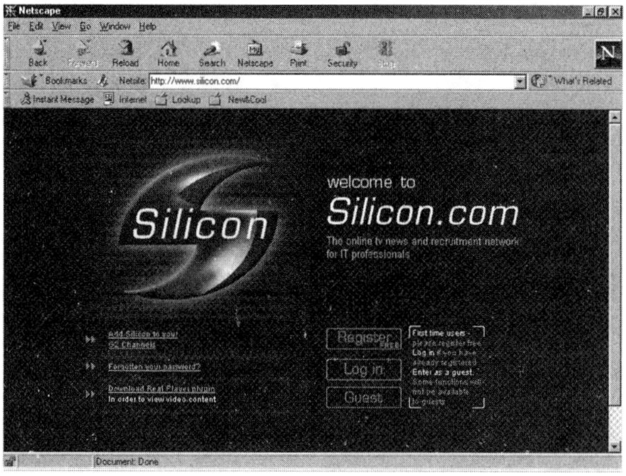

I have included a few Web sites which are not part of the KITE list, but all these sites display all the characteristics of Best Practices sites.

Since 1895 four successive generations of the Kelly family have created this thoroughly fine **Resort Hotel** in Rosslare, Ireland; they have most certainly moved with the times and as their customers move into the eWorld they can now interact with them. A good site and a great hotel. **http://www.kellys.ie/**

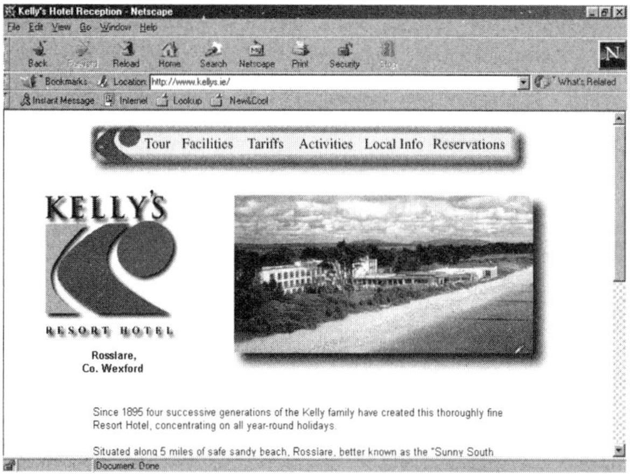

I was speaking at a conference in London recently and a fellow speaker was Stelios Haji-Ioannou, Chairman of the **easy** group of companies. His easyJet airline, through providing excellent service at a most reasonable cost, has grown in stature considerably in the past few years. Eighteen months ago he did not have a Web site for his airline. Today 65 per cent of his business comes from the eWorld. He said at the conference that his airline was 'The Internet's most favourite airline'. I suggested to him to change this to 'The eWorld's most favourite airline'. Let us wait and see if his marketing department adopt this slogan. His easyJet Web site is an example for everyone in its ease of use. **http://www.easyjet.com/**

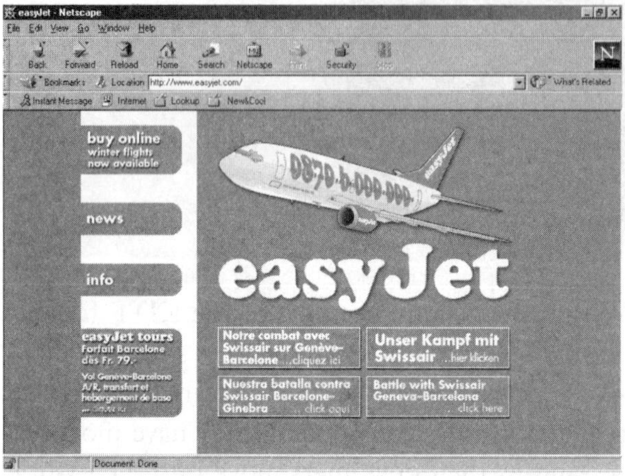

Stelios obviously sees the potential of the eWorld and has recently set up **easyeverything.com** which is the world's largest Internet cafe or cafes as there are many more in the pipeline. This is another site that is well worth a visit. **http://www.easyeverything.com/**

And finally a site you could literally spend hours on. This eBusiness was set up nine months ago by two most interesting individuals, Brent Hoberman and Martha Lane Fox, who have had the vision to see the possibilities in the eWorld. Their initial investment of £300,000 has grown in about a year to a market value of a conservative £400 million. They deserve every penny for having the foresight and determination to carry it through. Do visit this site as there is something there for everyone and at a bargain price. **http://www.lastminute.com**

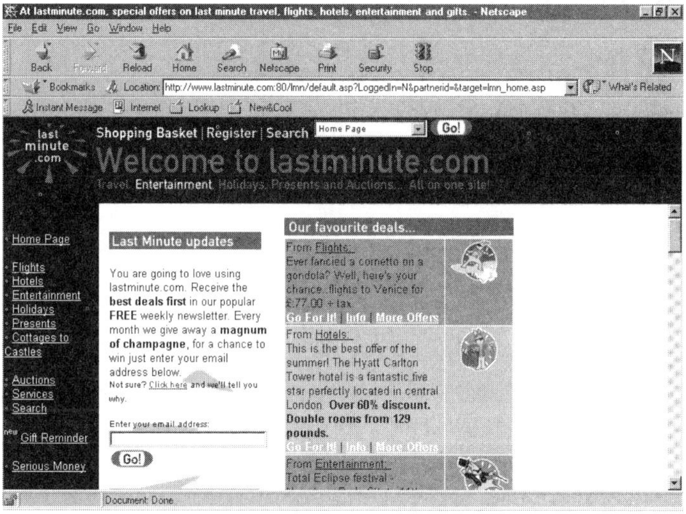

By taking the time to visit these sites you will have gained a clear insight into how culturally diverse organizations with a common business objective have found the most effective mechanisms to conduct business in the eWorld. Knowing now what constitutes a 'Best Practice' Web site, do not forget that a clear business strategy needs to be defined, to ensure the success of your eWorld business.

It is only by exploring eCommerce technology directly that you can begin to get insight into such issues. To do so, you should visit all of these sites online. By comparing the approaches and assessing what you have learned, you'll end up making a better decision as to your own needs.

23

Simplifying the eWorld for senior citizens

Few people know how to be old.

FRANCOIS, DUC DE LA ROCHEFOUCAULD
1613–80

- What is a senior?
- Don't hesitate to look and listen
- Why learn about the eWorld?
- The advantages
- What is happening around Europe
- America
- Some other sites of interest

In researching this section I have come to the conclusion that older people are not averse to using new technology, they are just unfamiliar with it. And once they have access to the new tools and the knowledge of how to use them, the eWorld can enrich their lives in ways that they would never have considered possible.

People over 50 are the fastest growing group in the eWorld, a virtual powerhouse of potential traffic and buying power who are now connecting to the vast potential of the eWorld. And yet the image of the eWorld remains one of youthfulness.

By 2000, seniors will constitute 45 per cent of the population. By 2006, 49.1 per cent of men and 72.6 per cent of women over 50, for whatever reason, will be retired. Seven per cent of people aged 50-64 have tried the eWorld compared to 3 per cent in 1996 and the numbers are still growing; however, still only 2 per cent of those over 65 have surfed.

What is a senior?

The word 'senior' is often misunderstood. Is it an age? An attitude? Is a 'senior' a 50-year-old or a 95-year-old?

At the beginning of the twentieth century, the average life expectancy was 46. Today, it is over 76. With advances in medicine and quality of life, it's not uncommon for people to start a new career at 60. With today's longer life spans, we must redefine our views of who seniors are and what they can accomplish.

The eWorld is giving people of all ages the ability to contribute to their community and the economy, rather than having to depend on it. The eWorld is helping to break down barriers, prejudices and misperceptions across generations.

Seniors and youth are discovering that they can grow and learn together, breaking stereotypes, creating friendships and sharing wisdom. The eWorld can bridge the generation divide for people of all ages.

Many seniors have memories of failed attempts to master a new skill, a new language, some new appliance or machine, and are not eager to repeat the experience. The computer is particularly intimidating to those first approaching it. Many still 'know' that it is obscure, mysterious, and prone to do totally unexpected things.

Always remember it is attitude that is important, not age.

Don't hesitate to look and listen

Internet sites are filled with health care information, financial news, film reviews, legal tips, jokes, maps and a multitude of newspapers and magazines. There are even tutorials online to teach us to use the Internet itself!

If you're not already online, the next time a grandchild wants to demonstrate something for you on the computer, or your son/daughter speaks about computers, don't hesitate to look and listen. Children and grandchildren are often highly sophisticated in the realms of computer expertise.

Even contemporary four-year-olds know that every mouse isn't Mickey. If your children haven't suggested it themselves, tell them when they plan to buy you a special gift or offer you a birthday holiday, that you'd rather have a computer. Tell them you'll give up the cruise to Barbados and cruise the eWorld instead. Ask a computer salesperson, 'Show me what this thing will do,' and be prepared to be amazed.

Dedication

Seniors often have an uphill struggle when venturing into new technologies. In addition to learning the technology, jargon, and inconsistent behaviour in software and hardware, they have their own unique issues confronting them. The young programmers who are writing some wonderful programs haven't always made things easy. They work in their own worlds with their own set of rules and standards. Many 'experts' in technology only really know the most complex natures of their field. They specialize in the complex, not the simple. This does not make it any easier for the senior citizen. Do not despair, more and more seniors are approaching the eWorld with intelligence, enthusiasm and a desire to master this new technology.

Why learn about the eWorld?

People use the eWorld for work and for leisure. Being able to use the eWorld gives you immediate access to a huge international network of people and resources. EWorld knowledge is becoming increasingly important for all of us, and everyone can learn it.

What is different about the over-50s?

The over-50s are those who are more likely to have had no experience of computers at work, school, college or at home. This makes integrating into the eWorld more difficult. When everyone else seems able to talk about Web sites and emails, it makes it all the more intimidating. Increasing numbers of this age group are retiring earlier, and in so doing so are moving away from environments where they may experience IT.

Barriers

The great barrier is the myth that 'old people are afraid of new techniques, old people are not interested in computers, old people do not have anything to gain from the eWorld'. But when you investigate what it's all about and get to know a little of the things that absorb so many of the youth of today, you start to realize something new and important is happening.

Ageing is changing

The image of ageing is changing. Old age is not what it used to be and, in the future, it will not be what it is today. Much has been written about the topic of geriatrics. We have long abandoned the concept that old age is an illness that we will all have to endure. Senior citizens do not all of a sudden become old when they reach that magic age of retirement. It is possible to live well into later years with a sense of enjoyment, productivity and general well-being. We all age biologically, psychologically and socially at differing rates, yet fundamentally we remain ourselves as we grow older. Senior citizens in the eWorld have the means and ability to create their choice of lifestyle for their future.

Tips, tricks and trivia

Reach for the stars

'As the flexibility in your body increases, life's possibilities will also grow!' So advises Carol Dickman's Stretch Central, at

http://www.stretch.com

Ms Dickman, a yoga instructor, has devoted her life to teaching people from all walks of life to stretch. Click through her Collection of 21 Stretches. Or send in a picture of your pet stretching, because as Carol says, 'Our friends in the animal kingdom stretch naturally all the time. Let's learn from them . . . '

The advantages

The eWorld can keep seniors in touch with the times in so many ways. Online networks can provide a genuine electronic community for seniors, helping them stay in touch with family and friends, thus avoiding depression and isolation.

The elderly have several advantages. The first is time. They have enough of it to be able to catch up with their grandchildren who are growing up with computers and who use them as naturally as any other household appliance. A recent survey revealed that many of the elderly started using the eWorld to send emails to distant relatives. They then connected on to the eWorld which then offered a myriad of online courses and self-help groups on everything from using the computer to flower arranging.

The possibility of online shopping also allows people to stay at home and still shop. Some wired seniors have found a second career in online consulting, offering advice on many subjects.

A whole group of dedicated chat lines have also provided the more isolated with a chance to participate in debates, conferences and generally to chat about mutual interests with other people all over the world. America is obviously ahead of Europe but Italian wired seniors are also starting to become a reality, contradicting the stereotype that the eWorld is only for the young.

A changing image

The image of the Net surfer is someone young and trendy who has been brought up with the latest technology. But this stereotype is going to change, for growing fast among those learning to love computers and all that they can do are the 'grey surfers'.

More and more pensioners are hooking up with the Internet and emails. Some Internet providers now have more pensioners on their books than people in their teens and twenties.

There are many reasons why pensioners are linking up to the eWorld. Some want to keep in touch with

Tips, tricks and trivia

The Scrabble Word Finder is just one of several puzzle word finders available at the Puzzle Depot site.

http://www.puzzledepot.com/wordfinder2/scrabble.html

families and friends, while others want to make new friends, share hobbies or find work.

Growing numbers of older people are becoming volunteer guides on eWorld services, looking after message boards in specific areas, such as gardening, and vetting abusive or unpleasant exchanges. They are bringing a new breadth of knowledge to the eWorld.

The important thing to remember is once you've mastered the basics of your computer, the eWorld and email are easy. There are so many magazines, books and telephone helplines to support you, you just can't go wrong. However, learning at an older age requires extra time and effort but it is worth it, as it will change your life.

Benefits of computers and the eWorld

Seniors use their computers for a wide variety of purposes.

- Finally writing that great novel or their own memoirs
- Tracing genealogical trees
- Starting up a home business
- Planning their finances
- Managing their investment portfolios
- Banking
- Getting hooked into a new world of information and friends in the eWorld
- Peer counselling
- Health monitoring and medical research data
- Just keeping up with their grandkids!

What is happening around Europe

SeniorNet Sweden is a national non-profit organization, set up to promote computer knowledge among Swedish senior citizens to respond to their claim to be full members of the information society. The government through the Swedish IT commission created SeniorNet. SeniorNet has its own Web site that will be developed continuously to provide a virtual home for Swedish citizens over the age of 55 years who are interested in IT. SeniorNet Sweden also hopes to develop cooperation with similar networks across the world. All material is published from a 55+ perspective. SeniorNet is a network where older people can learn to surf the Web, take a course in computers, or find virtual meeting places to communicate with their peers. The first SeniorNet club outside Sweden has now been established for senior Swedes living in Spain.

For further information: **http://www.seniornet.se**

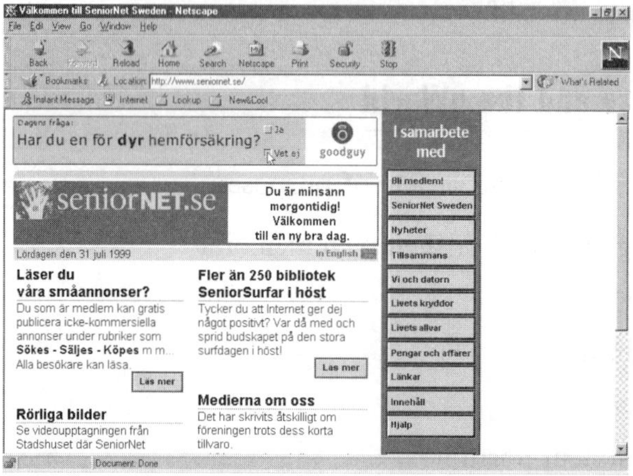

The eWorld requires new skills, which not all members of the public have, especially people over 50 years of age. For example, only three per cent of people in Germany who are over 55 years of age use a computer. Among online users only one per cent are older than 60 years. What older people know about the Internet is mainly limited to what is learned from radio and TV. However, many older people are interested in getting to know these technologies better.

In order to achieve this goal, together with the support from the Ministry of Economy and Technology as well as IBM, Vobis and other well-known companies, **VSiW** has organized a campaign 'Senior-Info-Mobil: Internet und Wohntechnik' (Senior-Info-Mobil: Internet and Home Technology). This provides seniors with the opportunity to inform themselves about the benefits and the use of these new technologies. A custom-made double-decker bus with a built-in Internet cafe gives seniors the possibility to learn about the eWorld and to test the first steps in using it. This 'mobile' Internet cafe travels all over Germany. Other European governments should take note.

The aim of the campaign is to support older people in forming their own opinion about the use of these new technologies and to strengthen their ability for self-help. **http://www.iid.de/vsiw/**

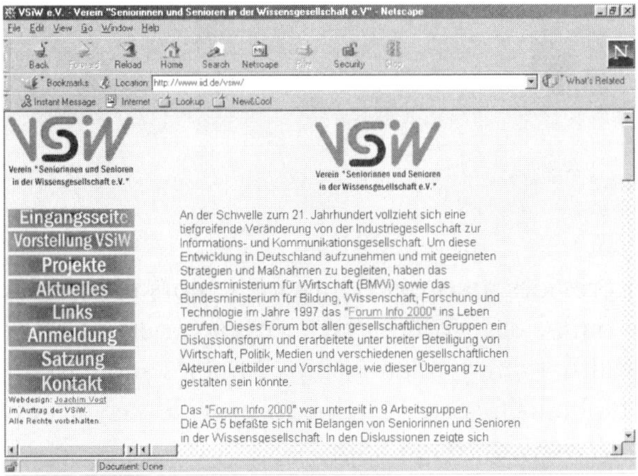

America

America has without doubt the most sites for senior citizens. Some to check out are Seniors-site.com, which is dedicated to helping senior citizens and their caregivers, and includes message boards, information about health issues, computers and the Internet, with links to a broad range of subjects, from Alzheimer's to grandparenting, and many other subjects of interest to older people. **http://seniors-site.com**

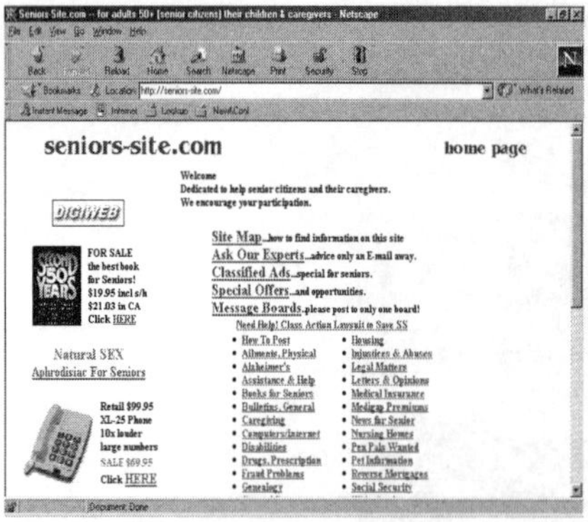

The biggest seniors site in the US is Aarp.org. **http://www.aarp.org/**

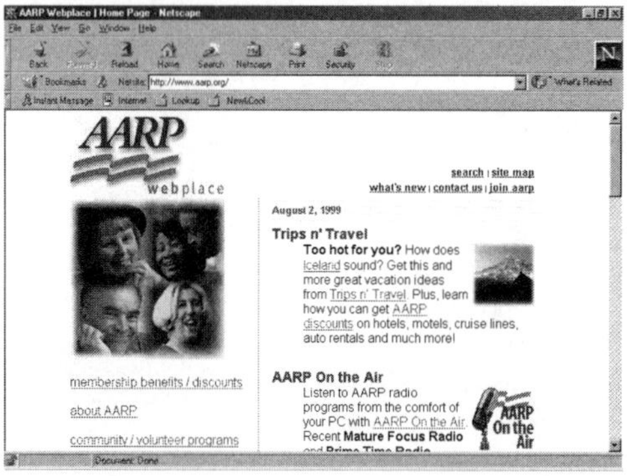

ThirdAge is a site which provides an opportunity for seniors to interact with each other through an online chat forum and access a variety of news about books, technology, health, money, relationships, hobbies and current events. ThirdAge also has its built-in search engine to provide easy access to many of its features. **http://www.thirdage.com**

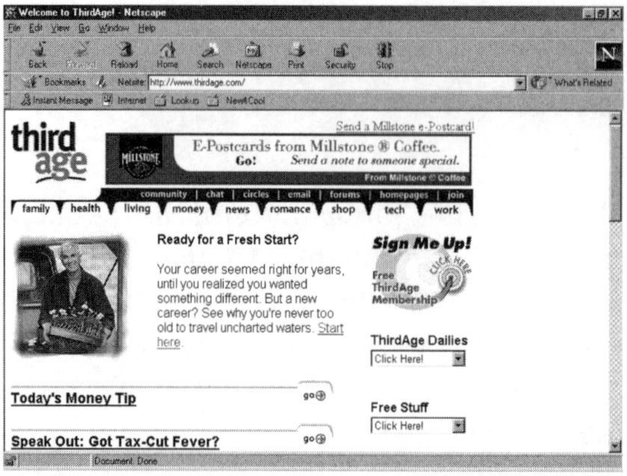

An interesting site is Computing Made Easy for Seniors. It is a non-profit Web site designed to help retired people understand how computers work and locate some resources for improving their computing skills. **http://www.ecst.csuchico.edu/~sheridan/seniors/computing.html**

Older would-be computer users will find many excellent 'do-it-yourself' computer learning sites available in the eWorld with many different tutorials for learning how to use the Internet, word processing, desktop publishing and other computer resources effectively.

Learn The Net, **http://www.learnthenet.com/english/index.html**, which I mentioned in Part I, has a string of tutorials on email, news groups, Web publishing and eWorld research and not just in English. The site also presents tutorials in German, Spanish, French and Italian.

The Internet Tutorial Site is an all-purpose site providing many useful resources for the new or advanced Internet user. **http://www.squareonetech.com**

Some other sites of interest

AGE CONCERN. A very well laid out site, offering a tour around, index, news, information and a huge collection of relevant documents and details of services that include insurance, available grants, training and fundraising. It's at **http://www.ace.org.uk/**. There's also a chat room for older people at the Baby Boomer Bistro: **http://www.babyboomerbistro.org.uk/**

ALTERNATIVE MEDICINE. A comprehensive list of sites and newsgroups in the eWorld. At: **http://www.pitt.edu/~cbw/altm.html**

ARP/50. The (British) Association of Retired and Persons over 50 local Web site for the East Anglia and East Midlands regions. ARP/50 provides 'a forum, a voice, and a range of money saving supplies and services' for those over 50. It looks interesting. This local site is at: **http://www.viridian.mcmail.com/arp/** but a national site is being developed at: **http://www.arp.org.uk/**

CANCER HELP. Helpful information and advice for patients as well as professionals from Birmingham University's Medical School. Well presented and matter of fact. At: **http://medWeb.bham.ac.uk/cancerhelp/**

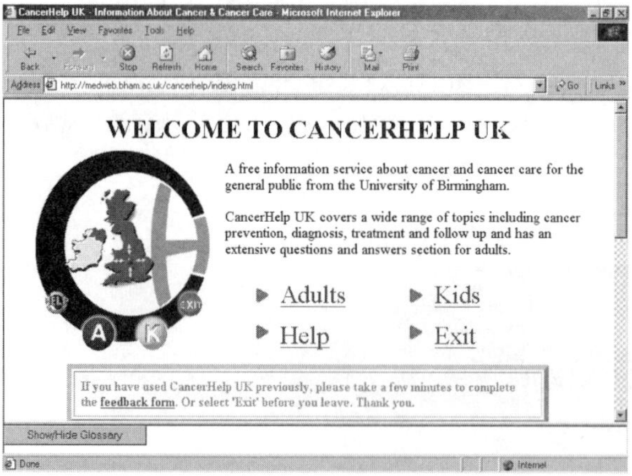

CARP (Canadian Association of Retired Persons). A non-profit organization that aims to safeguard rights of over-50s, provide useful information, and negotiate group discounts in Canada! A bit slow, and it needs a browser that can handle frames, but it sounds a very politically effective pressure group. You can find it at: **http://www.fifty-plus.net/**

CITIZENS' ADVICE BUREAU (Manchester). Very useful advice and information and a good database to search (there were, for example, 18 references to retirement). Also offers updates on changes in the law, Cloggie's (who's he/she?) advice on typical problems, and an email service to solve your problems. What more could you ask? It goes a bit over the top, though, with sound files that are slow to unload and which I, for one, had not got the necessary program to play. At **http://www.poptel.org.uk/cab/**. There is also a national CAB site that offers excellent online information and advice on a whole range of consumer subjects. It's at: **http://194.129.36.68/nacab/plsql/nacab.homepage**

HAIRNET. A London-based computer course, run by two young women, for people aged 50–90. Research suggests that only 3 per cent of 55–64 year-olds (and 2 per cent of those aged 65+) in Britain have even tried the eWorld, so this course aims to give more people the necessary knowledge and confidence. Their site, with some interesting links, is at: **http://www.hairnet.org/**

MISERABLE OLD GIT, THE. Philip Carr describes his site as 'warped humour for silver surfers'. It's a really amusing UK site that includes sections on famous MOGs, a personal appliances swap shop (!), rants and moans, famous last words, and even a so-called Salacious Sex Parlour. If you want help in growing old disgracefully, try: **http://fenet.net/mog/**

THE OLDIE, Upbeat and often entertaining. Edited by Richard Ingrams who enjoys being reactionary. It describes itself as 'A layby of sanity on the Information Superhighway'. Well worth a look. **http://www.theoldie.co.uk/**

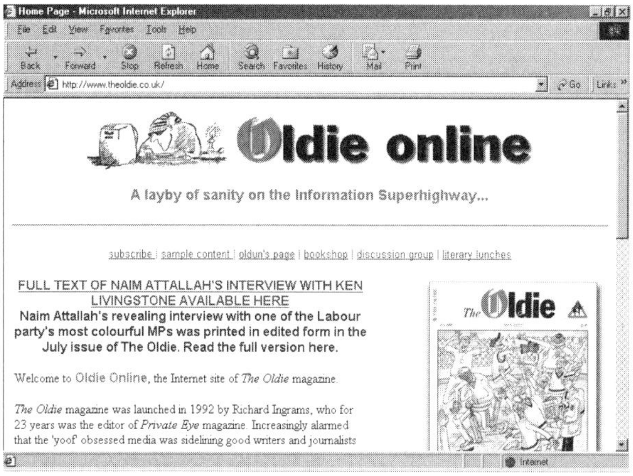

OPEN UNIVERSITY. Ever thought of doing a degree course in your spare time? They say you're never too old so, if you'd enjoy the challenge, it could be worth your while to find out more at: **http://www.open.ac.uk/**

REACH (Retired Executive Action Clearing House). Run by volunteers, this offers part-time, expenses-only jobs (taking up to two or three days a week) to retired business and professional people. All very worthy, but it's obviously a matter of luck whether there's an opportunity in your particular region that really suits you. Their Web site is: **http://www.volwork.org.uk/** and you can email them at: volwork@btinternet.com

SAGA. Caters exclusively for people over 50. You can join the Saga Club for £12.95 a year. It's worth considering. They have launched an Internet site, but it doesn't do much more than just plug the printed magazine. You'll find it at: **http://www.saga.co.uk/**

ST JOHN'S INTERNET CHURCH. Here's somewhere you can join in an act of worship any time of the day (or night), and can even take communion. Not everyone will approve of this, but it's a sensible well-presented site run by Rev. Dr. Everett A. Brown, a Methodist clinical psychologist in Rome, Georgia. It includes a chat room too. It's at: **http://www.religionnet.com/**

Sacred Space. In Dublin, the Jesuits have created a 'sacred space' Web site, Sacred Space can be found at **www.jesuit.ie/prayer**.

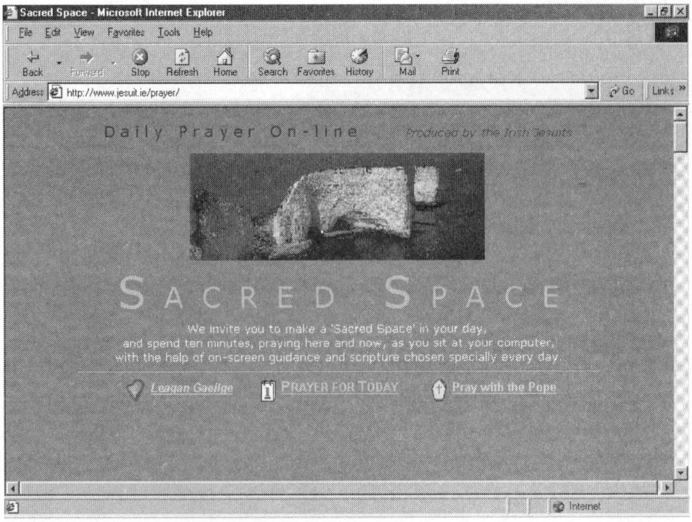

SENIOR COM. A very well set out site resembling a central square in a typical American home town, complete with city hall, advice centres and shops, all aimed at those over 50. There's advice on medical and (American) financial matters, travel and much else, with free offers and a chance to get in touch with other people. Visit it at: **http://www.senior.com/**

SENIOR FROLIC. An interesting and amusing American collection of links for older people arranged into 24 categories, ranging from Americana to Words, and including Cars, Diversions, Ingenuity, Intrigue and Senior Sites. I was impressed to find that it began by explaining that it did not provide medical sources, sociological information, or advice on how to lead a more productive life! But what it does, it does well. At: **http://www.geocities.com/Heartland/4474**

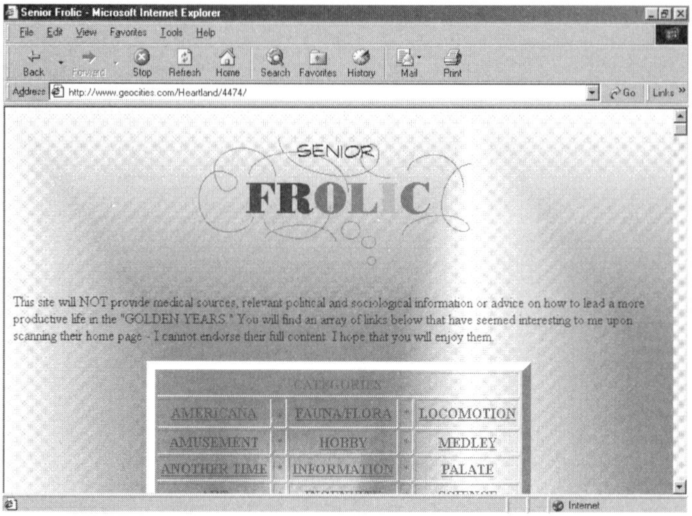

SENIORS' COMPUTER INFORMATION PROJECT. An excellent Canadian site offering an incredible variety of information and links including Ask Great-Granny about your sexual and other problems!, Health Line medical questions answered and a list of Seniors' Home Pages. But there's much, much more! Recommended by Joy Morrison who describes it as 'everything at your fingertips'. Pity about the title, though, which seems to suggest that it's all about computers! At: **http://www.mbnet.mb.ca/crm**

SOCIAL SECURITY, DEPARTMENT OF. If you have not yet retired, you can find out how much state pension you are likely to receive by filling in form BR19 (Pension Forecast Application Form) – obtainable from DSS offices, then posting it off to the Benefit Agency in Newcastle. Their Web site, however, is awful. You are passed from page to page with hardly any information on any of them! It's a slow and infuriating process, and probably not worth the effort. It's at: **http://www.dss.gov.uk/**

YAHOO SENIORS' GUIDE. Simple news, lots of chat, and useful links, although not quite as comprehensive a site as you might have expected: **http://seniors.yahoo.com/**

24

Using the eWorld to find what is new in Europe

Friends share all things.

PYTHAGORAS
582–500 BC

- Institutions
- People
- Policies
- Miscellaneous
- Issues

The European Union is using the eWorld as a way of distributing information and locations that can be accessed are increasing rapidly. The following selection you will find useful but it is by no means comprehensive. I have spent many hours researching various European issues. Having the following URLs will save you considerable time if you need to research into what is really happening in Europe.

Institutions

European Council

Finnish Presidency, July–December 1999

http://www.presidency.finland.fi

European Commission

The making of the new Prodi Commission (European Commission, 1999)

http://europa.eu.int/comm/index_en.htm

The Prodi Commission (European Commission, 1999)

http://europa.eu.int/comm/newcomm/index_en.htm

European non-governmental organizations

Directory of Interest Groups (European Commission: Secretariat-General, 1999)
http://europa.eu.int/comm/sg/sgc/lobbies/repertoire/indexrep_en.htm

European Citizen Action Service/ European Citizen's Association (ECAS)
http://www.ecas.org

European Evaluation Society (EES)
http://www.europeanevaluation.org

European Forum for Arts and Heritage (EFAH)
http://www.eurplace.org/orga/efah/index.html

European Solidarity Towards Equal Participation of People (EUROSTEP)
http://www.oneWorld.org/eurostep/index.html

European Commission: Committees and other consultative forums

Energy Consultative Committee (European Commission: DG V, 1999)
http://europa.eu.int/en/comm/dg17/openness.htm

National government and intergovernmental organizations (except EU)

Nordic Council/ Nordic Council of Ministers
http://www.norden.org/index_uk.html

Other EU agencies and bodies

Consumers in Europe Group (CEG, 1997)
http://www.ceg.co.uk/

UK organizations with a European dimension to their activities

Britain in Europe (UK movement supporting British participation in single currency) (Britain in Europe, 1999)
http://www.britainineurope.com

Business for Sterling (UK movement opposing UK participation in single currency) (Business for Sterling, 1999)
http://www.bfors.com

Euro Know (Bringing you the facts about the euro) (Organization against UK participation in the single currency)
http://www.euro-know.org

Federation of Small Businesses (FSB)
http://www.fsb.org.uk

Insitute of Directors (IoD)
http://www.iod.co.uk

New Europe (UK movement supporting UK membership of EU but outside single currency) (New Europe, 1999)
http://www.new-europe.co.uk/contents.html

People

Directory of Interest Groups (European Commission: Secretariat-General, 1999)
http://europa.eu.int/comm/sg/sgc/lobbies/repertoire/indexrep_en.htm

Policies

General information

A–Z of Europe: A concise encyclopedia of the European Union from Aachen to Zollverein (by Rodney Leach. Profile Books)
http://www.euro-know.org/dictionary/index.html

European public opinion (European Commission: DG X, 1999) (Eurobarometer and Europinion etc)
http://europa.eu.int/comm/dg10/epo/polls.html

People and politics

European Citizen Action Service/ European Citizen's Association (ECAS)
http://www.ecas.org

European public opinion (European Commission: DG X, 1999) (Eurobarometer and Europinion etc)
http://europa.eu.int/comm/dg10/epo/polls.html

Civil protection and environmental emergencies (European Commission: DG XI, 1999)
http://europa.eu.int/comm/dg11/civil/index.htm

The European Commission and special interest groups (European Commission: Secretariat-General, 1999)
http://europa.eu.int/comm/sg/sgc/lobbies/index_en.htm

Budget – financing the EU

Evaluation in the European Communities (European Commission: DG XIX, 1998)
http://europa.eu.int/comm/dg19/en/evaluation/index.htm

Economic and Monetary Union

Euro Know (Bringing you the facts about the euro) (Organization against UK participation in the single currency)
http://www.euro-know.org/

Britain in Europe (UK movement supporting British participation in single currency) (Britain in Europe, 1999)
http://www.britainineurope.com

Business for Sterling (UK movement opposing UK participation in single currency) (Business for Sterling, 1999)
http://www.bfors.com

New Europe (UK movement supporting UK membership of EU but outside single currency) (New Europe, 1999)
http://www.new-europe.co.uk/contents.html

Single market – competition

Regional state aid: Maps (European Commission: DG IV, 1999)
http://europa.eu.int/comm/dg04/regaid/1999/en/html/eu_page1.htm

Supplementary pensions (European Commission: DG XV, 1999)
http://europa.eu.int/comm/dg15/en/finances/pensions/index.htm

Employment – labour market

National Action Plans on Employment (1999) (European Commission: DG V, 1999)
http://europa.eu.int/comm/dg05/empl&esf/news/nap_en.htm

Social policy – social issues

Supplementary pensions (European Commission: DG XV, 1999)
http://europa.eu.int/comm/dg15/en/finances/pensions/index.htm

Structural policies – regional policy

Structural Funds: Latest developments (European Commission: DG XVI, 1999)
http://inforegio.cec.eu.int/wbnews/new_en.htm

Structural Funds: Objectives – Old (1995–99) and New (2000–2006)
http://inforegio.cec.eu.int/wbpro/mumm/object/obj_en.htm#graph
http://inforegio.cec.eu.int/wbpro/mumm/object/obj_en.htm

Regional state aid: Maps (European Commission: DG IV, 1999)
http://europa.eu.int/comm/dg04/regaid/1999/en/html/eu_page1.htm

Documents on spatial planning (including text of final version of ESDP, May 1999) (European Commission: DG XVI, 1999)
http://www.inforegio.org/wbdoc/docoffic/official/space_en.htm

Spatial development principles for the European continent (description and critical commentary on ESDP and Council of Europe equivalent CEMAT, plus links to other related sources) (Paul Treanor, 1999)
http://Web.inter.nl.net/users/Paul.Treanor/europlan.extra.html

Environment

EU environmental information and legislation database (Environmental Publications Ltd, 1997) (Irish focus)
http://kola.dcu.ie/environ/welcome.htm

Environmental economics (European Commission: DG XI, 1999) (includes database on environmental taxes in the EU + Norway & Switzerland)
http://europa.eu.int/comm/dg11/enveco/index.htm

Agriculture – Fisheries – Forestry

Towards a new direction for UK agriculture. Consultation exercise and conference on Agenda 2000 CAP reform (UK: MAFF, 1999)
http://www.maff.gov.uk/farm/agendtwo/agendtwo.htm

Research and development – Science and technology

R&TD Activites – 1999 annual report (covering 1998 activities) (European Commission: DG XII, 1999) (COM(1999)284 final (16.6.99))
http://europa.eu.int/comm/dg12/report99.html

Finnish EU Presidency R&D information service, July–December 1999 (CORDIS/ Finnish EU Presidency, 1999)
http://www.cordis.lu/finland/en/home.html

Education – Training – Culture

Cultural activity (European Commission: DG X, 1999) (includes Ariane, Raphael, Kaleidoscope and Culture 2000 Programmes)
http://europa.eu.int/comm/dg10/culture/index_en.html

European Forum for Arts and Heritage (EFAH)
http://www.eurplace.org/orga/efah/index.html

External relations

The Stabilisation and Association Process for countries of South-Eastern Europe (European Commission, DG Ia, 1999) (includes information on 'The Regional Approach')
http://europa.eu.int/comm/dg1a/see/intro/index.htm

Central Europe Online (European Internet Network) (Current news stories for CEEC countries)
http://www.centraleurope.com

EU–Cyprus relations (Republic of Cyprus, 1999)
http://www.pio.gov.cy/ir/cyprus_eu/recent_developments.htm

Countdown: Online information, documentation and communication centre on the EU's eastern enlargement (Vienna Institute for International Economic Studies (WIIW), 1999)
http://wiiwsv.wsr.ac.at/Countdown

Relations between the European Union and the Latin American–Caribbean countries. Key figures (Eurostat, 1999)
http://europa.eu.int/en/comm/eurostat/compres/en/6499/memorioen.htm

Miscellaneous

European programmes

ASIA-INVEST (European Commission: DG IB)
http://www.asia-invest.com

ASIA-URBS (European Commission: DG IB)
http://www.asia-urbs.com

Culture 2000 (European Commission: DG X, 1999)
http://europa.eu.int/comm/dg10/culture/program-2000_en.html

Newspapers, bulletins and other news-related services

Central Europe Online (European Internet Network) (Current news stories for CEEC countries)
http://www.centraleurope.com/

Periodicals and other series

Europe on the Move (European Commission, DG X, 1999) (Popular level series of brochures on the EU and its policies. Original texts from 1995)
http://europa.eu.int/comm/dg10/publications/brochures/move/index_en.html

Publishers of European information

EUROFI
http://www.eurofi.co.uk

Hart Publishing (including John Wiley's law list from Spring 1999)
http://www.hartpub.co.uk

Oxford University Press (OUP/Clarendon Press)
http://www.oup.com

Statistical sources

EFTA: Statistical Information
http://www.efta.int/docs/EFTA/Statistics/default.htm

OECD Statistics
http://www.oecd.org/std

Issues

Current awareness – keeping up to date

EUROPA: What's new
http://europa.eu.int/geninfo/whatsnew.htm

RAPID: Latest EU Press Releases and related documents from the European Commission and other EU Institutions
http://europa.eu.int/rapid/start/lastdocs/guesten.htm

News (from the EU Institutions)
http://europa.eu.int/news-en.htm

Midday Express (news from the Spokesman's Service midday briefing)
http://europa.eu.int/en/comm/spp/me/midday.html

Calendar of main EU activities
http://europa.eu.int/news/cal-en.htm

European Agenda (European Commission: UK Representation)
http://www.cec.org.uk/pubs/twie/index.htm

Background Briefings (European Commission: UK Representation, 1998)
http://www.cec.org.uk/pubs/bbrief/index.htm

Note: *Background Briefings* from the European Commission: UK Representation replace the *Background Reports*, which have now all been removed from the UK Representation's Web site.
European Voice
http://www.european-voice.com

POLIS: The starting point for European politics
http://www.polis.net

BBC World Service: Europe Today
http://www.bbc.co.uk/worldservice/europetoday

Yahoo: News Headlines: European Union (mainly links to Reuters and Associated Press)
http://search.news.yahoo.com/search/news/?p=%22European+Union

Europe in Prospect (Clifford Chance)
http://www.cliffordchance.com/library/newsletters

25

News and how to get it

The freedom of the press is one of the bulwarks of Liberty.

George Mason
1725–1792

- Getting your news
- Searching for news
- Computer and Internet news
- Links to news spanning the globe
- Online newspapers vs. printed newspapers
- Layout of an online newspaper
- What are the benefits of eWorld newspapers?
- The future

Could there be a day when the majority of people get all their news with a click of the mouse in the eWorld? It will not be long before this happens, when you consider that text, photographs and graphics will be joined with sound, video and animation in an online newspaper and this will influence many in their choice of news source.

This is where television has had an advantage over print. Broadcast journalists have always recognized how sound and video improve the words used in reporting a story. It will not be long before we see these features incorporated into online newspapers making eWorld newspapers truly multimedia.

The eWorld allows you to access your national and global news before the traditional media today. Normally an online edition is published just after midnight; you have to wait until 7.00 a.m. to get your copy from the newsagent. The news you get then may be well out of date. Online versions of national newspapers can provide you with timely information about your topic; some are even updated every hour. Many online newspapers also have searching capacities that will allow you to find the exact articles you are looking for.

Tips, tricks and trivia

AltaVista adds media search capability

AltaVista's new AV Photo & Media Finder lets you search for images, video clips and audio files. You can perform a basic search by entering a topic in the Search box. To refine your search, you can click Options. Doing so lets you look for colour photos, black and white images or art works, and search only 'premier' collections, as well as select what to display in search results. People over 18 can turn off the Filter option, which sorts out adult content from the search results.

Remember: You still must abide by any copyright provisions regarding images you download from the Internet.

http://image.altavista.com

If there is some topic that you do not understand, you can use the eWorld to research-more effectively. The most popular sites for news in the eWorld are science and health, technology and financial information. Almost half of those who go online for news check the weather.

Many users say they like having the large amount of information that the eWorld provides, while those who do not use computers feel 'overloaded' with information. The convenience of the eWorld is one reason for its increased use, as people can check the news anywhere they have access and at any time of the day.

The eWorld allows you to have access to those interesting background facts, and access to special interest news stories that seldom appear in

Tips, tricks and trivia

National Geographic News

http://www.ngnews.com

Here you get stories written by journalists who have taken the time to see things through to their conclusions. Plus, you get story enhancements, maps, previous features and so on, that only National Geographic can provide. An interesting feature is the site's Instant Delivery feature, which emails you a PDF (Adobe Portable Document Format) file of each day's stories.

traditional print. You may read newspapers, watch TV, and listen to radio, but in the eWorld you start to realize how limited the traditional news medium really is as it only gives you a small portion of the news. Many writers have experienced frustration when they have written articles of, say, 1,000 words but because of space constraints only 700 words are published. The depth of their article is greatly diminished. In the eWorld this is most unlikely to happen. The editors of print newspapers are not concerned about your particular interests. They serve a large group of readers with different interests.

Go online and discover the difference. Online news has an enormous breadth and depth. Besides 'popular' news, you will find stories that few editors bother to print. This may well give you a better insight into current developments, and in as much detail as you could possibly want.

Balance your news between traditional and eWorld presentations, letting one supplement the other. Get your news in whatever format and time frame suits your needs. Decide what stories are important based on your own interest, and enjoy the feeling of freedom, diversity and power. Most commercial online services offer news, and free news is abundant in the eWorld.

Tips, tricks and trivia

Why are all the butterflies dying?

The people at The Why Files, at

http://whyfiles.news.wisc.edu/index.html

claim to present 'the science behind the news'. Now, the stories into which they research – why corn pollen is killing butterflies, what monkeys have to tell us about maternal bonds – aren't exactly headlines, but that may be precisely why they can teach us more than any news programme ever will. My favourite part of the site was the Cool Science Images section, where I saw something called a Black Smoker. You'll have to find out for yourself what this is.

Often, you can read and search articles from magazines, newsletters and other special publications. Online news is a valuable resource for those whose jobs depend on up-to-date information. The ability to search today and yesterday's news makes it very effective. The eWorld allows you to access breaking news from major world wire services, enabling you to interact with the digital media as broadcast and print outlets bring their stories to the marketplace.

Getting your news

For a country-by-country listing of online newspapers throughout the world, check **http://www.Webwombat.com.au/intercom/newsprs/**.

There's a World News Index at **http://www.stack.nl/~haroldkl/** with links to daily news providers in the eWorld, covering the entire globe. International news, a provider of free daily global news, is at **http://www.artigen.com/newswire/world.html**.

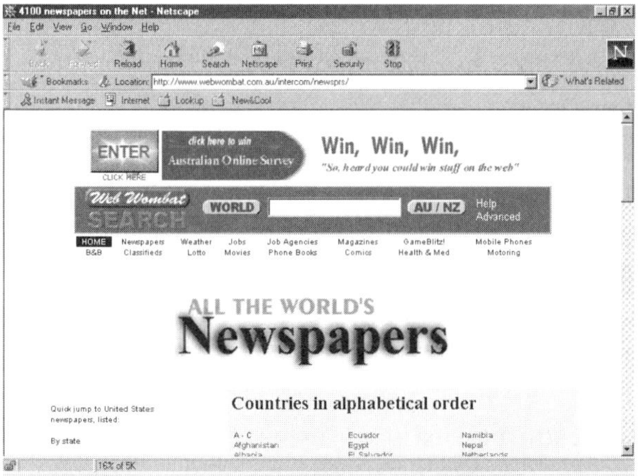

At Infoseek's News Centre **http://www.infoseek.com**, Business Wire and PR Newswire at **http://www.prnewswire.com** and Reuters at **http://www.reuters.com** you can search for specific names, phrases or words in the past 30 days of news stories.

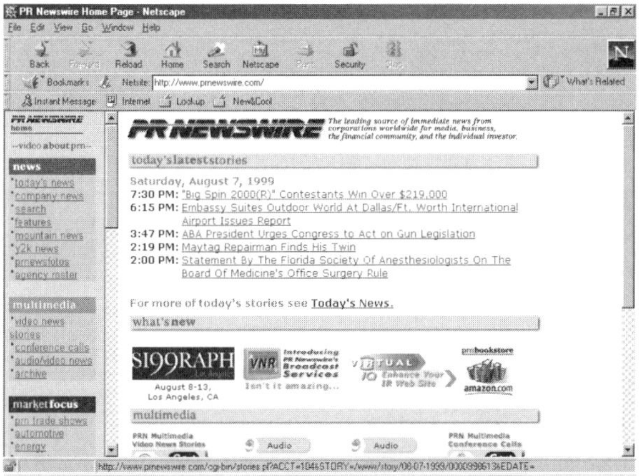

You can 'personalize' your news, and have Infoseek deliver only the news that interests you every time you return to the site. Also, you can have news headlines sent to you by email.

NewsPage provides commercial news at **http://www.newspage.com**. With more than 25,000 pages refreshed daily, and over 2,500 topic areas broken down into 240 categories within more than 20 industries, it covers a lot of ground.

They claim receipt of up to 20,000 news stories each day from over 700 English language sources – newspapers, magazines, trade weeklies, newsletters and press release wires. You can read pre-selected news by topic area, or create your own 'personalized' issue based on your own keywords.

For general news, start with major newswires, like Associated Press, Agence France-Presse **http://w3src.afp.com:80/AFP_VF/afpaccueil.html** or Reuters **http://www.reuters.com**.

Check links to broadcasting sources of news in many languages at **http://www.markovits.com/broadcasting/**. Choices include BBC, Channel 4 (United Kingdom), Deutsche Welle (Germany), Teletekst from NOS (Holland), Scandinavian broadcasters, Community Broadcasting Association of Australia, CBS, Radio Japan, the Internet Multicasting Service, US-based radio stations, CPB and NPR (USA), Radio Canada, Radio France, and many more.

The Current Awareness Resources using Internet Audio and Video page **http://gwis2.circ.gwu.edu/gprice/audio.htm** links to audio/video services that can be used in monitoring current events. It focuses on English language news/public affairs services. Most links will take you to the desired service.

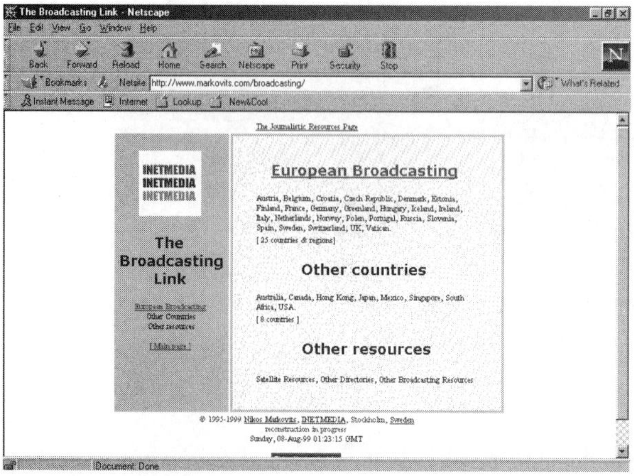

NOTE

To use these links, you'll need RealPlayer http://www.real.com/products/player/index.html from RealNetworks and Microsoft Media Player http://www.microsoft.com/windows/mediaplayer/default.asp.

Searching for news

News Index **http://www.newsindex.com/** is a news-only search engine. It indexes current articles from hundreds of sources from around the world. It is not an archive, but a resource for finding more information on current topics you are interested in. The news is broken up into various topics such as business, politics, sci-tech and opinion. Use it to read different versions of a story, and derive some semblance of what actually occurred. Use it to find multiple sources if your first choice wants to charge you for reading it. By following a large number of papers, you can follow ongoing stories as they happen. Use it to monitor what goes on within a topic of interest. Search

Tips, tricks and trivia

Finding magazines and newspapers on the Web

If you're looking for magazines on a particular topic or newspapers from a particular region, MetaGrid is a good place to start. The listing of links to media-sponsored Web sites is by no means exhaustive, however. The site has a basic search engine, but I found additional resources by browsing the relevant categories. I suggest you try both approaches if you don't find what you need at first.

http://www.metagrid.com

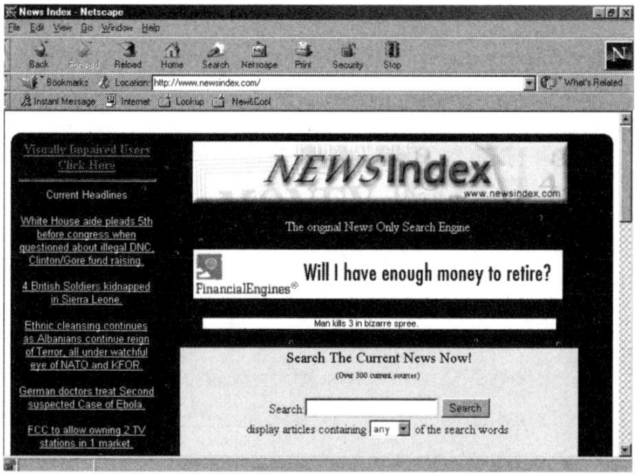

for a topic by submitting keywords. Hits containing all keywords are listed first. Click on the link to get an article's text. There are some other search engines focusing on today's news:

NewsBot	http://www.newsbot.com/
NewsTracker	http://nt.excite.com/
Lycos	http://www.lycos.com/news/
TotalNews	http://www.totalnews.com/

NewsTrawler at **http://www.newstrawler.com** is a meta search engine that allows you to search hundreds of news archives in the eWorld in tandem. The collection includes news, magazine and journal sources from a broad range of countries.

NOTE

While the search for information itself is free, a number of news resources provide free summaries but charge for the full report of information.

Computer and Internet news

The IM Europe Newsdesk provides links to news originating within the EU on information markets, multimedia, the information society, and information and communication technologies. The site **http://www.echo.lu/news/** can be accessed in English, French and German.

For free daily news about the eWorld, NewsLinx will give you updates on daily eWorld news. Check **http://newslinx.com/**.

NewsLinx features links to stories selected from the mainstream press, with an update posted each business day. There are many business or technology listings in the eWorld; this service provides links to the best stories, and it reports exclusively on the eWorld.

C|Net's NEWS.COM **http://www.news.com** is another brilliant source for this kind of news, as is The New York Times' Computer News Daily section at **http://computernewsdaily.com/**.

NewsPage **http://www.newspage.com** offers commercial news within these categories: Computer Hardware & Peripherals, Computer Software, Computer Professional Services, Data Communications, Interactive Media & Multimedia, Semiconductors, and Telecommunications. For information on computers, you should check out Newsbytes **http://www.nbnn.com**. This service gives headline news from around the world.

Links to news spanning the globe

Editor & Publisher Interactive collects data on just about every online newspaper in the world. For access, click on newspapers at **http://www.mediainfo.com/emedia/**. Here, you can list papers by continent by clicking on an Interactive World Map. You can full-text search to locate individual online publications or list papers by country.

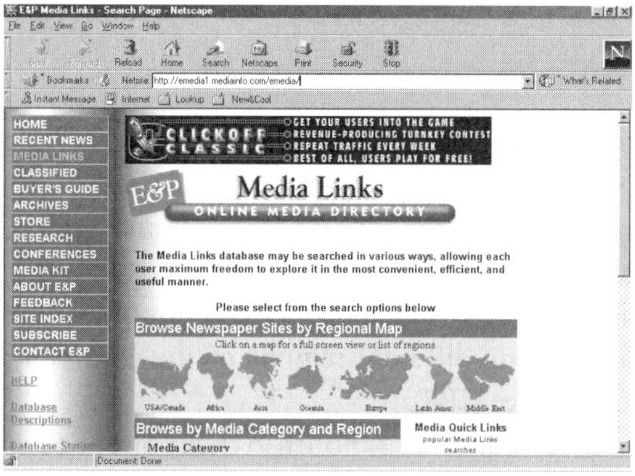

There's a competing service in the United States called HomeTown Free-Press at **http://www.GoThere.com/hometown.htm**. It offers free local news and information sites in Africa, Antarctica, Asia, Australia and New Zealand, Eastern and Western Europe, Middle East, North, South and Central America. Sites include newspapers, radio and television stations, schools, civic and civil organizations.

United Nations Daily Highlights: **http://www.un.org/News/dh/latest.htm**.

BBC Worldwide Monitoring **http://www.monitor.bbc.co.uk** draws upon radio, television and news agency reports from over 1,000 sources in over 140 countries to provide fast, reliable coverage of political and economic news.

Check **http://crayon.net/** for the free Creating Your Own Newspaper (CRAYON) service. Mark off your selected batch of information sources, and have a customized newspaper delivered to you.

Africa

Africa News Online **http://www.africanews.org** offers news from over 50 different sources, including 34 top African news organizations. The site is

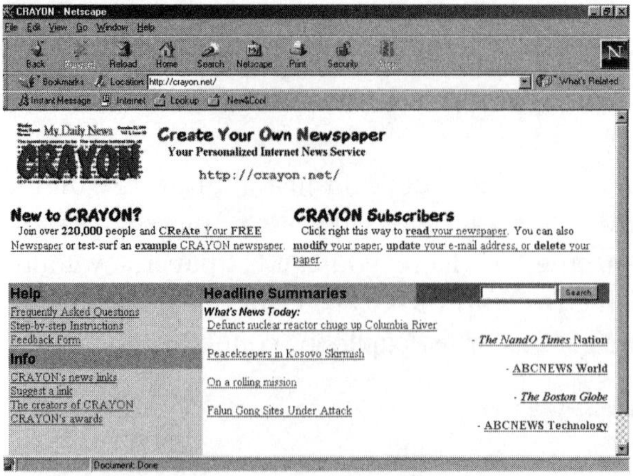

managed by Africa News Service, a non-profit agency. You'll find a wide range of country and topic-specific news, including stories relating to arts and entertainment, science and health, business and finance, and sports. An archive of past stories is searchable.

PeaceNet's World News Service **http://www.igc.org/igc/services/pwn.html** offers several digests on Africa, covering different regions of the continent, with coverage from the Inter Press Service (IPS).

The Weekly Mail & Guardian (Johannesburg, South Africa) offers news by email at **http://www.mg.co.za/mg/**. There is a searchable news archive.

China

China Daily On the Web **http://www.chinadaily.net/cndy/cd_cate1.html** delivers English language news from China under the headings Top News; Home News; China Business; World Business; Money; Opinion; Sport; Feature; World News.

China News Digest (CND) is a voluntary non-profit organization aiming at providing news and other information services about China-related affairs. All CND services are free of charge. Back issues of the China News Digest are at **http://www.cnd.org**. CND's English language publications include CND-Global (three issues per week), CND-US (one issue per week), CND-Canada (one issue per week), CND- Europe/Pacific (one issue per week), CND-China (two issues per month).

China News Service & Agency **http://www.chinanews.com/** offers daily business news from China, Hong Kong, Macao, and Taiwan to subscribers.

Japan

Japan Press Network **http://www.jpn.co.jp/** provides the latest news covering Japan's high-tech industries as well as finance, economics and the Japanese press.

The Japanese Journals Information Web **http://pears.lib.ohio-state.edu/ULJS/index.html** offers Current Awareness using access to tables of contents of current Japanese journals and magazines. In addition, it has The Union List of Japanese Serials and Newspapers (ULJSN) which currently includes information held by 20 libraries.

Middle East

The Middle East News Network publishes daily news, analysis and comments from 19 countries in the Middle East produced by the Arabic, Hebrew, Turkish and Iranian press. You can read this news through Reuters **http://www.reuters.com**.

Arabnet **http://www.countrylink.com/** brings up-to-the-minute Arabic news in Arabic characters. For Palestinian news, check the Birzeit University site **http://www.birzeit.edu/ourvoice/**.

Other countries in Asia and the Pacific

For interesting links to sources of political, social and economic news about mainland China, Hong Kong, Taiwan and Tibet, check **http://freenet.buffalo.edu/cb863/china.html**.

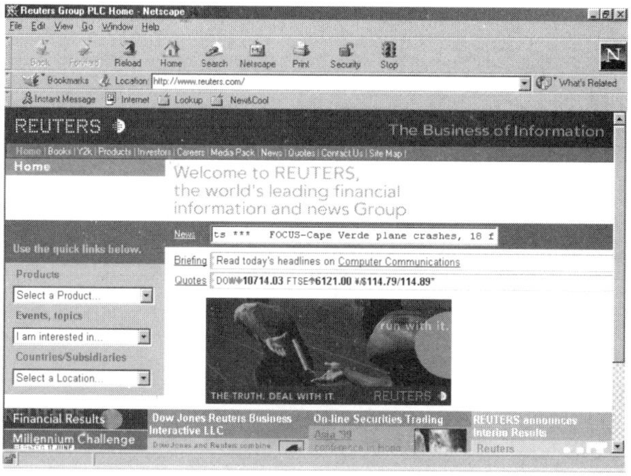

India and Pakistan

The INDIA-L mailing list **http://www.indnet.org/lists/india-l.html** distributes news from The India News Network, while the Pakistan News Service is at **http://www.paknews.org**.

Europe

You can search the Guardian OnLine Archives in England at **http://www.guardian.co.uk**, and the Economist is at **http://www.economist.com**. The Financial Times is another excellent UK site and well worth a visit at **http://www.ft.com**.

For Spanish news see El Periódico de Catalunya (Spain), at **http://www.elperiodico.es**. The Austrian 'Wiener Zeitung' claims to be the

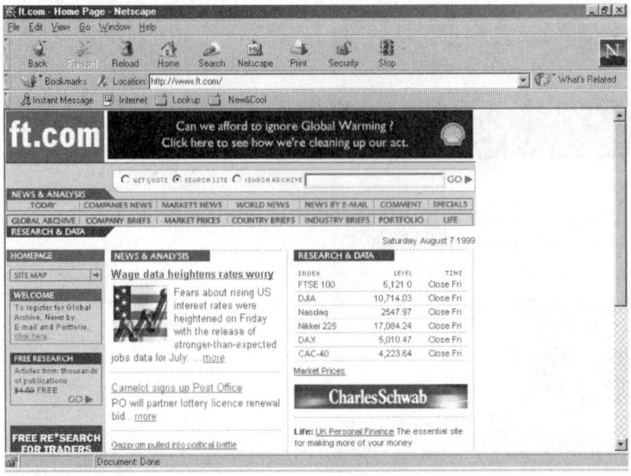

oldest existing daily newspaper in the world at nearly 300 years old. Its Web page covers domestic and world news in German, general information about Austria's government, the House of Parliament, the president, articles from the weekly computer page, and the Friday supplement, reviews of books, records and cultural events, a chess page, and more: **http://www.oesd.co.at/wz/wz.htm**. The Dutch language Internet newspaper InterNetKrant brings news from the Netherlands at **http://www.es.ele.tue.nl/ink/**. News about Flanders and Belgium Dutch is available from Rijksuniversiteit Gent (in Dutch). For information about how to subscribe, send an empty mail message to msr@elis.rug.ac.be with the word HELP in the subject line.

You may also want to try the News, Magazines & Information Servers page at **http://www.wb.utwente.nl/explore/news_main.html**. Der Spiegel (Germany) is at: **http://www.spiegel.de**. The HELLENIC NEWS database is at **http://www.greeknews.ariadne-t.gr/**.

Other links to international broadcasters: **http://www.wrn.org/stations.html**.

North America

There is a vast amount of online news sources covering North America. Some to check are:

The Wall Street Journal	**http://interactive.wsj.com/**
The Washington Post	**http://www.washingtonpost.com**
USA Today	**http://www.usatoday.com**
Los Angeles Times	**http://www.latimes.com**

Newslink **http://www.newslink.org** offers links to many US newspapers, broadcast networks and affiliates, magazines and publishers, and sites of special journalistic interest in the eWorld.

Russia

Press Rover **http://www.russianstory.com/rover/** offers free full-text search of an archive of Russian newspapers and periodicals. Your search may be limited to the following areas: Government & Society, Business & Economy, Culture & Arts, and Family & Entertainment. Payment is required for document retrieval only.

At **http://users.aimnet.com/ksyrah/ekskurs/rusnews.html**, there's a Russian News Links page with links to Federal News Service, Izvestia,

ITAR-TASS, InterFax/Maximov, Nezavisimaya gazeta, Pravda-5, and an extensive list of other Russian newspapers and magazines in the eWorld, including audio radio resources. It also has good coverage of other NIS countries, including Ukraine, Belarus, Armenia, Georgia, Kirghizistan, Azerbaijan and the Baltics.

A hypertext, English-language version of the St. Petersburg Press weekly is at **http://www.spb.su/**. This Web page also offers Severo-Zapad, a daily news source for information about North-West Russia.

Online newspaper vs. printed newspapers

The main objectives of both are the same, to offer timely information in an easily accessible manner to the highest possible number of readers. The differences are that these are two very different forms of media. In both cases it all begins with page one.

For a printed paper, page one is the attention seeker, the illustration of that day's paper's most important content, both visually and textually. On page one, a reader will also often find an index, with direction pointers to stories inside. The front page is the first step in a mostly linear process; once a reader reaches the end of a page, the most natural reaction is for him or her to turn to the next page.

'Page one' on a eWorld-based newspaper is a little bit different, and illustrates the difference in the ways a reader 'navigates' a Web site. One usually doesn't 'navigate' a printed newspaper, but a Web site's layout often makes 'page one' the main index. It provides the most recognizable way to move around from section to section, article to article. The basic idea is not all that different; even printed newspapers package content in various sections that have certain kinds of stories on each page,

Tips, tricks and trivia

Maybe you'd read the paper more if you knew *when* to read it

Let's face it: Spending a half-hour with the morning paper, once considered a daily necessity, is now a rare luxury. Fortunately, NewsAhead, at

http://www.newsahead.com

lets you pick your spots by telling you which news stories are coming up in the next month. Naturally, the service can only warn you about 'scheduled news', such as rocket launches, upcoming elections, and so on. But if you make a note to read about these items, who knows what 'actual news' you'll run across? I liked the idea.

sub-categories like sports, opinions, business, or entertainment, each accompanied with their own section directories.

An eWorld site might best be perceived as a directory tree similar to a table of contents with a comprehensive index list. Working from general to specific, users can find stories that interest them by working down the menus of the system. This isn't much different to turning pages through a certain section of a printed newspaper, though it is easier to find what you're looking for with the more receptive nature of 'point-and-click,' as opposed to flipping through dozens of pages.

In both cases, 'page one' has to be an attention seeker. Print papers' front pages feature the day's most commanding photographic or artistic elements along with the most important stories. This permeates through to the eWorld.

Layout of an online newspaper

In many cases, although the traditional rules of journalism are not completely neglected, eWorld publishers have recognized that the aesthetics for reading text on the screen are different from reading it on the printed page. As a result, some new standards have emerged and are quickly defining an acceptable model.

The pros and cons of hypertext

The use of hypertext is a critical part of online newspaper layout. Hypertext is not only a navigational tool, but also a means for 'three-dimensional reading,' allowing a reader to jump to new threads while in the middle of reading a story. Not surprisingly, online news sources make careful and often limited use of hypertext, as publishers are not inclined to link to pages that take their readers to different Web sites. The reasoning is obvious: linking elsewhere encourages users to leave your own site, which does not serve their own commercial interests. In the main, hypertext is used in cases of linking stories in a linear chronological process, to offer the reader options of viewing 'related stories' that are specifically relevant to the article. Such thoughts may well be subject to change given the nature of the eWorld.

The rules for printed media affect the way publishing ideas are implemented on the Web. Some rules carry over easily, but others are altered, or completely new rules are invented. And the effects may also go in both directions; as new standards appear online, some of these will inevitably find their way back into the printed realm.

What are the benefits of eWorld newspapers?

The news gets to the reader faster

This gives readers looking for more stories the opportunity to find something fresh, and the ability to offer instant updates allows people to learn about events that are particularly timely. These would include the likes of sports results, weather, or breaking news, without having to wait for the next printed edition, or even televised news broadcasts.

> **Tips, tricks and trivia**
>
> **News and reference in one search**
>
> Lycos and Versaware have joined forces to offer a quick way to find basic information about a topic. The Lycos Research Center allows you to search Funk & Wagnall's Multimedia Encyclopedia, Random House Webster's College Dictionary, Reuters News Wire, and an electronic media index through a single form. Or, if you prefer, you can select just one section for your search. If you're still having trouble finding relevant results, try the Power Search feature, which lets you limit your search terms to words in article titles and choose different sort orders.
>
> **http://www.funkandwagnalls.lycos.com**

Classified ads

Classified ads placed online will be an enormous cash generator, and will be available more often than not before the printed paper comes out. This is a benefit for people who might be searching for a home or used car. Indexes with hypertext make it much easier to find something by category.

Interaction

It's when getting into issues of interaction that the advantages of eWorld newspapers truly begin to become clear. Online publications must offer their audience the ability to interact in numerous ways. The simple but invaluable feature of an online opinion feedback form is vital. Offering users the chance to write letters to the editor or send complaints to circulation can replace the need to use the postal system or the telephone.

More advanced interactive features like opinion polls or online contests can attract readers to the Web site with the purpose of offering their point of view or trying to win a prize. People will use it if there's an obvious benefit involved. Pointing, clicking and pressing 'submit' are also easier than cutting the entry form out of the paper, filling it out, and then posting it.

Discussion forums

Discussion forums allow people from all over the world to discuss topics in a single virtual area. These are often no different than Usenet newsgroups in concept, but they do offer a specific arena to trade ideas, and also familiarize users who may be new to the eWorld with practical group discussion forums.

Online searchable news archives

The most valuable, useful and powerful interactive feature available to the online news media is the publicly available online searchable news archive. Who needs the library? Now a reader can launch a Web browser, type in a few keywords, and get back volumes of information. It's a major asset for research and a superb way of making information readily available to the public. Copies can't get lost or misplaced, and no one has to re-file the researched material. Quite possibly, newspapers may be the forerunner of the 'online libraries', with comprehensive and mostly reliable information easily available to anyone at any time.

Expands circulation beyond the local area

The obvious benefits of circulation beyond the local area as a result of worldwide access is a benefit, not only for readers, who may have moved out of their favourite paper's circulation range, but to the newspapers themselves, who can increase readership beyond the boundaries of their geographical areas.

In short, the benefits available on the eWorld are wide and varied, but it is important that publishing companies take advantage of these resources appropriately if they expect to capitalize on an eWorld Web site.

The future

Like any form of mass media, an eWorld newspaper must offer its readers a reason to view it in terms of design, content, interaction and usability. All these aspects must be bound together effectively to be useful. In the process, it must remain recognizable in terms of journalistic purpose, often calling upon the devices of traditional journalism, with which many people are familiar.

Newspapers will succeed because they understand the key transformation of turning information into readily understandable knowledge. While reporters have always been good at turning information into useful knowledge, they aren't rethinking how reporting could be done in this radically different medium.

What are these radical differences, and how might they change reporting?

Online journalism is hypertext, traditional journalism is linear. Too many electronic news products simply transfer the text used in the paper product and publish it in the eWorld. They have to rethink reporting as a different form of news presentation. News reporting for new products will have content with depth, not just by providing explanation, as has always been the reporter's strength, but by providing links to other relevant documents. Finding these relevant documents and providing links within the text of the story will be part of the reporter's job or, perhaps, will be the job of a whole new category of worker in the interactive newsroom.

There may be some entirely new models for the news story. Imagine this: in the publication of a news story, concerning any subject matter, the text of the article is displayed. Embedded in the text are hypertext links which explain the events written about, or the history of the proposals mentioned, or contrast the position on the topic as stated in previous articles, or give a brief biography on the people mentioned, and why they were mentioned. It is then left to the reader to decide what level of information they require from the main article.

This approach takes the superiority of the technology to achieve an unprecedented level of journalism, and provides a value-added feature that surpasses the other thousands of news providers' reporting of any subject.

The future for eWorld newspapers must be in the provision of hypertext journalism with no constraints.

26

Europe Internet search sites

AltaVista – Northern Europe
http://www.altavista.telia.com/

Euroferret
http://www.euroferret.com
25 million pages indexed.

Euro Index: The UK Business & Information Directory
http://www.euro-index.co.uk/

European Interactive Directories
http://www.euroyellowpages.com/index.html

European Search Engines
http://www.netmasters.co.uk/european_search_engines/page2.html

Europeonline
http://www.europeonline.com/
Europe Online – The European Gateway to the Internet, not impressive as it sounds but has a focus on quality over quantity. With a subject guide for most major European countries.

Euroseek
http://euroseek.net/
European search engine.

Lifestyle – Europe Search Engines
http://www.lifestyle.co.uk/cceu.htm

Search Europe
http://searcheurope.com
European wide search engine.

Yellow Web for Europe
http://www.yweb.com/
'The European WWW Source'. Recommended subject directory.

Eire Ireland online
http://home.iol.ie/1/
Subject catalogue for Ireland, including a Business section.

Irish Internet Yellow Pages
http://www.nci.ie/Yellow/

Part V

The future of the eWorld

27

Linux and open source software

A journey of a thousand miles must begin with a single step.

LAO-TZU
604–531 BC

When we look back five years, all the major companies, governments and telecommunication networks were announcing that the eWorld of the future would be founded on television technology and we would access this eWorld through our TV remote controls. We would be able to perform many of our daily functions through it. We could shop online, bank from home. Car rental, hotel reservations and airline tickets would all be available through pressing a button.

> **Tips, tricks and trivia**
>
> **Eye in the sky**
>
> NASA's Earth Observatory is a good resource for many earth sciences topics, including oceans, weather, and the ecosystem. The site offers detailed information on subtopics, such as cloud formation, accompanied by excellent graphics, including satellite imagery. For access to all the topic areas, click the Library option on the home page.
>
> **http://earthobservatory.nasa.gov**

A lot of this has come true. The eWorld has reinforced its position as the basis of the economy for the twenty-first century an unquestionably will become the most indispensable technology yet devised by the civilized world. It will change our economic systems as we proceed to a paperless society, with online shopping, ease of communication and all the other benefits the eWorld will bring us.

One of the reasons the eWorld is such a global success is because there is not one person, company or government who really controls it. As it evolves we shall see more government authorities regulating it but not controlling its evolution. Governments may wish to control it and it is obvious that companies like Microsoft are attempting to own and control as much of the eWorld as they possibly can. It is most certainly in nobody's interest to have a monopoly controlling this transformation of our lives.

Linux and the open source defenders have adopted a 'bring an end to Bill Gates' control' vision to their drive to make the eWorld 'uncontrolled' by any one person, organization or government. Simply put, control is handicapped by spreading the control.

There are millions of minds and imaginations in the eWorld population who have the intellectual capabilities and the programming skills to change the evolution of the eWorld, and their future and their children's future being controlled by any one organization or government is a serious motivation to them to achieve freedom from the shackles of 'closed' software. This is a clear example of the power of the eWorld, when you consider that Microsoft, with its colossal financial resources, will see its attempted control of the eWorld decrease in the twenty-first century, as more and more individuals and companies adopt the more stable, reliable and open source software that Linux offers.

The eWorld was not conceived in some enormous software company's laboratory but in the world's universities and research institutions where unsung heroes influenced and created what we now know as the Internet. The Internet evolved from the globally linked minds of the world's best computer analysts and programmers. It evolved as everyone connected with it freely and openly shared his or her experiences to create a technology that could be shared by all.

The majority of today's computers run on 'closed' operating systems like DOS, Windows and Macintosh, which means they are controlled by the company that created them. The companies who created them are the only ones who can modify these programs. Linux is the future, in the open software aspect of its configuration which allows any computer programmer to modify the inner workings of their computer just by using Linux as their operating system. The global support for Linux coupled with this capacity to change the operating system is set to change the whole concept of our eWorld.

The Linux concept is based on the fundamental principle that the best and most stable software comes from the global exchange of programming knowledge, where everyone is free to modify, develop, improve and then share the codes they have used, and not from the commercial aspects of companies like Microsoft and other software houses that offer closed systems and seek to control the eWorld's advancement. The global development of Linux is truly phenomenal in its extent and adaptation by thousands of supporters of open software. Linux is being developed, because of this combined global effort, at a momentous rate. If you visit any university's computer department or computer research institution you find the research is on Linux, not Windows or Macintosh systems. It is becoming more and more linked to the eWorld.

In major corporations we see Netscape giving away the source codes for their browser. IBM is adopting the same rationale, in support of their eCommerce initiatives, with their Apache Web server software. Apache is an open source Web server software program, which runs on half of Web servers in the world. Apache, like Linux, is being developed worldwide by companies and individuals. Linux, Netscape and IBM's Apache are all open source, as this is where our future eWorld will grow.

At the Open Source Web site, **http://www.opensource.org**, the following words on their homepage say it all: 'When programmers on the Internet can read, redistribute, and modify the source for a piece of

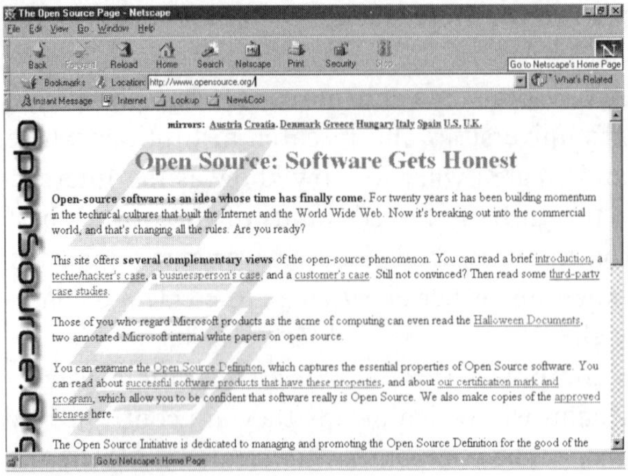

software, it evolves. People improve it, people adapt it, and people fix bugs. And this can happen at a speed that, if one is used to the slow pace of conventional software development, seems astonishing.'

How does Linux affect you?

What will be the effect of Linux and open source software? What are the implications for you? What should you be doing about it? The following pages try to give you some understanding of Linux and its history and how you can embrace Linux.

Linux

What is Linux?

Linux is an operating system, the software that allows computer hardware to run and serve the computer applications you use. It is like Unix; actually 'Unix, the Next Generation' would be a good way to put it. It is a direct replacement for MS Windows, Windows 95, Windows 98, Windows NT, or any other operating system for that matter. It does things that Microsoft has been talking about for years, but still has not delivered. It is stable in a way that no Microsoft software is. Years ago, Bill Gates made the statement 'Windows NT will be a better Unix than Unix.' Why wait? Linux already is. And it will only get better.

Linux delivers. Linux in some areas is still a little harder to use than equivalent Microsoft products, but it is catching up fast, and it is well worth learning because it is much more flexible.

Who invented Linux?

Tens of thousands of the best computer minds in the world developed it over decades. And millions alpha test, beta test and report problems to the developers directly. While many people think that the Finn, Linus Torvalds, must be a god to have developed Linux, and rich beyond belief, they are wrong. Linus did not invent or create the entire operating system known by many as Linux. He is a quiet software developer who wanted to share a fairly minor Unix-like program that he developed, which caught on and became the central hub for Linux. Then, after others began using it, a friend of Linus' dubbed his program 'Linux,' for 'Linus' Unix'. Since then hundreds have worked on the software, and thousands on the greater operating system that took on its name. Much of what is now known as Linux existed in the Unix world as much as a decade or more before Linus came on the scene. He was the right man with the right skills, the right motivations, and the right personality, appearing at the right time.

Linus continues to be the leader of the project, and the *de facto* leader of the Linux movement, which now involves tens of thousands of developers, all cooperating in a way that results in every component of Linux being as good as possible.

> **Tips, tricks and trivia**
>
> **It's Art**
>
> Among potentially uncomfortable and unpleasant social predicaments, nothing tops having to admit that you know nothing about modern art, and then having to listen to someone who does ramble on about the topic for hours, uninterrupted. Stop this horrifying nightmare from becoming reality by visiting Modern Masterworks, at
>
> **http://library.advanced.org/17142/**
>
> Learn the names of the major movements and painters; find out what makes modern art 'good' art; and expand your knowledge with links to reading lists, online discussions, and more. This site is part of ThinkQuest, an educational resource for teenagers, but you have a lot to learn from this site no matter how old you are.

But isn't Linux just for large computers?

This used to be true of Unix, but PC hardware today is more powerful than the 'big' computers of the past (the past being as recent as three years ago). Linux runs on everything from the 3Com Palm Pilot to parallel supercomputers. The famous water scenes from Titanic were rendered using a massively parallel Linux supercomputer, made up of many Digital Alpha processor-based PCs because no other operating system could handle the task within budgetary constraints. Linux is very personal, and very scalable in a way that corporations have been dreaming of – one consistent, capable and modular operating system from the smallest devices to the largest computing systems.

Is Linux hard to install and operate?

Well, some people think so. But then some people think DOS is hard too. Linux can actually be easier to install and use than Microsoft Windows. Many make the mistake of judging Linux by its installation, which can be a little complex, rather than its daily use. Isn't daily use what one does most often?

Does Linux crash?

Like the Mississippi, it keeps rolling along. There are people that have reported even early versions of Linux running for more than three years now without ever stopping. This kind of track-record is certainly hard to fault and may soon raise all our expectations – no more acceptance of crashing computers and loss of work.

But no one I know uses Linux!

Although it is possible that this is true, I doubt it. Ask around, see how many people use or know of Linux. In France Linux outsells Windows 98, and it looks like this may be true in the USA too, but I do not yet have enough evidence to tell for sure. A European automated Internet survey looks for machines online and asks what operating system they use; that survey finds that the majority are Linux systems. There are very few companies in the 'Fortune 2000' that have not bought Linux and Linux-related products.

But there is no support for Linux

This is absolute rubbish! There are Linux user groups that you can attend in nearly every community, consultants all over the world, companies that you can call for telephone support, and there is the free support available in many places on the Internet. Companies can even buy support contracts from many reputable sources. Many of the large computer manufacturers now support Linux.

■ But there are no big companies behind Linux

Netscape, Intel and IBM have invested in Red Hat. IBM just announced support for Apache, the default Web server in Linux. Compaq is involved; Dell has made announcements about Linux, as have Oracle, Corel, Sybase, Informix, etc. This gives an indication of how things are going. Every major computer and software manufacturer in the world, with one notable exception, is supporting Linux.

■ Don't I need to be a computer guru to use Linux?

No. There are things you may want to learn, or ask a friend to help you with, just like Windows. Once it is set up it is as easy to use as any other operating system. And it does use a GUI (Graphical User Interface). You can even buy computers pre-loaded with Linux, so you do not have to set it up yourself! The following screenshot shows a screen running with SuSE 6.2.

This GUI is running with KDE (Kontrol Desktop Environment) which is hosted in a German university. Their Web site is **http://www.kde.org/**.

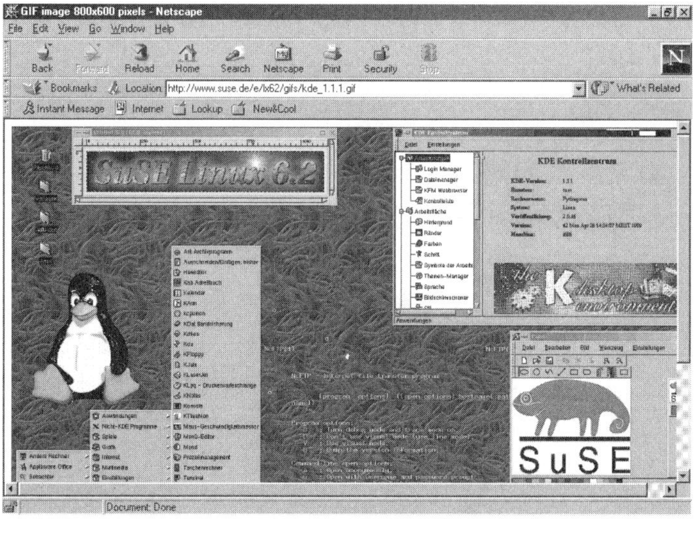

So why is Linux catching on so fast?

Linux has a technical excellence that might well challenge the supremacy of the Microsoft Corporation. The large and capable development team working on Linux is certainly impressive. Basically, Linux's potential is only just being realized – watch this space! For more information on Linux's rise to fame see the article 'Why Linux is Significant' at **http://www.LinuxMall.com/Allann/ lxsig.txt**, written in 1994. The predictions made in this article have been coming true right on schedule, and this article is as relevant now as it was then. Also see **http://www. LinuxMall.com/announce/netscape.html** for a number of resources that will help you understand what is happening and why. In fact, if you

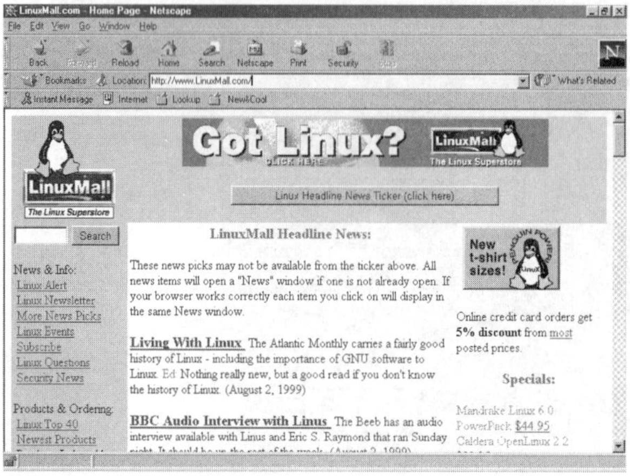

go through all the news archives on **http://www.LinuxMall.com**, you will see that they have consistently commented on future events which actually came to pass not too long afterwards.

If you really want to grasp the eWorld of the twenty-first century, the best advice I can give you is to take the time to research Linux. Take the time to install and learn Linux; once you understand it you will be convinced that Linux is the future. The following will give you the basic information you require.

Will my computer run Linux?

One of the best things about Linux is that it can run on just about any basic computer hardware.

Desktops

There are versions for hardware from Intel (and compatibles), PowerPC chips, Sun Sparcs, DEC Alphas and others. You don't need the latest and greatest system, either. Linux is very modular; it can be stripped down to run on as little as a 386 with 150 MB of disk space and 2 MB of RAM (though you'll want more disk space, processor power and memory for running graphical desktops, development tools and so on). Some developers have even created useful Linux versions that run off a single floppy disk.

Laptops

Linux can also churn along happily on many laptops, including most Apple PowerBooks, IBM ThinkPads and Toshiba Tecras. (You'll find a list of supported laptops, as well as installation tips and tricks, at Linux Online's laptop page.)

Tips, tricks and trivia

Good dog

If you've used a laptop, you know its chief drawback: it takes up your whole lap, leaving no room for papers, pens, books, or anything else you might need to use while working. The Lapdog, available at Shaun Jackson Design, at

http://www.sjdesign.com

solves this problem. A stylish carrying bag for your laptop, it unfolds on your lap to reveal side pockets that hold all your stuff while you work. Jackson has other products in development, each of which leads me to believe that he's spent countless hours in planes, trains and automobiles, wrestling with portable computing devices.

The odds are good that Linux will run on your Intel (or compatible) system or Mac, at least on the base hardware (motherboard, memory and processor). The biggest problem you may face is that you may not be so lucky with your peripherals.

■ Will my peripherals run under Linux?

Yes! And no. Most common peripherals, modems, printers, network adapters and so on work well under Linux. But some work better than others, and some don't work at all. Here are a few general guidelines for peripheral compatibility issues.

Older ISA cards

That NE2000-compatible network adapter, your old Sound Blaster 16 and the US Robotics Sportster modem you've used for years should function perfectly under Linux. In fact, that's part of what makes Linux great: you can take advantage of old hardware that would otherwise hit the rubbish bin.

PCI cards

As a rule of thumb, ISA is a better bet under Linux than PCI, at least for now. For instance, many PCI modems tend to be Windows modems, so they simply won't work under Linux. The latest PCI sound cards, such as the Turtle Beach Montego and Sound Blaster Live, aren't supported under Linux yet either, though developers are frantically working on the problem. It also helps to have the latest Linux version when trying to work with PCI cards. Also note that many PCI Ethernet and SCSI cards are supported. Check your distribution's supported hardware list for details.

Plug and Play

Plug and Play, though sometimes I think Plug and Pray would be a more apt name, can make life easier under Windows by allowing the computer to automatically assign resources to the various cards in your system. Linux can do Plug and Play, but the function isn't nearly as seamless. Check out this how-to for help with your own system. Depending on your hardware, you may have no problems, or you may have an awful lot!

Windows peripherals

To keep costs down, some hardware makers have started selling products such as modems and printers as Windows products. These devices tend to be less expensive than their more universal counterparts, but they won't work under Linux. Why? Because Windows devices (such as the 3Com/US Robotics Winmodem and the Lexmark Winwriter 200 printer) use software on the PC, and the system's CPU, to get their jobs done. Linux fans have managed to get some Windows printers up and running, at least partially.

USB

The market for USB peripherals is booming. Unfortunately, Linux hasn't caught up quite yet. At least one person is working on support for the bus. But as of the time of writing, it wasn't ready for release.

For fairly complete and somewhat up-to-date lists of supported peripherals, refer to the hardware section at Linux Online **http://www.linux.org** and the hardware compatibility how-to from the Linux Documentation Project **http://metalab.unc.edu/LDP/**.

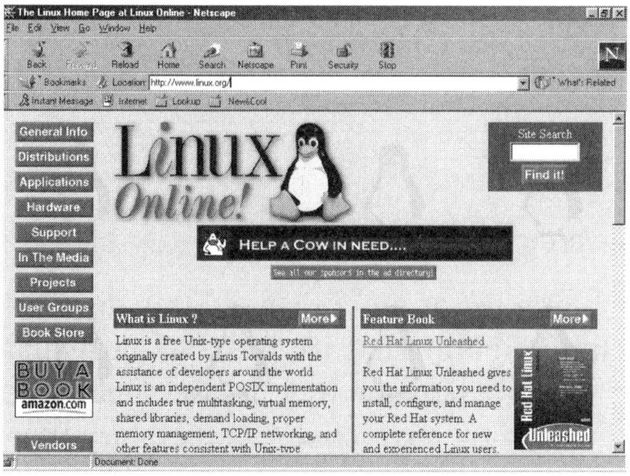

How do I download Linux?

First, some advice: don't download Linux to install it. Buy a copy.

Linux CDs

For around €40, you can get a good book like *Linux: Installation, Configuration, and Use* (Kofler, 2000) or *Hands-on Linux* (Sobell, Caldera Inc., 1998) that will include a CD-ROM full of Linux. These CD versions are far easier to install than the download, plus you get the added benefit of having written documentation. If you're new to Linux, you'll need the documentation.

Downloading the kernel

If you insist on downloading Linux, you have several options. If you're really looking to flex your technical muscles, you can simply download the kernel and build your own OS from the ground up. Unless you have a lot of time on your hands, don't. Instead, get a complete distribution. A distribution is a package that includes the Linux kernel and a variety of utilities and other software, useful things such as desktop managers, Web browsers and the like.

Linux distributions

You can go directly to the distribution makers:

SuSE	**http://www.suse.com**
Red Hat	**http://www.redhat.com**
Caldera	**http://www.caldera.com**
Debian	**http://www.debian.org**
Slackware	**http://www.slackware.com**

or visit a site like Linux Online for a list of more than a dozen distributions you can download. Each distribution has its fans and particular features. Once you decide which distribution you want to use, you'll need to check out the distributor's installation instructions, as they vary from vendor to vendor. One consideration to bear in mind regarding distributions is KDE, based in Germany. Star Office, which is the excellent office

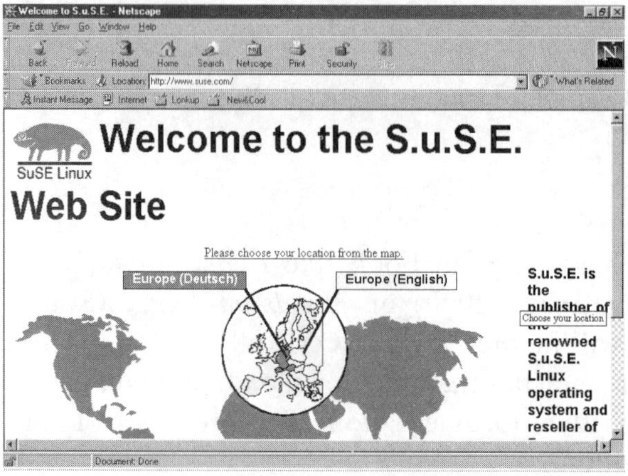

productivity suite including an alternative to Excel etc., is based in Germany. SuSE is also based in Germany and its US office has reported growth of 230 per cent in the first quarter of this year in the US. These fiqures are most certainly significant for a German software company selling in the US. All the other distributions use KDE and Star Office. Included in this Handbook is an Evaluation CD-ROM of SuSE 6.2. SuSE is my preferred distribution of Linux.

How do I install Linux?

Linux installations run from super-simple, done-in-30-minutes quickies to toss-your-computer-out-the-window frustration sessions. Why? First, Linux installation utilities generally require you to know more about your system than you'd expect. Secondly, Linux doesn't support all the hardware that you're bound to have.

Before you start

The best thing you can do to make things go as smoothly as possible is to create a list of your computer's components. Unlike Windows, which generally does a pretty good job of identifying hardware and configuring itself, Linux often needs some help. To be safe, jot down the following:

- the make, model and interface for your CD-ROM drive;
- the make and model of your SCSI adapter (if you have one);
- what type of mouse you have;
- the make, model and memory size of your graphics card;
- the make, model and refresh rates for your monitor;
- any networking information you may have kicking around (IP address, netmask, gateway address, DNS addresses, domain name and type of network card)

During installation, Linux may ask you for any or all of this info, and if you don't know it, you're going to pull your hair out.

Install a CD

As for the actual install, you have several options. Once again, the easiest way is with a CD-ROM version of Linux and a PC that supports booting from the CD drive (newer systems do). In that case, you'll often just have to drop the disk in your drive, set your system's BIOS to search for bootable CDs, and follow the installation instructions that pop up on the screen.

Install from DOS

If your system can't boot from the CD, you'll need to install from a DOS directory (if your distribution supports the option) or work from boot disks. Commercial distributions of Linux, including those from Caldera and Red Hat, come with 3.5-inch boot disks. Otherwise, you'll have to create the disks yourself (check this installation how-to for more information on creating the disks and installing Linux from a CD). You'll also probably need these disks if you plan on installing Linux from a hard disk or via Network File System (NFS).

Installing specific items

Your distribution's Web site should have all the details you need to know about installing specific items of Linux. If it doesn't, or if the documents are too difficult to understand, go with another distribution.

How do I get on the eWorld with Linux?

It's much harder to get on the eWorld with Linux than it is with Windows. Instead of simply clicking an Internet connection wizard and following the step-by-step instructions, for instance, Linux requires you to know a bit more about your connection than you might like. Fortunately, there are reams of documentation and some clever utilities that can help.

Before you start

First, you need to make sure that you installed all the necessary protocols, utilities and modules when you set up Linux. In many cases, you'll already have everything you need installed, such as TCP/IP, the basic network protocol; pppd, which connects you to your ISP; and chat, which tells pppd how to connect when you set up Linux. Check your distribution's documentation for details, or read the Linux networking how-to for step-by-step instructions.

Set up your connection

Once you have everything installed, you need to set up your connection. These PPP and ISP hookup how-tos hold all the details you need to configure your system to dial out and connect to your ISP.

Of course, that's the hard way. An easier way is to install any of the more user-friendly graphical PPP clients, such as X-ISP, kppp, GnomePPP or EzPPP. These utilities function much like Dial-Up Networking in Windows. You simply enter your login ID, password, ISP's phone number, DNS addresses, and such. The utility takes care of the rest.

Linux distributions

Better yet, many distributions, including SuSE, Red Hat, Debian and Caldera assume that you'll want to get eWorld connected, so they throw everything you need onto their disks and into their setup routines. You get all the protocols, Web browsers like Netscape Navigator and Lynx, email programs, and graphical setup and administration utilities without having to download anything.

How can I make Linux more like Windows?

There are some things you can do to make Linux more like Windows, at least from the standpoint of ease of use. Primarily, these consist of getting a good X Windows desktop manager and installing graphical utilities that make common tasks easier.

Desktop managers

The X Windows system has been around for 15 years. It provides the foundation for graphical user interfaces (GUIs) under Linux. Basically, you set up an 'X server' on your system so it knows about the capabilities of your graphics card and display. X-based 'desktop managers' can then run on the server. These desktop managers provide the graphical interface, and some of them look a lot like Windows.

Though dozens of desktop managers are available, a few have been getting lots of attention recently. The K Desktop Environment (KDE) **http://www.kde.org** is looking to build a complete set of graphical tools for Unix and Linux. With graphical file management, easily configured menus and loads of utilities, KDE can be a boon for those who want a graphical interface on their computing.

■ Free, user-friendly software

Some people don't like KDE for philosophical reasons. KDE is built using a commercial GUI toolkit called Qt. Some hard-liners in the freeware Linux community didn't like this, so they set out to create their own environment based entirely on free software. Thus, the GNU Network Object Model Environment (GNOME) **http://www.gnome.org** was born.

Which you choose will depend on how much you trust free software and which has the utilities you're looking for. But either one will let you make Linux look and feel a lot more like your old home, Windows, without the Microsoft logo. SuSE gives you the option of both KDE and GNOME.

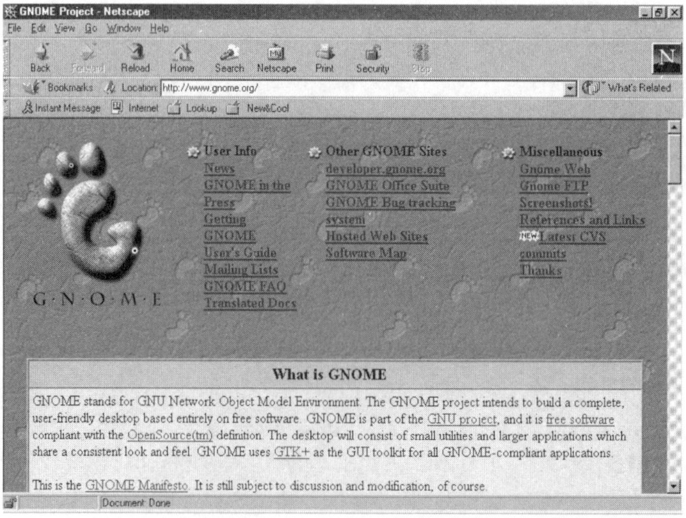

How do I run Linux with Windows?

If you want to run Linux but share your home with someone dedicated to Windows, you can run both operating systems on the same machine. You'll need to set up a dual-boot system that lets you decide whether to run Windows or Linux when you start the machine.

Run Windows or Linux

You can do this either by partitioning a fresh hard drive to have both DOS (Windows) and Linux partitions, or by repartitioning your existing drive with a utility that doesn't destroy your current data (V Communications' System Commander Deluxe or Partition Commander, for instance). You'll then need to install Linux on your new Linux partition and set up LILO (included with Linux) or another boot manager to let you choose either Windows or Linux on start-up. Many of the distributions, including SuSE, do this automatically when you install from a CD.

Tips, tricks and trivia

Let the Internet keep your schedule

You may have many reasons to consider using Jump as your personal information manager (PIM). For example, maybe you have tired of Microsoft Outlook or Lotus Organizer, one of which most likely came installed on your computer. Or you may be looking for a way to *share* your schedule with the other people working in your office without setting up some sort of network to do it.

Jump fits either bill and many others: It's an eWorld-based PIM that lets you share and/or manage your appointment book, contacts, to-do lists, email, and more with anyone (anyone you authorize, that is) who has an Internet connection. Plus, Jump is free, if you don't consider the timely ads that 'pop up' in your schedule to be a price to pay.

http://www.jump.com

Run Windows occasionally

If you only need to run a couple of Windows applications every once in a while, check out Wine. This freeware utility emulates Windows well enough to run many Windows applications under Linux. The Wine site provides a database of supported applications, so you can get an idea of what works and what doesn't.

Run Windows in Linux

If your application doesn't qualify, there's another option: VMware for Linux actually runs a copy of Windows 3.1, 95, 98, NT 4.0, or any of several other operating systems inside Linux. The product is currently in beta testing. The major issue with VMware is that it boosts your system requirements beyond what either Linux or Windows needs on its own. You'll need at least a Pentium with 64 MB of RAM, though VMware suggests a Pentium II with 96 MB for best performance. Still, if you love Linux but can't completely cut out Windows, VMware may provide a feasible option.

How do I run my Web site on Linux?

The eWorld provided most of the momentum that Linux has today, so it's not surprising that there are plenty of tools available to help you set up and run a Web site under the OS. In fact, many ISPs run their own servers on Linux.

Find a host

If you want to set up a site to run on Linux, your easiest option is to find a Web host that offers Linux servers, such as CI Host or Web Serve Pro. This way, you don't have to deal with the hassle of maintaining your own servers 24 hours a day and the cost of dedicated network connections.

If you do want to host your own site or you're planning to set up an intranet, rest assured that all of the most popular Linux distributions come complete with everything you need to get a Web site up and running.

Choose a Web server

The most important part, besides the OS itself, is the Web server. Usually, it will be Apache, the wildly popular server that's all most people will ever need. This feature-packed, speedy server has the power to run large corporate Web sites and, of course, your personal site. You'll find all the installation and configuration information you need on Apache's documentation page.

Connect

When you set up your Web server, you'll need to make sure that your system is properly connected to your network. You may also want to set up a firewall to protect your site from unauthorized entry by people with malicious intent. Whatever you need to do with your Web site, there are Linux tools to do it.

Where can I get technical support for Linux?

Whether you're an individual looking for free support or a corporation willing to pay extra for 24-hour technical help, Linux has plenty to offer. If you purchased a commercial copy of a Linux distribution from a company such as SuSE or Caldera, you're entitled to 90 or 30 days (respectively) of free installation support via email.

Community help

Run into problems later on? You still don't have to open your wallet. The Linux Documentation Project **http://www.metalab.unc.edu** maintains dozens of how-to files covering every imaginable subject, including installation, DOS emulation, networking, and using Cyrillic characters.

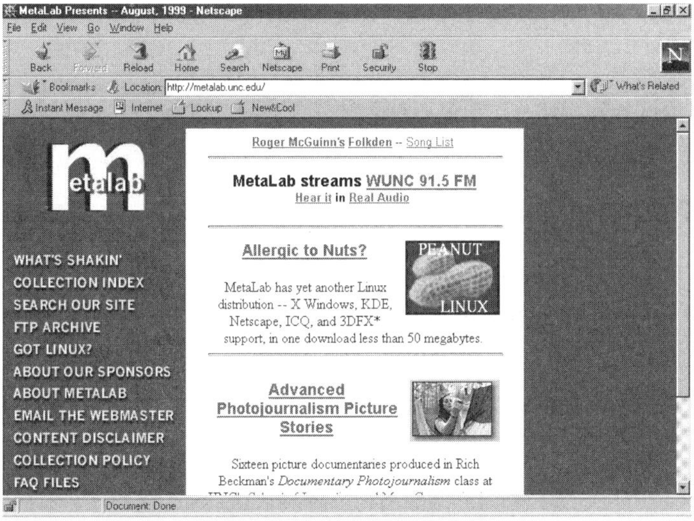

Newsgroups

Still can't find what you need? Check out the wide variety of Linux-based Usenet newsgroups, including comp.os.linux.misc, comp.os.linux.setup, comp.os.linux.questions, and alt.os.linux. If someone hasn't already asked and answered your question, you can always post it yourself. Linux users have a good track record of answering questions for newbies. There's even a Linux mailing list for beginners. Just send email to majordomo@vger.rutgers.edu with linux-newbie in the body of the message. You'll find a wide assortment of other Linux lists at Linux Online **http://www.linux.org**.

For additional Linux information try Slashdot **http://www.slashdot.org**.

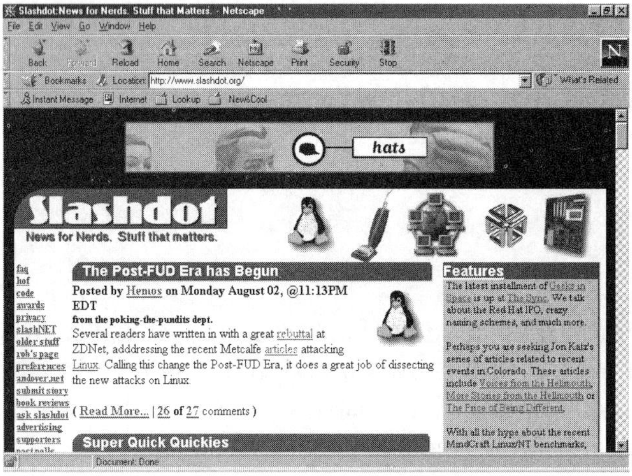

Fig 27.9

Applications

If you want to be truly amazed at the number of applications you can run on Linux visit **http://www.linuxapps.com/**. If you download them from this site they are free. Every conceivable application is there.

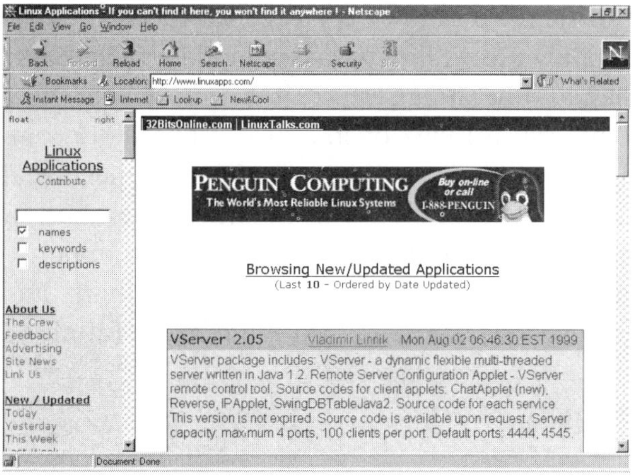

Conclusion

We are about to see a technology shift of spectacular dimensions. I believe Linux will affect the world economy and every computer-related industry in the world. The impact of Linux in the computing world will affect share prices, profits, margins and operating costs. The effects of it will be immense, as this completely new and distinct software model takes control. How will this be you may ask. The stability of the product and the economics of Linux, which is to all intent and purposes free, will ensure this. When you consider the costs to a small or even large business in running a Windows NT program, in some cases running into tens of thousands of euros, this cost is negated by the adoption of Linux as the operating system. The managers of the IT departments love the system. When the accountants from the finance department realize the cost savings involved, they will adore it, because the cost of Linux is a fraction of competing technologies.

> **Tips, tricks and trivia**
>
> **You'll see it, but you still may not believe it**
>
> If you've ever tried blowing out an egg (to leave a solid empty egg shell), you know how hard that is. Now imagine carving and sculpting the remaining shell into an elaborate and decorative work of art. Someone named Al Gunther does this and showcases his work at
>
> **http://www.webcom.com/24k/eggsculpture/**
>
> If you wish to see something truly remarkable then be sure to visit this site.

Companies will find it difficult to hold or even recruit the best in the programming world unless they are willing to accommodate their Linux religion. Linux is more than an operating system; it is a movement, with the explosive growth and interest in Linux of millions of hard-core computer developers around the world. Sony has recently announced that Linux will be the operating system that will run the next generation of interactive televisions. Linux will provide unprecedented business opportunity to those who take advantage of what it offers. It is the stability and economy of the system that will convince many that Linux is our future.

How will Linux affect you?

Linux and the open source movement have achieved such a global following that the impact on the future of the eWorld will become unquestionable. If you want to understand the eWorld of the future, get involved today to learn and appreciate what is going on.

Install and learn Linux

In the early days of the eWorld in 1993/94 it was a difficult and formidable task for those that were involved. But the eWorld changed this, providing a technology that anyone could use and anyone could learn. Linux is emerging like the early days of the eWorld. The potential of Linux is enormous: as you start to learn and understand it, it will grow on you. Visit all the Linux sites I have mentioned in this section. Read them and try to understand what it all means. I firmly believe that the future of the eWorld will be found in Linux and the open source movement as we enter the twenty-first century and encounter the many changes that will occur in all our lives. Any one person or any one organization should not control these changes.

28

The eWorld in the twenty-first century

All that is not a true change will disappear in the future society.

George Sand
1804–1876

- The strategic impact
- Dramatically improved operational and sales effectiveness
- Saving time
- New entrants
- Redefining your business
- Constraints for existing businesses
- Government
- Secondary effects
- Conclusion

The eWorld is going to change the evolution of the world. A strong statement, but a true one. In this chapter we will try to shed a little light on the implications that the eWorld will have on everyone's lifestyle in the twenty-first century. The eWorld is a global revolution, never previously seen in our civilized world. The reason for this is that the eWorld creates a means of human interaction that has never been possible in the history of mankind, a system of global communication in which knowledge and information travel the world at phenomenal speed.

The most important factor of the eWorld is its ability to link together all the computers in the world. It is going to affect us all in how we work, rest and play. The eWorld is completely changing everything it touches: commerce, education, science, research and government. The eWorld reduces the size of our world by making it as easy to communicate with someone from another continent as it is to speak to someone in another room. The eWorld is defining how business will function in the twenty-first century, offering the ability for small businesses to market their products and support their customers on a 24-hour basis no matter where they are situated in the world.

Consider being able to find new markets and new customers on a daily basis. Consider watching your sales increase weekly due to your eWorld business capabilities. The eWorld in education offers a prime opportunity for teachers and students alike. Simply put, the eWorld is the world's largest reference system. It will change our education system as we know it. The eWorld provides the ability to enhance our educational system by providing students with access to the entire breadth of human knowledge.

The eWorld will substantially alter the structure and operation of all our industries. I mentioned in my introduction the effect on our lives that the postal and telephone systems have had. The impact of the eWorld will be similar but its effect will be much faster.

For the management of any existing business the central question is not 'Will the eWorld be relevant to our business?' but 'How will it change our business?' and 'What do we need to do to profit from that change?'

The effects of the eWorld will take four to five years to replace existing patterns of social and business lives. However, the ultimate winners and losers will be those who take action during these formative years.

The strategic impact

The eWorld and its strategic impact are not technological issues. They are social and business issues. The particular impact will differ between businesses and people, so you need to identify the likely form of impact on your own business and your personal life and adopt suitable strategies. While each business will be unique in some ways, a number of general strategic risks are identifiable, especially the following:

- Using the eWorld, competitors become relatively more effective, e.g. reducing costs, improving service and increasing sales.
- Some important customers/suppliers proceed exclusively to the 'eWorld' and are inaccessible in any other way.
- The eWorld allows new entrants into the industry or into your markets. Some firms redefine their business in a fundamental way that threatens all existing competitors.

In fact, you will probably face a combination of the above. On the positive side, there are likely to be opportunities for your organization to take initiatives of these sorts in your existing industry or in others. The following pages will illustrate these strategic threats and opportunities.

Dramatically improved operational and sales effectiveness

Competitors achieve a significant cost reduction and/or improvement in service quality.

Online stockbrokers, such as E*Trade **http://www.etrade.com** and Ceres **http://www.ceres.com** in the US have existed for only a few years. They now offer an immediacy of order placement and completion, continuously updated customer accounts and extensive online market data, which a traditional competitor cannot match. Their fees are not just 10 or 20 per cent below traditional stockbrokers. They are actually 80 or 90 per cent less.

Lower costs

Costs are low because the whole process is computerized and customers do their own order entry. Consequently staff-related outlays, a major factor in traditional brokers, are drastically reduced. So these competitors offer dramatically lower prices and better-quality service for the reasonably informed investor.

Amazon.com's eWorld site **http://www.amazon.com** offers the largest list of books in the world. What's more, they are offered at discount prices. Customers can call up reviews on books, request lists of similar books, see comments made by other readers, and enter their own comments. Again, aided by computer, the customer moves through the information, enters their own order and shipping details. So amazon.com's staff requirements are kept down. So also are its stock costs. Customers do not see any physical stock, so orders placed on amazon.com can be automatically rerouted to publishers and distributors to ship to its distribution centre, compiled and shipped out to the customer. It also avoids the need for retail premises, which accounts for 10–12 per cent of a traditional bookseller's costs.

> **Tips, tricks and trivia**
>
> **Searching for rare books**
>
> Bibliofind, which was recently purchased by Amazon.com, is a database of more than nine million used and rare books and periodicals offered for sale by a number of book dealers. Searching the site is free, but ordering a book, of course, is not. You can search by title, author, price range, or date the book entered the database, and you can even limit the search to signed or first editions.
>
> **http://www.bibliofind.com**

Comparative developments are evident with online travel agents, which can make available a wealth of detail to customers at negligible marginal cost. They allow the customer to search through the selections, decide what they want and enter the order into a computer system via the eWorld.

Many banks and other financial services providers have introduced online banking systems for their customers. Customers can perform many transactions for themselves without involving bank staff and supporting equipment such as ATMs. At the customer end the equipment used is the customer's, not the bank's, and retail premises are not required. Originally some online banking was through established systems. But they are unattractive to customers compared with the flexibility of using the eWorld. When you consider that it costs a bank €1.4 million to open a branch and that for €1.4 million they can open an eWorld branch serving the world, it is not difficult to see which way they want to go.

Opportunities for cost reduction and service improvement are not confined to information-intensive industries, or to companies serving consumers. General Electric's cost-saving purchasing program from suppliers **http://www.tpn.geis.com** is strictly business to business. They have saved 30 per cent in faxes, mail and labour. The project, originally intended to be only 'in-house', has been so successful that a separate company has been set up to offer this service to other businesses.

Dell sells millions of dollars worth of computer equipment per day from its eWorld site to both consumers and businesses. Not only do the customers manage the connection and do the order entry but they can essentially custom-order the configuration they want, using an extensive menu process. Custom-tailored computers are provided at a low cost. Cisco, with its eWorld sales of network equipment, is serving customers at tangible cost savings over traditional sales methods. Dell and Cisco gain both labour and inventory savings from their eWorld sales, as well as enjoying direct customer contact.

Competitors are able to provide more effective sales effort

Competitors who deal direct with customers over the eWorld are in a position to build a much more informed relationship with their customers. This has always been accurate of direct marketing to some extent. However, the quality of the interaction possible over the eWorld and the virtually zero cost of personally tailored electronic communication has dramatically raised the prosperity and strength of possible relationships.

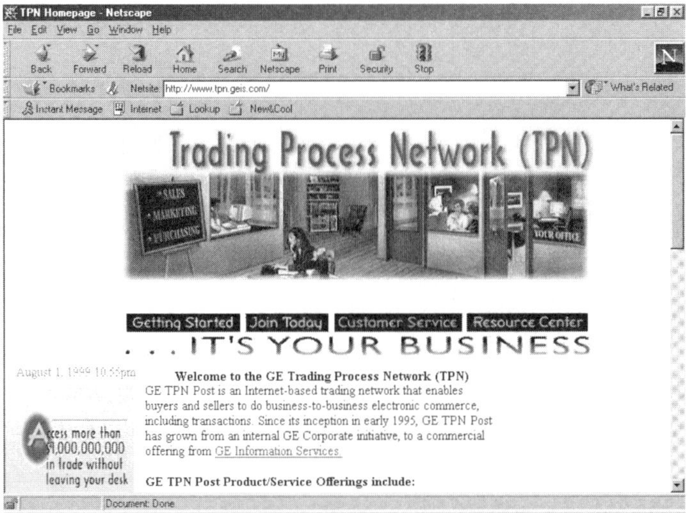

So CD-Now sends me a periodic email, computer generated, advising of new CDs and specials, and particularly mentioning offers which are similar to my previous purchases from them. Likewise amazon.com offers to inform me of the release of new books by my favourite authors, and by similar ones.

Recently I was in Australia speaking at the Australian Retailers Conference and sharing the podium with me was a senior manager from Net Perceptions. Net Perceptions is a leading provider of real-time relationship marketing solutions that enable eWorld retailers to market to customers on a personalized, one-to-one basis. With their software solutions, a retailer learns from each customer interaction and, based on the information received, adjusts marketing messages and offers product proposals to that customer in real time. This gives retailers that implement their software the ability to attract more customers, generate more products per order and increase customer loyalty.

Net Perceptions not only knows where you've been, it would like to tell you where to go. The company's collaborative filtering database software acts like an electronic salesperson, observing what visitors view and purchase at a Web site and then matching that information against data collected from other users. The software then offers shopping suggestions, provides targeted advertising, and makes personalized special offers. Their products are used by large online retailers and service providers such as Amazon.com, CD-Now and Business Week Online. Software companies like Net Perceptions will have enormous growth in the twenty-first century. Their Web site is at **http://www.netperceptions.com**.

Insurance and fund management companies whose eWorld contact with customers has enabled them to build a computerized picture of those customers' individual preferences can make offers tailored to those prefer-

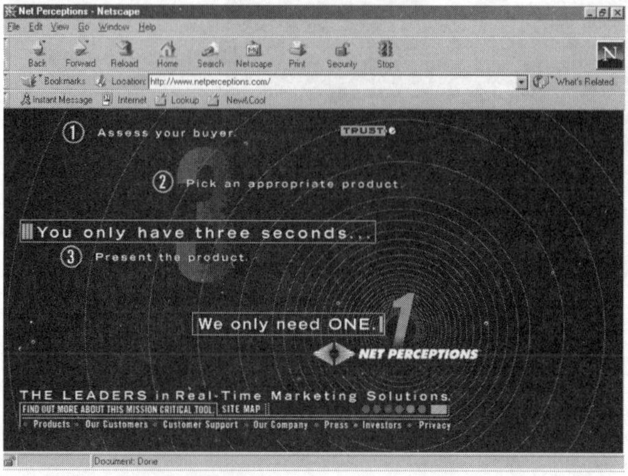

ences. Equipment suppliers receiving online orders for consumables and replacement parts can enhance that information with online automated dialogue with their customers to analyze and understand their use patterns and then offer advice specifically tailored to their circumstances.

Customers or suppliers migrate exclusively to the eWorld

There will be a significant group of people and businesses for whom the eWorld becomes the preferred form of commercial interaction. These customers or suppliers will become unavailable to businesses that lack an effective eWorld presence.

This movement to the eWorld will not be optional. Becoming an effective eWorld user takes time and effort. It is an investment. Fortunately, ability refined in the eWorld can be utilized for a great variety of tasks, and the eWorld offers a huge variety of sources and information, allowing more informed, effective and economical conclusions.

Saving time

In addition, the eWorld allows users to 'parallel process'. If I go to the bank to make a transaction and find a queue, which is not uncommon, I may be stuck there for 10 wasted minutes, unable to do anything else. If I am performing a similar transaction in the eWorld, and it is slow, I can simultaneously do other things.

I might, for example, check my stock portfolio, send someone an email, open and read my personally tailored news report, start downloading a software package, find a review of a film or car that interests me, etc. I can swap between these tasks and my banking transaction as I wish, proceeding with each

Tips, tricks and trivia

Northern Light beefs up

Northern Light has announced that it has indexed more than 150 million Web pages. The service has a subsection, called the Special Collection, that searches abstracts of full-text articles from more than 5,000 sources. Articles from the Special Collection are available for a fee. When you click the Power tab, you can choose to include or exclude the Special Collection when you search. The Power Search feature also lets you specify date ranges, topic areas, and source materials to narrow your search. Other tabs provide specialized search forms for industry and investment information, news, and source publications.

http://www.northernlight.com

when it is available. As a result the eWorld allows me to have a number of activities underway simultaneously, to proceed with them at my own pace, and thus avoid wasted time.

Many people value time and quality decision making. Once such individuals have become competent in using the eWorld they will prefer to use it rather than other distribution channels. If your business cannot satisfy them in their preferred manner, you will lose them.

New entrants

Barriers to entry are reduced, allowing smaller competitors to enter

In those industries where the difficulty of breaking into existing distribution channels has been a major barrier to entry, the eWorld offers a new, cheap, option. Numerous small software companies now offer their products directly over the eWorld, avoiding the need to physically package them and gain access to physical distribution channels.

Similarly, many speciality retailers will develop, selling directly over the eWorld and delivering via mail and couriers. In carving out many small niches they will cut into the business of more broadly based retailers.

In the same way, foreign firms with established home operations will break into overseas markets using the eWorld as their sales and service medium. Amazon.com doesn't sell books just in the US. Its reach is global. The same is true of CD-Now and of the US online brokers and online software suppliers. The same will be true of travel agents, financial services and many other businesses.

The cost of entering new markets can become very small when customers in those markets are simply accessing the same site you use for your local customers. It costs overseas customers no more to reach you than to reach someone in their own area. When substantial physical goods are involved you may need a distribution and service facility in the new market but often that can be subcontracted.

Until now, many service industries such as retailing, education and health have been largely shielded from foreign competition because of inherent features of their service delivery. The eWorld will remove that local protection for many of these industries.

School's never out in the eWorld

Distance education is a good example. The power of distance education lies in the course content and structure and, increasingly, in computer-based teaching processes. Developing high-quality distance education resources is costly but the marginal cost of each additional student over the eWorld is virtually zero. So some very powerful and successful distance education institutions will develop and operate globally. Many countries are currently building an education export industry using traditional methods.

These changes will ultimately impact on all education. When a degree through traditional, skilled-labour-intensive methods costs tens or hundreds of thousands of dollars, a degree that can be delivered consistently to tens or hundreds of thousands of students for a fraction of the cost, with equal or better results, will eliminate the old method. Look for a lot of surplus academics and disappearing educational institutions by 2006.

> **Tips, tricks and trivia**
>
> **A rose by a much nicer name**
>
> Once upon a time (not that long ago, in fact), computer-programmer types turned to a place called **www.computerliteracy.com** to buy books with titles like '*Professional Active Server Pages 2.0*' and '*Beginning Visual C++ 6.0*'. Well, the book titles are still the same, but the URL is now the ever-so-much-more-memorable
>
> **http://www.fatbrain.com**
>
> The discounts look good and the reviews are objective, but the biggest benefit here is specialization. If you're looking for a book on DHTML, you don't need to rummage through novels to find it.

In Australia worldschool.com.au offers pupils aged 9–19 study resources online. Students can log on for information relating to homework, projects or to gain assistance with exam study, normally provided by expensive

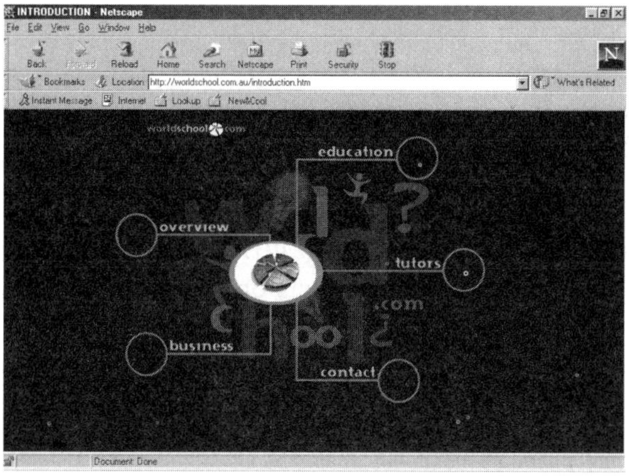

tutors. This eWorld school has been inundated with teachers, perhaps anticipating the changes, who are eager to take part. This is part of the changing face of education in the twenty-first century. The school's Web site is at **http://worldschool.com.au**.

It is likely that experiential components will still be important in many degrees, e.g. veterinary science, dentistry and performing arts. That simply means those degrees will be a mixture of low-cost eWorld-based teaching and relevant hands-on experience.

New competitors emerge and steal your customers

In the past five years in the UK, building societies have successfully challenged the stranglehold that banks held on banking services. Building societies will naturally want to capitalize on the customer relationships they have established. Offering other financial services is the most immediately obvious step. Credit cards, personal loans and insurance can be added without great difficulty and without the need for the eWorld. Transaction bank accounts are a little more difficult to service without branches, though not impossible. A credit card account can double as a transaction account and can be used to withdraw cash through other banks' ATMs and EFTPOS facilities.

However, account access over the eWorld enables the relationship, allowing the customer themselves to initiate and manage a range of transactions, such as bill payment on their account. The building society doesn't even need to develop and own this facility. It can be provided over the eWorld by a supplier in another country, invisible to the customer. Expect this cross-industry development to become common, involving new initiatives by power and telephone utilities, banks and many other businesses.

Redefining your business

If someone has come to your site, maybe your own little lonely 'electronic office', it is sensible to try to sell them other products or provide other services while they are there.

Provided the extensions are plausible to the customer, do not threaten your core business, and can be accommodated without imposing complexity costs on you or the customer, then they are likely to be successful. In many cases they will enhance customer convenience.

Costs of additional services will be kept low by transparently integrating electronically with specialist suppliers. So you capture the distribution value of your electronic office, and indeed enhance it, without the cost of developing and managing all the products and services it offers.

Any organization which is trusted by customers and has an eWorld site which individual customers access relatively frequently is in a strong position to extend its operations into new, complementary businesses. In a variant of this, Microsoft has used its name recognition to help it enter the travel industry (Microsoft Expedia) personal investment (Microsoft Investor) and car sales (Microsoft Carpoint) over the eWorld.

Tips, tricks and trivia

What exactly is the point?

The Webmaster at Icepick, whose clever motto is 'cool and to the point', started by connecting his doorbell to a computer so he could 'log' doorbell activity and then post it to his Web site. This allowed an entire world full of people hungry for doorbell ringing information to access it day and night. Encouraged by the results, his Web site now logs access to his refrigerator door, his toilet and his phone. It also tracks the times his cat goes into another room of the house to eat. And this is more than just data. You get pictures, frequency charts (including peak hour analysis), the works. Oddly, the question 'Why in heaven's name are you doing this?' has been omitted from the FAQ page.

http://www.icepick.com

Basic redefinition of the industry

New forms of competition arise and reduce your direct access to customers.

Brokers and other middlemen have long been part of the sales process for many industries. Frequently their business has depended on a network of personal relationships. The eWorld is giving rise to a system of impersonal middlemen. Their value and power flows from their ability to consolidate a mass of information relevant to purchasers. That allows purchasers the ability to find and compare alternatives much more efficiently.

Buying groups, which have always existed to some degree, may gain new power in a number of industries. This is because of the ability of the eWorld to bring a much higher level of efficiency and coordination to their activities.

While middlemen may exist in many industries, who they are and how they operate will change, destroying many established relationships and industry structures. In other industries they will assume much more importance than now, weakening customer relationships and 'customer ownership'.

Onsale **http://www.onsale.com** now sells millions of dollars of computer and personal electronic equipment a week by continuous auctions over the eWorld. PcOrder.com **http://www.pcorder.com** lets corporate buyers compare different vendors' prices for systems that meet the buyer's specifications. Auto-by-Tel **http://www.autobytel.com** and Autotrade match car buyers with vehicles and dealers, reducing the frustrations and difficulties now experienced by many car buyers. Mercedes Benz/Chrysler expects 25 per cent of its cars to be sold this way by 2001.

Physical commodity markets for farm products, grain, livestock and fruit will be at least partially changed by eWorld trading, allowing producers to cut out the costs of some of the brokers who are currently an important part of the sales and distribution process. Small producers will benefit from having an eWorld presence.

Using the eWorld someone redefines your industry

> **Tips, tricks and trivia**
>
> **Hypochondriacs' home page?**
>
> Have a pain in the neck, stomach, head or arm? Although it's no substitute for a doctor's advice, iBio helps you quickly research your symptoms. Don't rely on the site for a real diagnosis. Instead, use it as a tool to learn more about your condition and whether you should call a doctor. You can locate symptoms by clicking an organ group, such as Heart or Skin, and then browsing through a Symptoms list. Click on a symptom to see a list of possible diseases that may be at fault. Click a disease to see a brief self-assessment that can help you decide whether you should see a doctor about the problem. (Of course, if you have *any* doubt at all, see the doctor!) You can also click to see links to other sites dealing with the topic. The left side of the home page links to features on health, including the development of screening tests for serious diseases like cancer.
>
> **http://www.ibionet.com**

There are eWorld sites that exist today which offer lifestyle advice and health information. It is a natural step for some of them to interact with users and offer limited diagnoses and advice on medical problems. We can expect to see low-cost sensors attached to PCs, and so to the eWorld, that measure a person's physical condition. These won't be just measuring pulse, temperature and blood pressure. Developments now occurring in biochips, which are electronic sensors for chemicals, cells and their components, mean that in homes in the future, through the computer and connection to the eWorld, there will be far more sophisticated diagnostic facilities available than are in most doctors' surgeries today.

The strength of these facilities will come not just from the sensors but from the ability to collect information from the person, to match it against similar readings for the person built up over time, and to systematically and automatically analyze it by computer at an eWorld site, prompting further interaction with the user/patient where appropriate. Such facilities are likely to include automatic transfer to a doctor where the analysis indicates that is warranted.

These in-home facilities will not replace all doctors. They won't replace surgeons and intensive care wards and the sort of high-powered diagnostic facilities that will always exist somewhere. Nonetheless they will have a momentous impact on less traumatic medicine and on preventive health care. Health management organizations will use them aggressively to reduce costs and, because of the minimal cost and the convenience of each consultation, to actually improve health. The effects will be not just on the health delivery industry but on pharmaceuticals and medical equipment.

As with education, these services could be provided globally over the eWorld, shattering the protected structure of national medical systems. In fact many of these services may legally come from countries whose laws minimize the possibility of expensive professional negligence suits.

Home building in the eWorld

A less momentous example involves the design of custom-built housing, with techniques that cement a relationship between homebuilder and client. Some homebuilders will use online automated architects to lock in customers as they design their own home in detail. Such facilities would allow the user to 'walk through' the evolving design of their home, seeing their specifications in three dimensions from any position in or around the house.

Such an online architect would use knowledge of the proposed site to suggest alignment on the block and how to structure it to use the sun. Based on the structures proposed it would even estimate ongoing energy costs.

As the user explores alternative structures and fittings, the system would instantaneously revise price estimates and provide loan repayments. When the design is finalized the system would generate detailed construction plans.

Much of this could be done by a free-standing PC program. However, the eWorld allows continuous updating with prices and new materials. By allowing the customer to invest a lot of time in using its facilities, which retain the detailed information, the builder creates a significant deterrent to shopping around.

Constraints for existing businesses

In seeking to cope with the eWorld many existing businesses will experience difficulties not shared by new competitors. Again, the specifics will vary for companies but there are some general categories, including:

- threats to existing differential pricing;
- conflict of interests;
- inactivity of some customer segments;
- internal incapacity to realize or react to an eWorld future.

Differential pricing

Many global companies have financially beneficial differential pricing policies, enabling them to get the maximum profit from each of a number of different territories or segments. Typically the territories have been geographically based but are sometimes defined by customer segment, e.g. airlines' milking of business vs. holiday passengers. In Europe the pricing structure of cars in different countries is a perfect example.

When a single site is available to all possible customers, and customers can access good information about the price of alternative suppliers, it becomes very difficult to price differentially except to reflect true differences in the cost of serving various customers.

For firms that currently have differential pricing, this change can have a large adverse short-term impact. In many cases this will slow their adoption of eWorld commerce, creating opportunities for new or existing competitors without this constraint.

Conflict of interests

Many existing structures of brokers and distributors will be largely wiped out by the rise of eWorld commerce. Large amounts of personal and institutional capital will be destroyed in this way. However, this will not happen overnight. These relationships will remain important to many existing suppliers for a long time.

If a supplier openly starts to sell through the eWorld, existing customers are likely to see that as a threat to them and threaten to divert their business to other suppliers. Whichever choice the supplier makes is likely to impose some costs which new competitors do not bear.

Customer inertia

While some customers will quickly adopt eWorld commerce, others will not. This is a problem faced by banks with large branch networks. The customers who are not early adopters of new technologies want to be served in the way they are used to. But as other customers switch to the new technology the cost per customer of the old technology increases. Rationalizing branches inconveniences the more traditional customers, causing them to look for another supplier that still satisfies their preferences.

So as customers adopt eWorld commerce at different rates, existing suppliers need to maintain traditional and new distribution systems or lose some existing customers. New competitors do not have this split focus or face the loss of some existing business.

Internal limitations

People within an existing business sometimes find it difficult to imagine the business conducted effectively in a different way. This failure of vision, or of the willingness to attempt uncomfortable change, can impede existing firms from mobilizing themselves for the future.

Government

Operation of government agencies

Government agencies are not immune from the impact of the eWorld. A lot of government services are information-intensive. Users of those services will want to be able to access information directly over the eWorld without human intervention. It will be economical for governments to provide it this way. Government agencies are already doing this. However, the trend will be to go beyond simply

Tips, tricks and trivia

Federal Bureau of Investigation site

The FBI has created a Web site with a surprising amount of information, a far cry from the Hoover days. In fact, some of the files on people investigated by the Bureau in the old days are available in the FBI Headquarters Freedom of Information Act (FOIA) section. Some of the categories you can browse include Famous People and Unusual Phenomena. The FBI home page also links to sections on the most wanted criminals, high-profile investigations, jobs at the Bureau, crime statistics, and more.

http://www.fbi.gov

providing structured data. Automated interactions will be established, replacing clerks for much of the interaction with government agencies.

Revenue erosion

Tax offices are starting to recognize the adverse implications of eWorld commerce for many traditional forms of revenue. Sales and transaction taxes are already being eroded by eWorld commerce. It is certainly possible to tax these transactions but that will require the introduction of new mechanisms, some of which may be very cumbersome and inefficient. In addition, the US government has opposed taxation of eWorld commerce and is encouraging other countries to adopt this position.

Gambling has grown as a major source of revenue for many governments. Its shift into the eWorld, provided on sites outside a government's domain, will remove a lot of this revenue. Gambling sites can be easily established in low-tax localities. They are then able to offer their customers better odds than sites that carry a heavy tax rate.

The progress of these effects will fundamentally alter the revenue base for many governments. There will be attempts to derive more from remaining tax sources, which will hasten the movement of transactions to the eWorld. Ultimately eWorld activities are unlikely to escape some form of taxation. However, the governments able to collect revenue in this way may not be the ones losing it from existing sources. Consequently the eWorld's impact on commerce and taxation is likely to alter the shape of government.

Tips, tricks and trivia

Researching games

Games Domain aims to be a megasite for people who love computer-based gaming. You can find tips and even 'cheats' for your favourite games, reviews of new products, downloads, and lists of best-selling games. Fortunately, the site has a search engine (powered by Excite) that makes sorting through all this information much easier.

http://www.gamesdomain.co.uk

Regulatory control

Legal agencies will have to direct a lot of effort to eWorld-based crime, since crime follows other human activities, although in the eWorld crime is much easier to detect. Many regulatory actions which have been relatively simple within national boundaries become enormously complex when one party to the transaction is in another country with quite different legal requirements. In Scotland there is a firm of solicitors,

MacRoberts, at the forefront in IT law. The 'Publications' section of their Web site **http://www.macroberts.co.uk/** is well worth a visit. The detail in their articles on global IT matters is most informative.

There are implications for what regulations are possible within one's own boundaries. If local regulatory requirements impose a sales or cost burden on local firms, which is not borne by competitors operating from offshore locations, local firms may be driven out of business.

If regulations are to be imposed, they will be ones that suit the countries with the strongest economies. Even more than today, the US will create *de facto* regulations for many other countries.

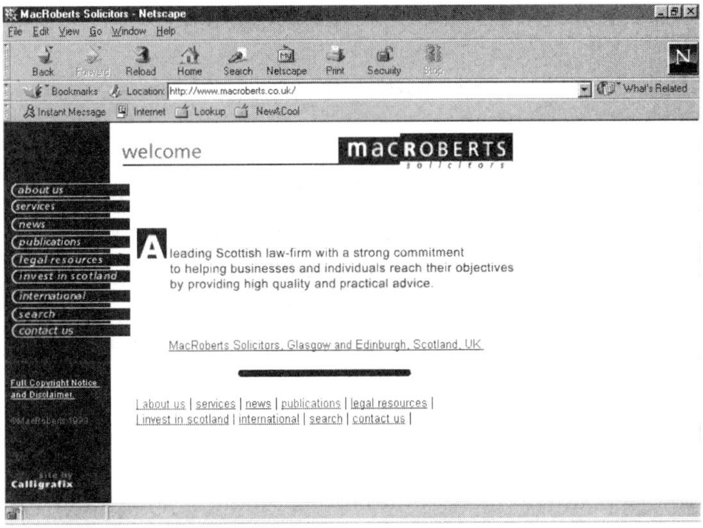

Secondary effects

Many of the examples above illustrate the first effects of the eWorld. They are what will occur when businesses take the initial obvious steps to exploit the eWorld. As they occur they will change the overall business environment and those changes will lead to secondary effects as people respond to the changed environment.

Transportation and distribution provides an example. The eWorld is already directly used by transport companies such as DHL, with its online package tracking service **http://www.dhl.com**. Beyond that, as people and companies use the eWorld to easily find new sources of products, at a distance, the demand for flexible transport systems able to cheaply cope with a multiplicity of small deliveries will rapidly increase. That will put a premium on consolidating those deliveries but without incurring significant delays.

Other secondary consequences will arise from the attempts by governments to protect their revenue base as the eWorld produces major changes in the pattern and domicile of transactions and assets. The response by governments will destroy some business opportunities and create new ones. The same will be true of governments' struggles to regulate many activities while the eWorld renders much regulation ineffective.

Conclusion

Your livelihood and lifestyle will be affected by the eWorld. There is a good chance that it will be fundamentally changed. The examples put to you are meant to illustrate some of the diversity of change that will occur. They are in no way comprehensive. Millions of imaginations will be adjusted to doing business in other ways, exploiting the eWorld and the changes it will produce.

You need to come to grips with likely forces, effects and consequences. You need to determine strategies that will enable you and your company to survive. And you will need to set the foundation for the strategies in the near future, not five years from now.

Finally, we need to keep in mind that the eWorld is just a tool. The capabilities to consider, investigate, query and debate will continue to be the crucial skills. The eWorld is not an end in itself, but a beginning.

Part VI

Keep in touch

Appendix

Useful European WWW addresses

Austria

Bank of Austria **http://www.austria.eu.net/oenb/ english/index_e.htm**

Vienna Stock Exchange **http://www.wbag.at/e_index.html**

Austrian Press Agency **http://www.apa.at/eu/welcome-e.htm**

Austrian EC Presidency **http://www.presidency.gv.at/index.html.en**

Foreign Ministry **http://gov.austria.info.at**

Federal Ministry of Finance **http://www.bmwa.gv.at**

Central Statistics Office **http://www.oestat.gv.at**

Austrian Federal Economic Chamber
http://www.wk.or.at/aw/aw_intl /index.htm

Government Information Service **http://www.austria.gv.at/e/**

Belgium

Brussels Stock Exchange **http://www.beurs.be/index.html**

Belgian Futures and Options Exchange **http://www.belfox.be/**

Ministry of Finance **http://www.minfin.fgov.be**

Belgian Bankers Association **http://www.abb-bvb.be/en/**

Federal Government Information **http://www.belgium.fgov.be**

Euro site **http://www.euro.fgov.be**

Denmark

Danish Central Bank **www.nationalbanken.dk**

Copenhagen Stock Exchange **http://www.xcse.dk/uk/index.htm**

Centre for Labour Market and Social Research **http://www.cls.dk**

Danish National Research Foundation **http://www.dg.dk**

Ministry of Finance **http://www.fm.dk/english.htm**

Ministry of Economic Affairs **http://www.oem.dk/eng/ministry/index.html**

Ministry of Business and Industry **http://www.em.dk/engvers.htm**

Statistics Denmark **http://www.dst.dk/internet/startuk.htm**

Ministry of Foreign Affairs **http://www.um.dk/english**

Finland

Bank of Finland **http://www.bof.fi/env/startpge.htm**

Helsinki Stock Exchange **http://www.hse.fi/**

Helsinki Exchanges **http://www.hex.fi/**

Euro site **http://www.euro.fi**

Council of State **http://www.vn.fi/vn/english/index.htm**

President's Home Page **http://www.tpk.fi/eng/index.html**

Ministry for Foreign Affairs
http://www.vn.fi/um/ministry/english/umeng.html

Ministry of Finance **http://www.vn.fi/vm/english/mof.htm**

Government Institute for Economic Research
http://www.vatt.fi/eng/default.htm

Research Institute for the Finnish Economy **http://www.etla.fi**

Statistics Finland **http://www.stat.fi/sf/home.html**

Ministry for Foreign Affairs
http://www.vn.fi/um/ministry/english/umeng.html

France

Banque de France **http://www.banque-france.fr/us/home.htm**

Paris Stock Exchange **http://www.bourse-de-paris.fr/**

French Banking Association **http://www.afb.fr/**

Prime Minister **http://www.premier-ministre.gouv.fr/GB/index.htm**

Foreign Ministry **http://www.france.diplomatie.fr**

Permanent Representation to the EU
http://www.rpfrance.org/english/index.htm

Ministry for Economic Affairs **http://195.101.154.69/Sommaire.htm**

Statistical Office **http://www.insee.fr**

Confederation Nationale du Patronat Francais **http://www.cnpf.fr**

French minting authority **http://www.monnaideparis.fr**

Germany

Bundesbank **http://www.bundesbank.de/index_e.htm**

Frankfurt Stock Exchange **http://www.exchange.de/index.html**

German Banking Association **http://www.bankenverband.de/**

Finance Ministry
http://www.bundesfinanzministerium.de/default_us.htm

Federal Ministry of the Economy **http://www.bmwi.de/**

Federal Ministry for Foreign Affairs **http://www.auswaertiges-amt.de/**

Federal Government PressOffice **http://www.bundesregierung.de/**

German Statistical Instituten **http://www.statistik-bund.de/e_home.htm**

Bundestag **http://www.bundestag.de/btengver/e-index.htm**

Konrad Adenauer Foundation **http://www.kas.de/englisch/index.html**

Greece

Bank of Greece **http://www.greekgov.ariadne-t.gr/gov/uk-bank24.html**

Athens Stock Exchange **http://www.ase.gr/**

Ministry of Foreign Affairs **http://www.mfa.gr**

Ministry of Press **http://www.minpress.gr/**

Athens News Agency **http://www.ana.gr/**

Ireland

Bank of Ireland **http://www.treasury.boi.ie**

Central Statistics Office **http://www.cso.ie**

Emu Business Awareness **http://www.emuaware.forfas.ie**

Department of Finances **http://www.irlgov.ie/finance/default2.htm**

Department of Foreign Affairs **http://www.irlgov.ie/iveagh/**

Government of Ireland Information **http://www.irlgov.ie/irlgov/contents.htm**

Government Information Services **http://www.irlgov.ie/gis/**

Prime Minister's Office **http://www.irlgov.ie/taoiseach/**

Revenue Commissioners **http://www.revenue.ie/**

Italy

Milan Stock Exchange **http://www.borsaitalia.it/**

Italian Association of Private Banks **http://www.assbank.it**

Italian Association of Cooperative Banks **http://www.bcc.it**

Ministry of Treasury **http://www.tesoro.it**

Ministry of Finance **http://www.finanze.it**

National Institute of Statistics **http://www.istat.it**

Foreign Ministry **http://www.esteri.it/eng/indexeng.htm**

Cittadini d'Europa **http://die.pcm.it/opuscolo/**

Luxembourg

Luxembourg Stock Exchange **http://www.bourse.lu/uk/gb-home.htm**

Luxembourg EU Presidency **http://www.etat.lu/uepres**

Finance Ministry **http://www.etat.lu/FI/**

Government Information **http://www.etat.lu/CIE**

Netherlands

Central Bank **http://www.dnb.nl**

Amsterdam Stock Exchange **http://www.aex.nl/**

Ministry of Economic Affairs **http://info.minez.nl/ezenglish/index.htm**

Finance Ministry **http://www.minfin.nl/**

Netherlands Foreign Investment Agency **http://www.nfia.com**

Dutch Foreign Ministry **http://www.bz.minbuza.nl/**

Statistics Office **http://www.cbs.nl/indexeng.htm**

Parliament **http://www.parlement.nl**

Portugal

Bank of Portugal **http://www.bportugal.pt/default_e.htm**

Lisbon Stock Exchange **http://www.bvl.pt/**

Council of Ministers **http://www.pcm.gov.pt**

National Statistics **http://www.ine.pt/index.html**

Treasury **http://www.dgt.pt/dgte.html**

Ministry of Finance **http://www.dgep.pt/menprinci.html**

Spain

Banco de Espana **http://www.bde.es/welcomee.htm**

Madrid Stock Exchange **http://www.bolsamadrid.es/**

National Institute of Statistics **http://www.ine.es**

Sweden

Central Bank **http://www.riksbank.se/eng**

Stockholm Stock Exchange **http://www.xsse.se/eng/**

Government Information Server **http://www.sb.gov.se/info**

Parliament **http://www.riksdagen.se/index_en.htm**

Swedish Institute **http://www.si.se/eng/eindex.html**

Finance Ministry
http://www.sb.gov.se/info_rosenbad/departement/finans/finans.html

Statistics Office **http://www.scb.se/indexeng.htm**

Exchanges

London Stock Exchange **http://www.stockex.co.uk**

LIFFE **http://www.liffe.com**

London Metal Exchange **http://www.lme.co.uk/cgi-bin/php/main1.htm**

Central government

UK Euro Web site **http://www.euro.gov.uk**

10 Downing Street **http://www.number-10.gov.uk**

Foreign Office (FCO) **http://www.fco.gov.uk/**

UK EC Presidency Web site **http://presid.fco.gov.uk/homepage.html**

UK Permanent Representation, Brussels **http://ukrep.fco.gov.uk/**

HM Treasury **http://www.hm-treasury.gov.uk**

Department of Trade and Industry (DTI) **http://www.dti.gov.uk**

Bank of England **http://www.bankofengland.co.uk/**

Central Office of Information
http://www.coi.gov.uk/coi/depts/deptlist.html

Her Majesty's Stationery Office (HMSO) **http://www.hmso.gov.uk**

Office for National Statistics **http://www.ons.gov.uk**

Local government

Local Government Association **http://www.lga.gov.uk**

Local Government Information Unit **http://www.lgiu.gov.uk**

Local Government Directory **http://www.tagish.co.uk**

Political parties

Conservative Party **http://www.conservative-party.org.uk**

Labour Party **http://www.labour.org.uk**

Liberal Democrats **http://www.libdems.org.uk**

Alliance Party **http://www.unite.net/**

Green Party **http://www.greenparty.org.uk/**

Liberal Party **http://www.libparty.demon.co.uk**

Plaid Cymru **http://www.plaidcymru.org/**

Scottish National Party **http://www.snp.org.uk/**

Sinn Fein **http://www.irlnet.com/sinnfein/index.html**

Social Democratic and Labour Party **http://www.indigo.ie/sdlp/**

Socialist Party **http://www.socialistparty.org.uk**

Ulster Unionist Party **http://www.uup.org**

UK Independence Party **http://www.independenceuk.org.uk/**

Ulster Democratic Unionist Party **http://www.dup.org.uk**

Parliament

Houses of Parliament **http://www.parliament.uk**

House of Commons
http://www.parliament.the-stationery-office.co.uk/pa/cm/cmhome.htm

House of Lords
http://www.parliament.the-stationery-office.co.uk/pa/ld/ldhome.htm

BBC UK Politics News
http://news.bbc.co.uk/hi/english/uk_politics/default.htm

Special interest groups

British Chambers of Commerce **http://www.britishchambers.org.uk**

Confederation of British Industry (CBI) **http://www.cbi.org.uk**

Institute of Directors **http://www.iod.co.uk**

Federation of Small Businesses **http://www.fsb.org.uk/**

Consumers' Association **http://www.which.net**

Trades Union Congress (TUC) **http://www.tuc.org.uk**

Citizens' Advice Bureaux **http://www.nacab.org.uk**

National Council for Voluntary Organisations (NCVO)
http://www.vois.org.uk/ncvo

Think tanks, research, lobbying

Adam Smith Institute **http://www.cyberpoint.co.uk**

British Council **http://www.britcoun.org**

Centre for Economic Performance, LSE **http://cep.lse.ac.uk**

Centre for Policy Studies **http://www.cps.org.uk**

Centre for Economic Forecasting, LBS **http://www.lbs.ac.uk/cef**

Centre for the Study of Financial Innovation
http://www.csfi.demon.co.uk

Charter 88 **http://www.gn.apc.org/charter88/home.html**

Demos **http://www.demos.co.uk**

Economic and Social Research Council **http://www.esrc.ac.uk**

European Movement **http://www.euromove.org.uk**

Federal Trust **http://www.compulink.co.uk/~fedtrust**

Institute of Economic Affairs **http://www.iea.org.uk**

Institute for Fiscal Studies **http://www.ifs.org.uk**

Institute of Public Policy Research **http://www.ippr.org.uk**

Labour Research Department **http://www.lrd.org.uk/labres.html**

National Institute of Economic and Social Research
http://www.niesr.ac.uk

Political Studies Association **http://www.lgu.ac.uk/psa/psa.html**

Political Economy Research Centre
http://www.shef.ac.uk/uni/academic/N-Q/perc

Royal Economic Society **http://www.res.org.uk**

Royal Institute for International Affairs **http://www.riia.org**

Business help

Business Link **http://www.businesslink.co.uk**

Enterprise Zone **http://www.enterprisezone.org.uk**

European Information Centres (EICs) **http://www.euro-info.org.uk**

Training and Enterprise Centres (TECs)
http://www.tec.co.uk/tecnc/index.html

DTI Overseas Technologies Service **http://www.dti.gov.uk/ots**

Trade UK **http://www.tradeuk.com**

DataOp Alliance **http://www.dataop.com**

Expert Access System **http://www.xas.co.uk**

Europe Online **http://www.europeonline.com/biznet**

Business directories on the Web

The Business Information Zone **http://www.thebiz.co.uk**

The Business Bureau (UK) **http://www.u-net.com/bureau**

Yahoo! Small business info
http://www.yahoo.com/business/Small_Business_Information

Opinion polling

Gallup **http://www.gallup.com**

MORI **http://www.mori.com**

NOP **http://www.nopres.co.uk**

Glossary

Glossary of search terms

This glossary contains terms applicable to searching the eWorld. For ease of use by the beginner, the definitions are brief and in simple language.

Bookmark A page on the Netscape Browser that lists URLs or Web addresses. Bookmarks serve as links for easy access to Web addresses. Internet Explorer's equivalent is called Favorites. To bookmark a Web page on your screen, click Bookmark on the bar, and when it is displayed, click Add Bookmark. The link is then added to the bottom of the Bookmark Listing.

Boolean search A keyword search that uses Boolean operators for obtaining a precise definition of a query.

Browsing In the eWorld, browsing refers to a directory search. In popular use, browsing, or surfing, means casually looking for information on the Internet.

Browser A computer program used to connect to Web sites on the World Wide Web and access information.

Concept search A query that implies a term's broader meaning, rather than its literal meaning.

Data Information such as text, numbers, images and sound contained in a form that can be processed on a computer.

Database Stored information at a search tool's Web site. For search engines, a robot is used to keep the database current by an automated procedure called spidering. For directories, the database is kept current through reviews conducted by qualified people.

Directory search A hierarchical search starts with a general heading and proceeds through selection of increasingly more specific headings or subjects. It provides a means of focusing more closely on the object of the search. It is also referred to as subject search, directory guide or directory tree.

eWorld My term for ***everything*** that is connected to the Internet.

False drops Documents that are retrieved but are not relevant to the user's interest.

Fields Components of a Web page such as a title, URL, summary, text and images often displayed by a search engine to help narrow a search.

Full-text indexing A database index that includes all terms and URLs. In practice, each search tool uses a filter to remove words it considers unnecessary.

Hierarchical A ranking of subjects or things from the most general to the most specific.

Hits A list of links or references to documents that are returned in response to a query, also called matches or matching queries.

Home page The first page of a search tool's Web site.

Hypertext link A highlighted word or image [shown in colour] on a Web page that, when clicked, connects or links to another location with related information. Links provide an easy way to move about the Internet.

Index or catalogue A file that designates the location of specific data in a search engine's database.

Internet The Internet, with an upper case I, refers to a worldwide system of linked computer networks that serve as a communication system. Not to be confused with intranet, a term used to mean a group of interconnected local networks.

Keyword A term that a computer can recognize and use as the basis for executing a search.

Keyword search A search that utilizes terms that define the user's interest.

Link More accurately hypertext link. It is a connection between two Web pages or sites that have related information. For example, highlighted data such as text and graphics at one Web site, when clicked, provide related information residing at another Web site.

Location box, also address box A designated place within a browser for an address [URL]. It is the starting point for accessing a Web site.

Multi-engine search A search that uses a number of search engines in parallel to provide a response to a query.

Operator A rule or a specific instruction used in composing a query.

Phrase search A search that uses a string of adjacent, related words enclosed in quote marks as the query.

Popular items A search category created to cover frequently sought subjects and services. Search tools list popular items on their home page.

Precision A standard measure of information retrieval, defined as the number of relevant documents obtained divided by the total number of documents retrieved.

Proximity Proximity is how closely words appear together within a document. In this context, adjacency or phrase usually means that words must appear exactly in the order specified with no intervening words.

Query A search request. A combination of words and symbols that defines the information that the user is seeking. Queries are used to direct search tools to appropriate Web sites to obtain information.

Query by example Use of an example to solicit more like information.

Ranking A means of listing hits in the order of their relevance. It is usually determined by some selection of the number, location and frequency of the term in the document being searched.

Relevance The usefulness of a response to a query.

Robot The software for indexing and updating Web sites. It operates by scanning documents on the Internet via a network of links. A robot is also known as a spider, crawler or indexer.

Search box A place within a search engine's Web site to enter a query. Also called a location box and address box.

Search engine A host computer that serves a Web site and provides information from within its own sites and via links with other Web sites. This is accomplished by using the keywords of a query to match index terms in the search engine's database.

Search tool A computer program which conducts a search on the World Wide Web.

Site The location of a page on the Internet. In the WWW, it is called a Web site and identified by its URL.

Spider To spider is the process of scanning Web sites to add new pages and to update existing ones. A spider is the same as a robot.

Stemming The use of a stem [i.e. root] of a word to search words that are derived from it. For example, 'child' would retrieve information on child, children, childhood, childless and so on.

Term A single word or combination of words used in a query.

Truncation See *stemming*.

Uniform Resource Locator (URL) Uniform Resource Locator is the Internet designation of a Web address.

Web page The address of a Web site. It can also refer to a page within a Web site. When Web pages are part of the same document, they are also collectively known as a Web site.

Web site In search use, it is a specific address or URL on the WWW. In function, it is a computer system that is set up to distribute documents stored in its database. Web sites range in size from as little as one page to a vast number of pages, such as those of a search engine's database or a full textbook.

World Wide Web (WWW or the Web) A global computer communication system that uses the Internet to transmit data [i.e. text, numbers, images and sound].

Email terminology

Address book An area in which to store email addresses so that you don't have to remember and type them in each time you want to send a message.

Alert A method of letting you know that you have new mail. Most often a text box that appears on your screen and/or a sound.

Attachment A file sent along with an email message, which can be text, a graphic or even an application.

Contact An address book entry, which you can select to enter the address in an outgoing message.

Filter An email management tool that enables you to determine in advance how certain incoming email messages will be treated.

Forward Send a copy of a message you have received to someone else. Usually the original message is presented as a quotation so that you can add a message of your own which will be distinguishable from the original content.

Inbox A folder where copies of received messages are stored.

Mail server The computer and computer program located at your Internet service provider that transmits, receives and stores email messages.

Nickname A distinguishing name for an address book entry that you can select to enter the address in an outgoing message.

Outbox A folder where copies of sent messages are stored.

POP (Post Office Protocol) The rules and procedures used by computer networks to enable email to be sent, received and stored by a mail server.

Queued messages Messages written but not sent are stored (queued) in the Outbox folder until you are ready to send them.

Quotation All or part of a received message included in a reply. Each line is preceded by a '>' (right angle bracket) to distinguish it from the new material.

Recipient The person to whom you send a message.

Redirect Send a message you have received as is to someone else. Differs from 'Forward' in which the original message is presented as a quotation so that you can add a message of your own.

Reply A message sent in response to a received message. Normally, all or part of the received message is quoted (each line preceded by a '>' (right angle bracket) to distinguish it from the new material).

Signature A message that will automatically be added at the bottom of each outgoing message, used by the sender to personalize messages.

TCP/IP (Transmission Control Protocol/Internet Protocol) The computer network rules and procedures which run the Internet. Email is one of the functions made possible by TCP/IP.

Index

Accompanying CD-ROM SuSE Linux 6.2

SuSE Linux 6.2 installation

First and foremost, before installing SuSE Linux 6.2 – back up all your data. Also ensure that you have enough space on your hard disk to install SuSE Linux 6.2. You can get by with about 300/400MB but I suggest, approximately 1GB. If you are sharing your hard disk with Windows then run the defrag program under Windows. To create space you may wish to use 'fips', a dos utility (directory dosutils) which you will find on this CD. Before you use it you should read the file InfoSuSE that is located in the same directory. With this program you can re-size Windows partitions, to create more space for SuSE Linux. Remember to back up your files first.

1. If your computer is equipped with a modern BIOS you can boot directly from the SuSE Linux 6.2 CD. After approximately 3 seconds Linux will start automatically. If you cannot boot from your CD-ROM, then write your own boot disk. The default boot disk image is called 'EIDE01'; it can be located in the directory \disks on the CD-ROM, also read the file README.DOS in the same directory. To write the boot disk you need to use the program 'rawrite'; this is available in the directory\dosutils\rawrite. For further information you can find it in the documentation.
2. The utility Linuxrc starts up and offers a selection of menu option. Select 'Language', 'Kind of Display' and 'Keyboard Mapping'.
3. If required, load the kernel modules for the SCSI-host adaptor and for accessing the installation system (CD-ROM drive, network card or PCMCIA). This can happen either automatically or manually. With some modules you can also specify parameters. To return to the higher-level menu use 'Back'. *Important*: If you have an ATAPI CD-ROM drive you do not need to load any special drivers. ATAPI drives are

supported by the (E) IDE hard disk driver. Support for the Adaptec SCSI Hostadapter aic7xxx is included in the kernel.

4. Select 'Start installation/system' and then 'Start Installation' in order to start YaST (Yet Another Set-up Tool). The source 'CD-ROM' which you should select. NOTE: By pressing *F1* you can access on-line help for YaST at any time.
5. On the Initial YaST screen you should choose the menu option 'Install Linux from Scratch'.
6. As this is a new installation of Linux you need to select 'partitioning'. You are now presented with another 'partitioning' selection (it has been used in two consecutive menus) to create Linux Partitions. Please do not forget the swap partition! You have to set the type explicitly with *F3*. If you are not sure just create one partition for swap (approx. 32-64 MB or more) and one other large partition. *Warning*: YaST is able to create Linux partitions automatically. If you select 'Entire Disk', ALL DATA on the hard disk will be deleted, including any other operating systems installed. If you choose 'Entire disk' you can ignore the following two points.
7. If you have manually created the partitions and they have been successfully created, select 'Continue'. On the next screen you assign mount points to the partitions. If you are creating just one partition mount point should be / . Use *F6* to determine whether and how the Linux partitions should be formatted. Usually 'normal formatting' suffices.
8. Select 'OK' and YaST will format the Linux partitions.
9. Choose 'Load Configuration' if you want to pre-select your software.
10. In 'Change/create configuration' you can select or de-select individual software packages. If you want to set up X Window System you can choose the X server for your graphics card from the series 'xsrv' at this point. If you have any doubts you can also do this at a later stage. Return to the installation menu by pressing *F10*.
11. Start loading the software you selected by choosing 'Start Installation'.
12. Close YaST by returning to the main menu and selecting 'Finish up installation'.
13. Choose the kernel with which you wish to boot your system in the future.
14. Create a special boot disk with which you can start Linux. This disk will be invaluable in emergencies.
15. You can now install the Boot Manager LILO.
16. Assign a name to your machine and select the type of network. Your computer will then continue to boot and you can log in to your Linux

as 'root'. Remember your password – if you forget it you will not be able to access your computer.

17. Add the finishing details to your system by configuring mouse, mouse, etc. Configuration scripts are processed in the background. You can view the output of these scripts on Console 9 (Switch over with *Alt-F9*). Do NOT switch off your machine before the processing of these scripts have been completed. You can now log in as 'root', start YaST (by typing yast in the command line) and create users via 'System administration'. You can set up the graphical interface (the X Window System) with *SaX* (SuSE Advanced X-Configuration) after selecting 'Configure Xfree86' from the menu.

You should now have SuSE Linux 6.2 on your computer. This is a very brief installation guide for you. On the *eWorld Handbook* Web site **http://www.eworldhandbook.com** you will find a much more detailed and informative installation procedure.

If you have any problems, in the directory docu you will find the complete SuSE Linux 6.2 manual in English, German, French, Italian and Spanish (as text or as a PostScript file).

Another excellent source of help is the SuSE Support database, which you can find at **http://www.suse.de/Support/sdb_e/**

This CD, included in the *eWorld Handbook* contains Kernel 2.2.10, KDE 1.1.1 (K Desktop Environment), Xfree86, SaX, Star Office 5.1, Corel WordPerfect 8, GIMP and much more.

Up until recently Linux was extremely difficult to install on a desktop. The last six months have seen dramatic changes in the ease of installation and this is changing daily. Installing and using Linux will require an investment of time, as there's a bit of a learning curve, but it is worth it and it will get simpler.

I firmly believe in software accessibility and affordability, and am convinced Linux is a mature, robust operating system, which more people should be able to use without having to face technical barriers. There is no doubt in my mind that in a very short period of time we will find Linux pre-installed, as the default standard installation in every computer manufactured in the world.

I believe it is worth investing the time to understand and appreciate Linux as I consider it to be the 'Aladdin's Cave of Computing Technology'.

Some SuSE Linux – FAQs

After the Installation I always get the error message 'login:'. What am I doing wrong?

You have done nothing wrong – The installation is complete you now log into your computer with your user name and password; initially only 'root' exists.

How can I enter commands under KDE?
Click on 'K' – 'Tools' – 'Terminal'. Or you can press Alt + F2 and then enter xterm. Then you will have a 'Terminal' – often mistakenly referred to as the DOS- window, in which you can enter commands.

I can't find many programs in KDE
You can start all programs from a terminal window (xterm) by entering the program name and pressing enter.

Is my hardware supported?
To check this out go to **http://www.suse.de/cdb/**

Do I need to compile my own kernel?
NO most certainly not. I strongly advise inexperienced users NOT to re-compile the kernel.

Do I need to worry about viruses in Linux?
No. In Linux there are no critical viruses to speak of. Viruses cannot cause any significant damage to your system as long as they are not invoked as root. The only virus scanners which exist in Linux are for searching mail for Windows viruses – when Linux is serving as a router.

I would like to remove Linux, how do I do this?
Delete the Linux partitions with the command fdisk; you may need to run fdisk under Linux (the Linux version of fdisk). Then you should boot from the MS-DOS floppy and enter the command fdisk /mbr under DOS or Windows.

No warranty

As this CD is licensed free of charge, there is no warranty for the program, to the extent permitted by applicable law. Except when otherwise stated in writing the copyright holders and/or other parties provide the program 'as is' without warranty and liability of any kind, either expressed or implied, including, but not limited to, the implied warranties of merchantability and fitness for a particular purpose. The entire risk as to the quality and performance of the program is with you. Should the program prove defective, you assume the cost of all necessary servicing, repair or correction.

In no event unless required by applicable law or agreed to in writing will any copyright holder, or any other party who may modify and/or redistribute the program as permitted in the licence, be liable to you for damages arising out of the use or inability to use the program (including but not limited to loss of data or data being rendered inaccurate or losses sustained by you or third parties or a failure of the program to operate with any other programs), even if such holder or other party has been advised of the possibilities of such damage.

Accompanying CD-ROM
The IBM HomePage Creator™

The IBM HomePage Creator™ – installation and highlights

The IBM HomePage Creator™ self-loads. Simply insert it and follow the very easy-to-use instructions.

What it includes

- Information about eBusiness and how IBM can help you get started
- An introduction to IBM HomePage Creator™ for eBusiness
- Examples of Web sites built with IBM HomePage Creator™ for eBusiness
- The small business guide to the Net
- Guides and a manual from the IBM HomePage Creator™ for eBusiness sites
- Software Tools and goodies

AT&T Business Internet Services

AT&T

AT&T Business Internet Services

Whether you're on the road or in the office, you need easy, reliable Internet access to your e-mail, the Web, news, file transfer and search tools. More and more, growing businesses like yours want global reach, an Internet presence and electronic business capabilities to compete in a global market. AT&T Business Internet Services does it all–with superior network reliability, easy installation and use, flexible billing options, security features and world-class customer support.

Internet access as easy as dialing a local number

Designed for your ease-of-use, AT&T Business Internet Services provides more than 1,350 local points-of-presence around the world – all accessed through a single, high-speed connection.

Easy installation and software enhancements bring you the latest technology

You can quickly "Internet-enable" everyone in your company with reliable access using our Setup Wizard, designed to make dialer installation easy and convenient. In addition, our Internet access kit features industry-leading Web browsers to enhance navigation and e-mail access. You caneasily download the most recent AT&T software and files, including enhancements to the dialer program, local dial access numbers and modem lists.

Paying for dial access is simple and convenient

Both credit card billing and invoice billing are available. You make the choice, depending on your users, usage and needs.

Credit Card Payment: Set up a personal account, use one of the major credit cards and get immediate access to the Internet. You'll need to have your card number ready for input during the installation process.

Corporate Invoice Payment: If you have five or more employees, you can establish a standard billing agreement resulting in a single monthly invoice covering all user IDs. You will be given a customer account number to enter during the installation process.

Long distance charges apply to those outside local dial access areas.

The internet access kit CD-ROM contains additional program license terms to which you must agree before software installation. If you do not agree to the terms, do not install the software. Either return or destroy the program package.

Why AT&T Business Internet Services?

- industry-leading network availability
- global high-speed access in 50+countries
- award winning performance
  PC World "Best ISP"
  PC Magazine annual
  Reader's Choice
- flexible billing options
- Multilingual world class customer support available 7 days per week

There when you need us: a network engineered for reliability

This commitment is supported by AT&T Global Network Services, engineered to provide world-class service and reliable transport for your important business information. We've built in high levels of redundancy, including duplication of key network components, such as control centres and transmission links.

At the same time, AT&T Global Network Services keeps you well-connected with sophisticated network monitoring for exceptional performance levels. And AT&T Business Internet Services just keeps getting better as we rapidly deploy newly emerging, leading-edge technologies.

Recommended System Requirements

Everyone and everything working together in a whole new way. To make your business succeed.

Microsoft® Windows® 3.1

IBM-compatible PC with 386 or higher microprocessor
Windows 3.1 or higher running on Microsoft DOS or IBM PC-DOS version 5.0 or later
14.4 Kbps or higher modem
8 MB of random access memory (RAM)
20 MB of available disk space for Netscape Navigator
Mouse or compatible pointing device

Microsoft® Windows® 95/98

IBM-compatible PC with 486 or higher microprocessor
14.4 Kbps or higher modem
24 MB (RAM)
20 MB of available disk space for Netscape Navigator
40 MB of available disk space for Netscape Communicator
70 MB of available disk space for Microsoft Internet Explorer
Mouse or compatible pointing device

Microsoft® Windows NT® 4.0

IBM-compatible PC with Pentium 60 or higher microprocessor
Windows NT Service Pack 3 required prior to installation
14.4 Kbps or higher modem
32 MB (RAM)
20 MB of available disk space for Netscape Navigator
40 MB of available disk space for Netscape Communicator
70 MB of available disk space for Microsoft Internet Explorer
Mouse or compatible pointing device

AT&T Global Network Dialer for Windows –
Credit Card Accounts

1 Insert CD-ROM into appropriate disk drive.
2 Windows NT, Windows 98 or Windows 95 – Wait for the AT&T Global Network software to launch automatically, then click on Install Software. OR, Click Start on the task bar, then select Run and type 'x':\setup.exe (replace 'x' with the drive letter of your CD-ROM).
Windows 3.1 – From the Program Manager, click on File and then click on Run. Type 'x':\setup.exe (replace 'x' with the drive letter of your CD-ROM).

Please review the Program License Agreement before continuing installation.

3 Follow the instruction prompts to install the software.
4 Select "I would like to open a personal account".
5 Your computer will connect to the AT&T global network and you will be prompted to complete your registration online using your Web browser.
6 Select a service plan and user ID.
7 Once your account is created, you will receive an account ID, user ID and password.

AT&T Global Network Dialer for Windows –
Corporate Invoice

1 Insert CD-ROM into appropriate disk drive.
2 Windows NT, Windows 98 or Windows 95 – Wait for the AT&T Global Network software to launch automatically, then click on Install Software. OR, Click Start on the task bar, then select Run and type 'x':\setup.exe (replace 'x' with the drive letter of your CD-ROM).
Windows 3.1 – From the Program Manager, click on File and then click on Run. Type 'x':\setup.exe (replace 'x' with the drive letter of your CD-ROM).

Please review the Program License Agreement before continuing installation.

3 Follow the instruction prompts to install the software. Once you have completed installation, shut down and restart your computer
4 Double click on the dialer icon
5 Click on "Yes, I have a business account".
6 Enter your AT&T Account and user ID information.
7 Follow the instruction prompts to connect to the AT&T global network.

World Class Customer Care

If you should need assistance with AT&T, online help is available to quickly answer your questions. The online help service also provides links to newsgroups and our help desk Web Site.

The following URL's are valuable resources for retrieving the latest information about AT&T. For quick reference, please save them in your Web browser.

Help Centre
http://www.attbusiness.net/hlpctr/index.html

Internet Tutorial
http://www.attbusiness.net/hlpctr/netorial.html

Software Centre
http://www.attbusiness.net/softctr/index.html

Local Access Numbers
http://www.attbusiness.net/hlpctr/accessnum.html

If you require further assistance, the AT&T Global Network Dialer provides menu access to our helpdesk phone numbers.

w w w . a t t . c o m / g l o b a l n e t w o r k